THE INFERNAL MACHINE

By Steven Johnson

THE INFERNAL MACHINE

A True Story of Dynamite, Terror, and the

Rise of the Modern Detective

STEVEN JOHNSON

CROWN

NEW YORK

Hardback ISBN 978-0-593-44395-8
Ebook ISBN 978-0-593-44396-5

Library of Congress
Names: Johnson, Steven, 1968- author. Title: The infernal machine :
a true story of dynamite, terror, and the rise of the modern detective /
by Steven Johnson. Description: First edition. | New York : Crown,
an imprint of the Crown Publishing Group, [2024] | Includes bibliographical
references and index. Identifiers: LCCN 2023047189 (print) |
LCCN 2023047190 (ebook) | ISBN 9780593443958 (hardcover) |
ISBN 9780593443965 (ebook) Subjects: LCSH: Anarchists—New York
(State)—New York—History. | Detectives—New York (State)—
New York—History. Classification: LCC HX846.N7 J646 2024 (print) |
LCC HX846.N7 (ebook) | DDC 335/.8309747—dc23/eng/20240205
LC record available at https://lccn.loc.gov/2023047189
LC ebook record available at https://lccn.loc.gov/2023047190

Excerpted lyrics from "Ludlow Massacre" words and music by
Woody Guthrie. © Woody Guthrie Publications, Inc. Used by permission.
Page 91 photograph: The History Collection/Alamy Stock Photo.

Printed in the United States of America on acid-free paper

crownpublishing.com

9 8 7 6 5 4 3 2 1

First Edition

Book design by Jen Valero

For Clay

When compared with the suppression of anarchy, every other question sinks into insignificance. The anarchist is the enemy of humanity, the enemy of all mankind.

—*THEODORE ROOSEVELT*

Disobedience, in the eyes of anyone who has read history, is man's original virtue. It is through disobedience that progress has been made, through disobedience and through rebellion.

—*OSCAR WILDE*

The bomb is the ghost of your past crimes.

—*ALEXANDER BERKMAN*

CONTENTS

CAST OF CHARACTERS

(in order of appearance)

ALFRED NOBEL (1833–1896): Swedish chemist, engineer, inventor, businessman, and philanthropist who is best known for inventing dynamite and founding the Nobel Prize.

PETER KROPOTKIN (1842–1921): Russian geographer, sociologist, and naturalist who played a major role in the development of anarchist theory through books such as *Mutual Aid* and *The Conquest of Bread*.

ALPHONSE BERTILLON (1853–1914): French police officer and biometrics researcher who first developed an identification system for law enforcement based on physical measurements.

ALLAN PINKERTON (1819–1884): Scottish American abolitionist, detective, and entrepreneur who founded the Pinkerton National Detective Agency, the first private detective agency in the United States.

CZAR ALEXANDER II (1818–1881): Emperor of Russia from 1855 to 1881 who is most famous for his emancipation of the Russian serfs in 1861.

SOFIA PEROVSKAYA (1853–1881): Russian revolutionary and member of the People's Will who was executed for her role in the assassination of Czar Alexander II.

EMMA GOLDMAN (1869–1940): Russian-born anarchist and writer who immigrated to the United States in 1885. One of the leading intellectuals of the early twentieth century, Goldman is known for her advocacy for free speech and women's rights and for founding the political journal *Mother Earth*.

ALEXANDER BERKMAN (1870–1936): Russian-born anarchist who immigrated to the United States in 1888 and became a prominent advocate for free speech and labor rights. He served fourteen years in prison for his attempted assassination of Henry Clay Frick.

JOHANN MOST (1846–1906): German American anarchist and writer who is known for his radical views and advocacy for violence as well as for popularizing the phrase "propaganda of the deed" to describe terrorist actions.

HENRY CLAY FRICK (1849–1919): American industrialist who played a key role in the development of the steel industry through his partnership with Andrew Carnegie. He was the target of an assassination attempt by Alexander Berkman in 1892.

ÉMILE HENRY (1872–1894): French anarchist who is known for his advocacy for violence. He was executed for his role in the bombing of the Café Terminus in Paris in 1894.

OWEN EAGEN (1857–1920): American firefighter who led the New York City Fire Department's Bureau of Combustibles and is famous for defusing more than seven thousand bombs over the course of his career.

LEON CZOLGOSZ (1873–1901): Polish American anarchist who assassinated President William McKinley in 1901.

THEODORE ROOSEVELT (1858–1919): American statesman, conservationist, and twenty-sixth president of the United States. He served as police commissioner for New York City from 1895 to 1897.

JOSEPH FAUROT (1872–1942): American police detective who introduced the use of forensic science, particularly fingerprinting, to the NYPD, and played a leading role in investigating the anarchist bombings of the 1910s.

ARTHUR WOODS (1870–1942): Boston-born schoolteacher, entrepreneur, social reformer, and commissioner of the NYPD who led the modernization of the police force during his tenure as commissioner from 1914–1917.

BECKY EDELSOHN (1892–1973): Latvian American anarchist who is known for fierce political activism and her underage relationship with Alexander Berkman.

JOSEPH PETROSINO (1860–1909): Italian American police officer and detective who created and led the NYPD's Italian squad, investigating the Black Hand, an Italian American crime syndicate.

HANS SCHMIDT (1881–1916): German priest, rapist, and suspected serial killer who was executed in 1916 for the murder of his wife, Anna Aumüller. Schmidt was the only Catholic priest to be executed in American history.

JOHN EDGAR HOOVER (1895–1972): First director of the Federal Bureau of Investigation (FBI) who is known for his anti-communist and antiradical views and for his focus on using information science to fight crime.

JOHN D. ROCKEFELLER JR. (1874–1960): American businessman and philanthropist who was the son of John D. Rockefeller, the founder of Standard Oil.

JOHN PURROY MITCHEL (1879–1918): American reformer and politician who served as mayor of New York City from 1914 to 1917. Mitchel was the first NYC mayor of Latin American descent.

THOMAS TUNNEY (1875–1952): Irish American police officer who joined the NYPD in 1903 and later led the NYPD's Bomb and Anarchist Squad.

AMEDEO POLIGNANI (1892–1932): Italian American police detective and member of the Bomb and Anarchist Squad whose undercover work broke up a plot to bomb St. Patrick's Cathedral.

MITCHELL PALMER (1872–1936): American politician who served as attorney general of the United States from 1919 to 1921. He is known for his antiradical views and for his role in the Palmer Raids, a series of raids against suspected anarchists and communists.

PREFACE

July 5, 1915

Police headquarters, Centre Street, Manhattan

The bombs came in all kinds of packages.

Often they arrived in tin cans, emptied of the olive oil or soap or preserves the cans had originally been manufactured to contain, now wedged tight with sticks of dynamite. Sometimes they were wrapped with an outer band of iron slugs, designed to maximize the destruction, conveyed to their target location in a satchel or suitcase, "accidentally" left behind in the courthouse, or the train station, or the cathedral. Many of those devices were time bombs running on clockwork mechanisms. The more inventive ones utilized a kind of hourglass device, releasing sulfuric acid into a piece of cork, the timing determined by chemistry, not mechanics: how long the acid took to eat its way through the cork, until it began dripping onto the blasting cap below. Many were swaddled in old newspaper pages. One of the most notorious bombing campaigns sent the devices through the mail, dressed up in department-store wrapping.

And sometimes the bomb was just a naked stick of dynamite, with a fuse simple enough to be lit with the strike of a match, ready to be flung into an unsuspecting crowd.

Many bombs were delivered anonymously. But others were accompanied by missives sent to a local paper, or left on a doorstep: threats, intimations of further violence, delusional rants, and more than a few manifestos. The smaller bombs—the ones detonated by a storefront, a few notches up from fireworks—were the mobster version of an "account overdue" mailing: the big stick of the extortion business. A few came from clinically insane individuals without a cause, propelled toward the terrible violence of dynamite by their own private demons. But most of the explosions that made the national news during those years were expressions, implicit or explicit, of a political worldview.

The political bombers were a diverse bunch: socialist agitators, Russian Nihilists, Irish republicans, German saboteurs. But of all the bomb throwers of the period, no group was more closely associated with the infernal machines—as the press came to call the bombs—than the anarchists. The forty-year period during which anarchism rose to prominence as one of the most important political worldviews in Europe and the United States—roughly from 1880 to 1920—happened to correspond precisely with the single most devastating stretch of political bombings in the history of the West. Indeed, the whole modern practice of terrorism—advancing a political agenda through acts of spectacular violence, often targeting civilians—began with the anarchists.

What was anarchism, really? Start with the word itself. Today the word *anarchy* almost exclusively carries negative connotations of chaos and disorder. But when the political movement first emerged in the middle of the nineteenth century, the word's meaning was much more closely grounded in its etymological roots: *an-*, meaning no, and *-archos*, the Latin word for "ruler." The anarchists believed that a world without rulers was possible. At times, they convinced themselves that such a society was inevitable; imminent, even.

The anarchists maintained that there was something fundamen-

tally corrosive about organizing society around large, top-down organizations. Human beings, its advocates explained, oftentimes at
gunpoint, had evolved in smaller, more egalitarian units, and some
of the most exemplary communities of recent life—the guild-based
free cities of Renaissance Europe, the farming communes of Asia,
watchmaking collectives in the Jura Mountains of Switzerland—
had followed a comparable template, at a slightly larger scale. These
leaderless societies were the natural order of things, the default state
for *Homo sapiens*. Taking humans out of those human-scale communities and thrusting them into vast militaries or industrial factories, building a society based on competitive struggle and authority
from above, betrayed some of our deepest instincts.

At its finest moments, anarchism was a scientific argument as
much as it was a political one. It had deep ties to the new science
that Darwin had introduced, only it emphasized a side of natural
selection that is often neglected in popular accounts: the way in
which evolution selects for *cooperative* behavior between organisms,
what Peter Kropotkin—anarchism's most elegant advocate—called
"mutual aid."

As a theory of social organization, anarchism was equally opposed to the hierarchies of capitalism and the hierarchies of what
we would now call Big Government. For this reason, it lacks an
intuitive address on the conventional left-right map of contemporary politics, which partly explains why the movement can seem
perplexing to us today. Whatever you might say about Emma Goldman and Alexander Berkman and Peter Kropotkin—the three
main anarchists in this book—they should never be mistaken for
free-market libertarians. They wanted to smash the corporate regime as much as they wanted to smash the state.

But the other confusion about the movement lies in the language
itself. The main reason that the word *anarchy* now carries the implicit connotation of troublesome disorder is because a century ago,

a wave of anarchists insisted on blowing things up, again and again and again, in the name of the movement.

That sense of unruly chaos that the word *anarchy* triggers in our mind today is the aftershock of all those explosions, part of the debris field they left behind. For the anarchists, it was arguably one of the most disastrous branding strategies in political history. They turned a *word* against their cause.

Why exactly were the anarchists so intent on blowing things up? That is, by definition, a technological and scientific question as much as it is a question about radical ideologies: How did anarchism and dynamite—born in the same decade but otherwise unrelated—come to be so closely intertwined? Dynamite gave small bands of humans command of more energy per person than they had ever dreamed of having before. Dynamite, quite literally, gave them power. The anarchists happened to be the first political movement to embrace that new power. But why were they compelled to make that choice? Could they have made a more persuasive case through less destructive means? To even begin to answer those questions, we need to understand where the anarchist's appetite for political violence originally came from, its complex symbiosis with the everyday violence that industrialization had unleashed into the world. For every death at the hand of a bomb-wielding anarchist, a hundred or more would die from factory accidents.

We also need to understand what that appetite for violence— enabled by the energy density of the dynamite-based explosion— helped bring into the world. When the anarchists began dreaming of a society unfettered by institutional authority, there were no forensic detectives, no biometric databases of identity, no anti-terror agencies. Where official police forces did exist, they were usually in bed with urban crime syndicates and political machines; national and international investigatory bodies like Interpol or the FBI or the CIA were decades from being created. But in the end it turned out to be those institutions that triumphed over the stateless dream of the anarchists. In many key respects these techniques and organizations were prodded into being by the emerging threat of the infernal machines, like an immune response to an invading virus. The innovation of dynamite-driven political terrorism created a counterreaction from the forces of top-down authority, one of those stretches of history where some of the most powerful institutions in the world are shaped by the activities of marginal groups, working outside the dominant channels of power. In this case, though, the legacy of the anarchist movement ultimately possessed a kind of tragic irony: the dream of smashing the state helping to give birth to a regime of state surveillance that would become nearly ubiquitous by the middle of the twentieth century.

In the summer of 1915, the site in the United States that best represented that new regime was the Identification Bureau of the New York Police Department, created originally by a cerebral detective, Joseph Faurot, and eventually overseen by Commissioner Arthur Woods, a well-born Bostonian turned social reformer. The bureau was on the ground floor of the NYPD headquarters in Lower Manhattan, lined with file cabinets containing tens of thousands of photographs and fingerprints, organized by intricate classification schemes. In a predigital era, the Identification Bureau was the closest thing imaginable to the U.S. government's plan for "Total Information Awareness" that would become so controversial in the months after 9/11.

The Identification Bureau had an equally revolutionary idea at its core, one that had first developed in Paris and London at the end of the nineteenth century before Faurot and Woods brought it stateside: the idea that crime and sedition were fundamentally problems that could be solved with *data*. The way to combat individuals or groups who were intent on disrupting society was not to overwhelm them with physical force. Such naked expressions of power only inflamed the passions of the radicals. It was better to contain dissent through more subtle means: file cabinets filled with information, undercover operations, a web of invisible oversight stretching across the country and, increasingly, across the world.

This book, then, is the story of two ideas, ideas that first took root in Europe before arriving on American soil at the end of the nineteenth century, where they locked into an existential struggle that lasted three decades. One idea was the radical vision of a society with no rules—and a new tactic of dynamite-driven terrorism deployed to advance that vision. The other idea—crime fighting as an information science—took longer to take shape, and for a good stretch of the early twentieth century, it seemed like it was losing its struggle against the anarchists. But it won out in the end. How did that come to happen? And could the story have played out differently?

The history of the struggle between those two ideas involves a global cast of some of the most fascinating characters of the age: most of all Berkman, Goldman, Kropotkin, Woods, and Faurot. But doing justice to that story demands that we take a wider view of the historical timeline: venturing back to the original invention of dynamite itself and its first deployments as a political weapon in czarist Russia, the growth of anarchism as a political worldview in the late 1800s, the pioneering innovations of forensic science in Paris that evolved in part to counter that growth—all the way up to a terrifying, but now mostly forgotten, stretch of New York City's history in the early twentieth century, when the metropolis experienced thousands of bombings over the course of just two decades.

If you had to select the one point on that timeline that marked the apex of the struggle between anarchism and the surveillance state, the point where you might get even odds as to how it was all going to turn out, you could make a good case for the night of July 5, 1915. Despite the late hour, the Identification Bureau was bustling with activity. A bomb had detonated two days earlier in the U.S. Capitol building; the financier J. P. Morgan, Jr., had been attacked at his home in suburban Long Island the following morning; and the detectives had just discovered that the suspect in both crimes had recently purchased two hundred sticks of dynamite in New York, only six of which had been accounted for. For weeks Joseph Faurot had been receiving death threats in the mail from anarchist groups, reminding the detective of the fast approaching one-year anniversary of one of the most devastating explosions in the city's history, a blast that destroyed an entire apartment building on the East Side, the work of anarchists plotting an attack on another titan of industry. That damage had been wrought with only a few sticks of dynamite. The trove of explosives currently missing threatened to make the previous year's blast look like a bottle rocket by comparison.

But the clash between the anarchists and the NYPD was not only visible in the frenetic activity inside the Identification Bureau itself. To see it in its full scope, you needed to leave the file cabinets and the fingerprint studios behind, walk out the plate glass doors into the hall, venture down a set of fire stairs into the darkened hallways of the basement. There you would have seen a cheap suitcase, leaning against a doorway. Below the muffled hum of activity in the Identification Bureau directly above, if you listened very intently, you might just have heard the quiet metronome of a ticking clock.

PART ONE

Fuse

1866–1892

CHAPTER 1

The Controlled Explosion

August 1866
Krümmel, Germany

Seen from afar, the dunes rising up over the River Elbe, cradling the ruins of the nitroglycerin factory, appeared to be composed of ordinary sand. Only their vivid white coloring betrayed their true origins. Millions of years before, they had been living organisms: diatoms, the single-celled algae that produce more than a third of all the oxygen on earth. In the dunes looming over the Elbe, all that remained of these creatures were their exoskeletons, forming a soft powder easily carried by the wind. The Germans who first discovered it called it *kieselguhr*. Under a microscope, kieselguhr turned out to possess a secret geometry of intricate honeycomb-like fragments. A few years earlier, Darwin had extolled the splendor of these ancient skeletons in *The Origin of Species*. "Few objects are more beautiful than the minute siliceous cases of the diatomaceæ," he wrote. "Were these created that they might be examined and admired under the higher powers of the microscope? The beauty in this latter case, and in many others, is apparently wholly due to symmetry of growth."

Each morning in the final weeks of August, a brooding, bearded man in his midthirties made his way along the edge of the dunes to a barge anchored just offshore. The barge was a floating chemistry lab, cluttered with the tools of his trade: vials, beakers, pipettes, microscopes, thermometers, Bunsen burners, scales, powders, oils. All through the long, warm days of late summer, the man labored over his workbench, measuring and weighing and tinkering. Once or twice a day, he would venture back on land and set off what seemed from afar to be fireworks. The construction workers rebuilding the nitroglycerin factory a few thousand feet away would hear the booms reverberating across the kieselguhr dunes. Each time, they would pause for a few seconds, glance at each other nervously, wondering if Alfred Nobel had finally managed to blow himself up.

The nitroglycerin detonations that Nobel was triggering were still a relatively new phenomenon in the mid-1860s. The compound had only been discovered two decades before, by the Italian chemist Ascanio Sobrero, who nearly killed himself when a small amount of nitroglycerin oil detonated in his face in 1846. Sobrero's discovery had been a momentous one. Humans had been using chemistry to create explosions for more than a thousand years, dating back to the Chinese invention of gunpowder circa 800 CE. Occasionally, this new capability was employed for peaceful purposes: in fireworks displays or mining operations. But mostly gunpowder was used for military ends, making the invention of guns, cannons, and rockets possible. But over that entire period, up until Sobrero first started investigating nitroglycerin in the mid-1840s, gunpowder remained the primary means of triggering a manmade explosion. The ingredients changed slightly over the centuries, as people tinkered with the formula to make it more powerful. But gunpowder effectively had no rivals for a thousand years.

Sobrero is now mostly a footnote in the history of nitroglycerin, in large part because he walked away from his creation after that brush with death in his lab in 1846. Nitroglycerin is far more unstable than gunpowder; to this day, it is considered one of the most explosive materials known to man. Gunpowder required a spark or an active flame to trigger its explosions. But as Sobrero discovered, above a certain temperature, a nitroglycerin detonation could be triggered just by jostling it in a glass vial.

The power of nitroglycerin was evident from the very beginning. The problem was how to control that power, how to deploy it reliably. That was the problem Alfred Nobel was wrestling with in his floating chemistry lab on the Elbe.

The summer of 1866 was not the first time Nobel had set up a working lab on a boat. Two years before, he had retreated to a barge on Lake Mälaren outside of Stockholm after the death of his beloved younger brother, Emil. Nobel had been born in Sweden and had spent his early life shuffling back and forth between Stockholm and Saint Petersburg, where his father had built a lucrative business as an arms merchant. It was in Saint Petersburg that a teenage Nobel first developed his obsession with chemistry: watching his father tinker with new gunpowder-based devices in the lab, and studying with two dynamic science tutors who were professors at a local university. One of those tutors introduced nitroglycerin to Nobel in the late 1840s, pouring a droplet of the compound on an anvil and then slamming a hammer on it. Nobel later recalled that the hammer strike produced a "report like a pistol shot." The experience left a deep impression on the young man, and in the following years, he began an investigation into the mysteries of the substance that would continue the rest of his life.

Taming nitroglycerin involved two primary challenges. The first was figuring out how to reliably trigger a detonation. Gunpowder's explosive force relies on combustion, effectively a very fast form of burning, which makes it easy to detonate with a lit fuse. But nitroglycerin does not burn. Its power derives from supersonic shock waves generated by atoms of oxygen, nitrogen, and carbon rearranging themselves to form more stable bonds after a physical disturbance.

In 1862, Nobel first demonstrated a solution to the detonation problem through the invention of what he called a blasting cap. He had spent years trying to figure out how to create the kind of pressure wave that would cause the nitroglycerin to explode. Ultimately, he realized that the solution lay in the very material he was trying to make obsolete: gunpowder. While gunpowder relied on combustion to do its work, the explosion generated by that rapid burning was itself a pressure wave. Nobel's blasting cap placed a small amount of gunpowder next to the nitroglycerin and connected the gunpowder to a traditional fuse. Igniting the gunpowder unleashed the supersonic shock wave of the nitroglycerin.

Those investigations gave Nobel his first commercial product, but they came at a terrible cost. In 1864, his brother was killed in an explosion in a laboratory Nobel had designed on the family estate in Stockholm. The accident was a public scandal and a private tragedy; the blast itself was audible in many parts of the city and the papers had covered it extensively. Within weeks of the explosion, Stockholm officially banned the manufacture of nitroglycerin inside the city limits, and landlords outside the city laughed in Nobel's face when he inquired about leasing space for further experiments.

There is a version of Nobel's story in which he fits the familiar mold of the tenacious entrepreneur who plugs away at a promising but somehow fraught new idea and eventually succeeds in making it a reality. (To his credit, Nobel had little interest in nitroglycerin as a weapon, despite his father's line of work; he thought its primary use would be as a blast agent for engineering projects.) But there is another version of Nobel's life that can be told, one that probably has just as much truth in it, which is a story about a man so obsessed with an idea that he is willing to sacrifice a staggering amount of human life to bring it into the world. Conjuring up a new technology so unstable that it directly caused the death of your own brother would have dissuaded most budding innovators. But not Alfred Nobel. Prohibited by city ordinance from continuing his investigations on land, Nobel retreated to the barge on Lake Mälaren, which turned out to be a literal lifeboat for his struggling company in those first months. Nobel juggled many different roles: managing director, accountant, chemist, head of publicity. He began officially selling "Nobel's Patented Explosive Oil" for 2.50 crowns per pound, the equivalent of fifteen dollars today, all of it manufactured with primitive tools on Lake Mälaren. Somehow, he managed to keep himself and the barge in one piece.

The blasting cap made it possible for the first time to detonate nitroglycerin on command, from a distance. By the mid-1860s Nobel was selling his oil to industrial companies all around the world. It was roughly five times more efficient than traditional gunpowder-based explosives, making it far easier to blast through rock to build the railroads that were spanning the continents of Europe and North America. But the material itself remained dangerously volatile. While you could trigger an explosion reliably thanks to the blasting cap, transporting the oil was still a deadly business. Headlines around the globe announced accident after horrific accident: fifteen dead in an explosion at a Wells Fargo office in San Francisco; eighty-four killed on board a German ship bound for New York; dozens dead after a warehouse explosion in Sydney.

The nitroglycerin accidents were particularly troubling because of the gruesome damage they did to the bodies of their victims. Even on the field of battle there was very little precedent for that level of carnage. Cannons would occasionally explode if they were poorly maintained. Primitive mines could maim, and gunpowder reserves would accidentally ignite from time to time. But nitroglycerin explosions introduced a whole new level of physical destruction. The news reports of accidental detonations would often refer delicately to the fact that the remains of the victims were not readily identifiable, a polite way of pointing out that the bodies of people near the explosion had been separated into dozens of bloody fragments. This was, historically speaking, a new outcome for the human body. Humans had been stabbed, poisoned, impaled, burned, shot at, and hung. But getting blown to bits was a novel way to die.

In the summer of 1866, during a promotional tour of the United States, Nobel got word that the new nitroglycerin factory that he had just constructed in Germany had been destroyed in an accidental explosion. He cut short the American trip—which was already failing to assuage his critics—and returned to the factory rubble by the Elbe. The rising body count from his invention—at home and worldwide—had made it clear that solving the detonation problem was only half the job. The dream of the controlled explosion would never be realized until Nobel figured out a way to store and transport the compound safely as well.

The solution turned out to be all around him, as he labored on the barge on the Elbe: in those white kieselguhr dunes rising over the river. The diatomite powder was highly porous, and through a series of experiments conducted that August, Nobel discovered that mixing nitroglycerin and diatomite created a paste that made the blasting oil far less prone to accidental explosions. And the paste could be sculpted into semisolid forms, perfect for customizing into a range of products, each optimized for a different industrial use.

Nobel ultimately settled on a ratio of three parts nitroglycerin to one part diatomite. He packaged it in convenient and portable cylinders, using the blasting cap that he had perfected five years before as a detonator. On September 19, 1866, Nobel filed a patent in Sweden for his new invention. In the application, he wrote: "My new explosive . . . is simply nitroglycerine in combination with a very porous silicate, and I have given it a new name, not to hide its nature, but to emphasize its explosive traits in a new form; these are so different that a new name is called for."

In actuality, Nobel gave his invention two names. One was a variation on his earlier product's branding, with an emphasis on its newfound stability: Nobel's Safety Powder.

But it was the other name that stuck: Dynamite.

CHAPTER 2

Mutual Aid

As Alfred Nobel toiled on his floating laboratory, a thousand miles to the east another man with longstanding ties to Saint Petersburg rode on horseback through the dense forests of larch, spruce, and pine that wind between the towering granite peaks of the Yablonovy Range in southeastern Siberia. While Pyotr Alexeyevich Kropotkin was only twenty-three years old, he had already spent four years exploring the vast and hostile terrain of Russia's eastern provinces. He had rowed two thousand miles down the Amur River, nearly drowning several times in the massive waves kicked up by the typhoons blowing in from the East China Sea. He had traveled through the tundra of northern Siberia in the depths of winter, wrapped in fur and lying in a horse-drawn sledge, surviving temperatures fifty degrees below freezing. Now, in what would prove to be his final expedition, Kropotkin was attempting to find a navigable route through the Yablonovy Range, connecting the gold mines north of Irkutsk to the warm, cattle-rich plains of Transbaikalia, on the present-day border of Mongolia and China.

Kropotkin had been born into an aristocratic family, with a bloodline that reached back to the Rurik dynasty that ruled Russia for seven hundred years, before the rise of the Romanovs. As a child, he had been formally known as Prince Peter Kropotkin, though he dropped the honorific at the age of twelve, under the spell of a tutor who described French aristocrats renouncing their own titles during the revolution. While the gesture was a hint of the radical thinking that was to be the hallmark of his future intellectual life, Kropotkin spent most of his childhood surrounded by the power elite of czarist Russia. When Alexander II—the reform-minded Romanov most famous for liberating the serfs in 1861—heard that Kropotkin had overruled his father's objections and secured a post on the Siberian frontier, the czar had shrugged and given a lukewarm blessing: "Well, go; one can be useful everywhere."

Kropotkin was not the first Russian to seek a route through the Yablonovy Range. Several expeditions had previously attempted to find a pass, most of them coming from the south, but all had given up hope upon confronting the "dreary mountains spreading for hundreds of miles," as Kropotkin later described them. For his expedition, Kropotkin was accompanied by a zoologist and a topographer, along with an indigenous guide—"an old Yakút hunter"—who claimed to have traversed the desolate region twenty years earlier. Before departing the gold mines, Kropotkin had stumbled across a crude map

Pyotr Alexeyevich Kropotkin, 1864

carved with a knife into a piece of birch bark, delineating a path through the river valleys and gorges of the Yablonovy Range. The map "so struck me by its seeming truth to nature," Kropotkin wrote in his memoirs, "that I fully trusted to it."

The trust paid off. "For three months we wandered in the almost totally uninhabited mountain deserts and over the marshy plateau,"

Kropotkin wrote, "till at last we reached our destination." He gave most of the credit to the Yakút hunter. "He really accomplished this wonderful feat," Kropotkin noted, "even though there was no track of any sort to follow, and all the valleys that one sees from the top of a mountain pass, all equally filled with woods, seem, to the unpracticed eye, to be absolutely alike."

The czar's benediction—"One can be useful everywhere"—turned out to be an understatement. Kropotkin's adventures uncovered much more than a navigable route through the Yablonovy Range. After his return to Saint Petersburg, Kropotkin would propose a radical new understanding of the orientation of the mountain ranges he had explored, literally redrawing the map of Asia. (The editors of the *Encyclopaedia Britannica* would later invite him to write the entry on Transbaikalia for their 1888 edition.) But Kropotkin had also been puzzled by the many Paleolithic remains he had encountered in the "dried beds of shrunken lakes" in the desiccated mountains of southern Siberia. Subsequent surveys of glacial moraine in Sweden and Finland would lead him to an insight that he considered his most meaningful scientific contribution: the idea that glaciers had once extended down through most of the Eurasian steppes as far as the 50th parallel, and in retreating had left behind a network of lakes and marshes that had been inhabited by early humans until the changing climate turned them into barren deserts. According to environmental historian Mike Davis, Kropotkin's theory—originally published in the mid-1870s—was "the first scientific attempt to make a comprehensive case for natural climate change as a prime mover of the history of civilization."

Kropotkin's long sojourn in Siberia did not just contribute to geography and the emerging science of climatology. It also profoundly shaped the way he saw the world, planting seeds in his mind that would continue to germinate for the rest of his life. Kropotkin had embarked on the trip under the spell of Darwin's recently pub-

lished *The Origin of Species,* with its radical new account of natural
selection operating through the competitive struggle for reproduc-
tive success, quickly paraphrased as the "survival of the fittest" by
Darwin's ally, the sociologist Herbert Spencer. But in the extreme
conditions of Siberia, Kropotkin witnessed a different kind of
struggle—not the struggle *between* different organisms but rather
the shared struggle against the environmental conditions themselves. "Real competition and struggle between higher animals of
the same species came very seldom under my notice," he later wrote,
"though I eagerly searched for them." Instead, Kropotkin saw abundant evidence of a different kind of interaction: networks of cooperation among and between species, what Kropotkin would later
call "mutual aid." Inhabiting such an extreme ecosystem for so many
years left Kropotkin with a sense of wonder at all the ingenious
ways that organisms managed to survive despite the environmental
obstacles—and at how much of that survival depended not on fighting off rivals but instead on lending them a hand. Kropotkin detected the pattern of mutual aid at all scales: in insect colonies, in
flocks of fallow deer crossing the Amur River, in communities of
seabirds gathered on archipelagos in the Arctic Sea—and even in
the small human villages that formed organically in the more remote regions of Siberia.

Spending time in those remote villages also set in motion another, related idea—an idea that would go on to inspire a generation
of radical thinkers and activists around the world. Part of Kropotkin's original assignment in Siberia had been to assist in a forced
settlement scheme, where groups of convicts and former serfs had
been rounded up and dispatched to the eastern front. This was not
the Siberian exile that would become such a flagrant emblem of
Soviet-era repression; the men (and women, though there were far
fewer of them) sent to Siberia were delivered there not as a form of
punishment but rather in the hopes that they would plant roots on

the eastern steppes, slowly but steadily building up a local supply of workers to extract the region's copious natural resources. But everywhere Kropotkin looked, he saw the folly of these top-down administrative interventions. Most of the communities planned out in exquisite detail back in Moscow and Saint Petersburg didn't survive their encounters with the tundra and the desert mountains of northeast Asia. But the indigenous tribes of the region, who had settled there through their own migrations thousands of years before, had built a sustainable relationship of mutual aid with the unpromising wilds of Siberia, entirely without the help of a domineering centralized state. "To live with natives, to see at work all the complex forms of social organization which they have elaborated far away from the influence of any civilization, was, as it were, to store up floods of light which illuminated my subsequent reading," he wrote more than thirty years later, in his autobiography, *Memoirs of a Revolutionist*. "I lost in Siberia whatever faith in state discipline I had cherished before. I was prepared to become an anarchist."

CHAPTER 3

A Nature-Copy of the Forever Unchangeable

Right at the moment that Peter Kropotkin and other radical minds of the 1870s began dreaming of stateless societies modeled on the mutual aid of the natural world, another idea began to take shape in Europe that would ultimately consolidate state power, not eradicate it. The first incarnations of that idea did not initially seem to have anything to do with political philosophy or governance systems at all. They were merely observations about a strange quirk of human physiognomy: the spiral grooves of skin on our fingertips.

In February of 1880, Charles Darwin received an unusual letter postmarked from Tokyo, written by a Scottish doctor and missionary named Henry Faulds. The letter shared some puzzling discoveries that Faulds had made regarding what he called "the skin furrows of the hand," more commonly known as fingerprints. He had come to the topic through a serendipitous finding: a fingerprint accidentally left on a piece of prehistoric Japanese pottery, with the distinctive loops and whorls preserved in paint. Inspired by this ancient trace of identity, Faulds developed a series of techniques for capturing and studying the unique marks of these "skin furrows." Faulds had a specific reason to share these findings with Darwin: he believed a comparative study examining the fingerprints of lemurs might offer some new insight into the evolutionary origins of *Homo sapiens.* But he also noted, at the end of the letter, that these markings could potentially be useful for criminal investigations. "When bloody finger marks, or impressions of clay, glass, etc. exist, they may lead to the scientific identification of criminals." He even suggested the idea of maintaining an archive of fingerprints that could be used in forensic investigations. "There can be no doubt as to the advantage of having, besides their photographs, a nature-copy of the forever unchangeable finger-furrows of important criminals."

The idea of a "scientific" mode of identification was a novel one. Well into the nineteenth century, law enforcement agencies were chronically inept at—almost indifferent to—keeping track of the identities of potential or suspected criminals. Only a few brute-force methods were deployed. France maintained a practice until 1832 that allowed the state to brand individuals convicted of crimes with a red-hot iron, marking them as criminals for life. But those "finger-furrows," Faulds suggested, could do the same work far more accurately. Branding someone a criminal merely told you that he had at one point been a criminal in the eyes of the law. Fingerprints, on the other hand, could help solve a new crime.

Faulds's vision of biometric-based identification—and its application to law enforcement—were of little interest to Charles Darwin, who was near the end of his life and more concerned with completing (and defending) his grand unified theory of natural selection than with the nascent science of forensics. He never took up Faulds's offer to collaborate on a fingerprint study, but he did take the time to pass along the letter to his cousin Francis Galton.

Galton was a brilliant multidisciplinary thinker who made a number of important contributions to fields as diverse as statistics, meteorology, and psychology. He was also, as it happens, an appalling racist of the worst order: the founding father of the eugenics movement, largely inspired by his reading of Darwin's books on evolution. (Galton coined the term *eugenics* itself.) Darwin knew that his cousin had been making exact measurements of the human body, looking for statistically interesting patterns in the data he collected, a pseudoscience then known as *anthropometry*. Faulds's observations about the unique nature of the skin furrows seemed to offer another potential biometric that Galton could explore in his research.

Galton's research agenda at the time was less about using biology as an identification system than about revealing some innate property of the person being measured. In this respect, Galton was building on a long line of inquiry into the connection between crime and physiological traits that had inspired some of the most preposterous and openly racist scientific investigations of the nineteenth century. Anthropometry, like its close cousin phrenology, rested on the idea that certain personality types—particularly the "deviant" ones—had distinctive physiological features. It was a poisonous intellectual tributary that would flow directly into the pseudoscience used to rationalize the Final Solution.

What exactly Francis Galton did with Faulds's letter is a matter of heated debate among historians of forensic science. Some believe that he deliberately buried it; others think the note from his cousin planted the seed of an idea that unconsciously took root. Galton himself never acknowledged receiving the letter, but a little more than a decade after Darwin forwarded it, Galton published the first scientific treatise on those skin furrows that had so fascinated Henry Faulds. It was called, simply, *Finger Prints*. (The original cover of the book featured a full set of Galton's own prints.) In the book, Galton proposed a classification scheme for the distinctive patterns that make up a human fingerprint—what are now called "Galton details." Drawing on his statistical training, he claimed that the odds of two people having the same fingerprint pattern was one in sixty-four million.

And while Galton made many attempts over the course of his career to link biological traits to criminal ones, in his fingerprint study he came to the conclusion that there was no correlation between the whorls and loops and an individual's psychological profile. In modern terms, they were closer to the seemingly random numeric string of your Social Security number than your DNA. But if you captured the salient properties of each fingerprint, Galton realized, and translated those properties into some kind of standardized code, you could build a reliable system of identification based on the "forever unchangeable" furrows of skin on our fingers.

In one of many similar cases of simultaneous discovery in the annals of science, just as Henry Faulds was contemplating using the biological traits of fingerprints as unique identifiers, an equivalent thought was taking shape in the mind of a young clerk at the prefecture of police in Paris: Alphonse Bertillon. The son of a statistician, Bertillon had discovered through a series of photographic experiments that a systematic series of measurements of the human body could provide a biometric identifier equivalent to Faulds's skin furrows. During his spare time, Bertillon began measuring inmates at La Santé, the famous prison in Montparnasse. (Predictably, his superiors saw the twenty-six-year-old Bertillon's penchant for wandering around a maximum-security prison with a ruler and a notepad as more than a little eccentric.) In Paris, Bertillon developed a parallel approach based on body parts, standardizing around five key measurements: the length and breadth of the head, the length of the middle finger, the length of the left foot, and the length of the *cubit*—the ancient unit that corresponds to the distance between the elbow and the tip of the middle finger. String those measurements together and you had a biological identifier that was almost as unique as the fingerprint itself.

While European pioneers like Bertillon were beginning to imagine a new paradigm in fighting crime using the soft power of data as a weapon, across the Atlantic the state of law enforcement was much less promising. National investigative institutions were effectively nonexistent, and local police forces were appallingly corrupt and inefficient. For the first half of the nineteenth century, crime prevention in cities like New York had been the responsibility of a loosely organized group of constables—effectively, watchmen whose lack of training was matched only by their meager compensation. Even after the official creation of the municipal police force—the predecessor of the NYPD—in 1845, murder rates in the city remained roughly five times higher than they are today. In part, the crime problem reflected the poisonous connection between the police department and machine politics, with many officers of the law functioning as a kind of crime syndicate of their own. Tammany Hall officials would appoint their cronies to prominent positions in the police force, where they took in a steady stream of bribes from underworld figures in return for turning a blind eye on their prostitution rings, gambling parlors, and opium dens. But the police also lacked the institutional and methodological techniques required to fight crime. Patrolmen were simply muscle on the street, glorified security guards. Not only did they lack the science of forensics, which hadn't been invented yet, but the very act of collecting and analyzing evidence in the service of solving crimes was simply not part of the job description. New York City, for instance, would not have a dedicated detective bureau until the 1880s.

Despite their absence on the payrolls of big-city police departments, detectives had played an outsized role in the European and American imagination for much of the nineteenth century. In many ways the idea of a detective first took root in fiction, and only later migrated over to the real world. Edgar Allan Poe's Auguste Dupin— the sleuth in stories such as "The Murders in the Rue Morgue," published in 1841—is generally considered the progenitor of the literary detective, followed by Dickens's Inspector Bucket in *Bleak House* and Wilkie Collins's Sergeant Cuff in *The Moonstone*—a lineage that would ultimately lead to Conan Doyle's Sherlock Holmes and the whodunit genre that continues to enchant readers and viewers well into the twenty-first century.

For many Americans in the 1800s, the first encounter with actual detectives came courtesy of a Scottish émigré named Allan Pinkerton, founder of the Pinkerton National Detective Agency. While the agency would ultimately become tarred as a private army working to destroy the labor movement on behalf of industrial titans, Pinkerton himself had progressive roots, fighting for universal suffrage in Scotland as a Chartist as a young man in the early 1840s before immigrating to America, where he became an active partici-

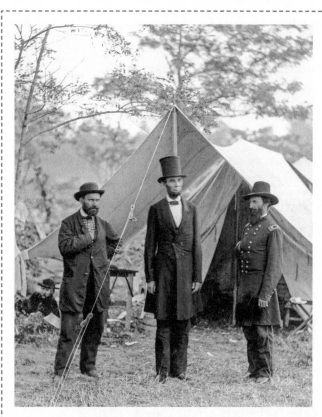

Allan Pinkerton, President Abraham Lincoln,
and Major General John A. McClernand, 1862.

pant in the abolitionist movement. He rose to national fame providing private security for Abraham Lincoln, allegedly breaking up a plot to assassinate him in Baltimore on the way to his first inauguration, and went on to oversee espionage efforts for the Union Army during the Civil War.

But Pinkerton's big break commercially arrived as a secondary effect of the country's westward expansion: with gold mines and oil fields opening up on the American frontier, large quantities of vulnerable cash and other securities had to be transported via railroad through desolate, generally lawless territories. Embezzlement and graft flourished. To fill the law enforcement vacuum, Pinkerton sold his company's services to the railroads, both supplying security forces to protect the transport of valuable goods and investigating crimes when they occurred. (The security force side of the business, as we will see, eventually metastasized into a mercenary army.) While the Department of Justice had been officially created in the early 1870s, it lacked a proper investigative force; rather than train its own detectives, the government effectively outsourced the work to the Pinkertons, making them de facto representatives of state power.

The relentless surveillance of the Pinkerton detective was famously embodied in the all-seeing eye of the corporate logo and its vaguely menacing slogan: "We never sleep." Like Poe's Dupin, Pinkerton detectives were not so much scientists as they were rationalists, capable of outfoxing the suspect through the sheer power of their intellect. (The "scientific" detective, using data analysis and physiology to solve crimes, would be a twentieth-century phenomenon.) "Crime can and must be detected by the pure and honest mind obtaining a controlling power over that of the criminal," Pinkerton wrote. The agency also helped lay the groundwork for another crucial role that would become standard in police departments: the undercover agent. While Pinkerton stressed that his detectives must have "a keen analytical mind," he also demanded that they be social chameleons: "[The detective] must possess, also, the player's faculty of assuming any character that his case may require . . . His movements should be quietly conducted; his manner should be unobtrusive, and his address agreeable. He should be able to adapt himself to all persons, in all the various grades of society."

Though he probably employed more actual, practicing detectives than any other human in the nineteenth century, Pinkerton also advanced the profession through another means: storytelling. Starting in 1874, Pinkerton published more than a dozen nonfiction thrillers documenting the exploits of his force. The first, *The Expressman and the Detective,* was a suspenseful picaresque that followed a team of undercover Pinkertons traveling through the American south in an attempt to expose a thief accused of stealing $10,000 from a private delivery company. Thanks to the reading public's growing fascination with fictional detectives, the books were runaway bestsellers. Between the glowing press coverage of the firm's triumphs and Allan Pinkerton's sideline work as an author, the agency became one of those brand names that is used interchangeably with the product category: Kleenex tissues, Xerox copiers, Pinkerton detectives.

Pinkerton died in 1884. He had one of the great career arcs of the century: from agitating for voting rights to overseeing a de facto Secret Service to commanding his own private army. He transformed the detective from a fictional character into a legitimate job description. And in his spare time, he helped invent the genre of true crime.

The alliance with the railroad made Allan Pinkerton a wealthy man, and in the long run helped perpetuate the idea of the detective operating in the service of reason, an idea that would flourish in the decades after his death. But for the agency itself, throwing its lot in with the industrial magnates proved to be a Faustian bargain. Before long, the Pinkerton men would find themselves on the wrong side of it.

CHAPTER 4

The Dynamite Club

Peter Kropotkin's journey through the Siberian frontier didn't just lay the groundwork for ideas that would ultimately be deployed against centralized state power, it also helped transform the identity of the Russian nation-state. A few decades after Kropotkin returned to Saint Petersburg, the tracks of the Trans-Siberian Railway—to this day the longest contiguous rail line on earth—were laid along the exact path that Kropotkin mapped through the Yablonovy Range. Before the Trans-Siberian line, Russia was effectively a midsized European nation with an immense, distant frontier that might as well have been its own country—much like the United States before the building of the Transcontinental Railroad. Connecting the dense, affluent cities of Moscow and Saint Petersburg to the agricultural and mineral riches of the Asian steppes was one of the defining acts that created the modern Russia we know today.

Epic engineering projects like the Trans-Siberian Railroad were not just dependent on fearless explorers and surveyors like Kropotkin and his guide. Even the most promising mountain pass required moving massive amounts of earth and stone to make way for the march of iron and steam. And where no viable pass could be located, tunnels needed to be carved through granite and gneiss and schist.

Alfred Nobel's dynamite made all this possible.

No chemistry experiment conducted in the nineteenth century shaped the infrastructure of the world as profoundly as Nobel's mixture of nitroglycerin and diatomite. Perhaps because his father had been in the munitions business, Nobel's critics often accused him of being an accomplice to the war machine. But dynamite turned out to be a peripheral player in the history of warfare. Its primary application proved to be in the realm of engineering and public works, allowing an unprecedented surge in the creation of rail tunnels, sewer systems, and subways around the world—major engineering projects that would have been impossible to pull off without the controlled explosions of dynamite. Almost all the iconic engineering triumphs of the period—the London Underground, the Brooklyn Bridge, the Transcontinental Railroad, the Panama Canal—relied extensively on the new explosive. (Nobel's invention even partially enabled Allan Pinkerton's detective agency, given the latter's dependence on the rapid expansion of the railroad networks.) Mining operations, too, benefited from Nobel's Safety Powder: new reservoirs of coal to power the industrial age became accessible thanks to Nobel's invention. By the mid-1870s, Nobel was selling his explosives in markets all around the world. The ambitious young chemist had become a titan of industry.

Drawn to the literary and philosophical scene thriving in Paris, Nobel moved to France and bought a palatial home near the Bois de Boulogne, with a glassed-in winter garden and a state-of-the-art laboratory. The days of mixing compounds on a floating barge were long behind him. In Paris, Nobel cultivated relationships with intellectuals like Victor Hugo, who based a character on the industrialist in his book *Le Ventre de Paris*. But Nobel's immense commercial success had little impact on his temperament. He retained his Nordic melancholy and was prone to spells of deep depression. Nobel spent countless hours alone in his Paris laboratory, tinkering with his latest innovations. He was known as "the loneliest millionaire."

In part that gloom derived from the fact that Nobel could not free himself—and his name—from the gruesome violence that had long haunted his nitroglycerin obsession. Even if its military use had been negligible, the compact format of the dynamite canister enabled an entirely new form of political violence. "As a weapon, it required little skill or effort," the historian Beverly Gage writes.

> Dynamite was cheap, available, and easy to use. Like a gun or a knife, it could be easily hidden, carried around for deployment at strategic moments. Dynamite gave its owner the ability to act anonymously; bombs could be planted on an enemy's doorstep or tossed from afar. Most of all, it provided the working class with firepower to match the armies of the state.

Nobel's invention enabled a different kind of destruction, perpetrated in the cities and palaces of Europe, carried out not by soldiers but by political revolutionaries and anarchists—many of them inspired by the writings of Peter Kropotkin. The press dubbed them "the Dynamite Club."

And as it happened, the very first head of state to be killed by Alfred Nobel's invention was the man who had sent Kropotkin off to be "useful" in Siberia so many years before: Czar Alexander II.

The young carpenter Batyshkov cut a striking figure in the servants' quarters of the Winter Palace. Just twenty-two years old, he was tall with a mane of thick hair, rosy cheeks, and a ready smile. Batyshkov was the son of a peasant, not versed in the urban sophistication of Saint Petersburg, but he was a first-rate carpenter, and he quickly found himself assigned to repair work throughout the enormous compound, the seat of Romanov power since 1734. He seemed to enjoy his new employment, flirting with the chambermaids and roaming through the immense royal chambers on the second floor of the palace, restoring furniture and performing other handiwork where needed. A few weeks into the job, in the fall of 1879, his co-workers noted that he had come down with some kind of seasonal flu: his flushed cheeks turned gray and clammy, and he complained of headaches. But then one day he announced to his roommates that he was engaged to be married, lugging an oversize trunk to house his bride-to-be's trousseau into his cramped quarters in the cellars beneath the palace. He lived frugally, using all his extra cash to purchase nightgowns and petticoats for his fiancée, storing them in the trunk. The imminent nuptials seemed to improve his health: the color returned to his cheeks and the headaches disappeared.

Batyshkov's work soon gave him an intimate knowledge of the palace's elaborate structure, more than a thousand rooms strung out along the banks of the River Neva. The retinue of the royal family—all the ladies-in-waiting and courtiers and extended relatives of the Romanovs—lived and worked on the grand second floor of the palace, while the cellar and the first floor contained kitchens and workshops and servants' quarters. A troop of fifty Finnish guards lived on the first floor directly above Batyshkov's quarters in the cellar; above the guardroom, separated by thick slabs of granite flooring, lay the Yellow Dining Room, where the czar sometimes entertained guests in an intimate setting. (Intimate, at least, compared to the palace's immense main dining room, which could host more than a thousand guests for a seated dinner.)

That distinct configuration of palace rooms was of special interest to the handsome young carpenter living in the cellar for one reason: beneath the lace garments of his fictitious future wife's trousseau lay several hundred pounds of Alfred Nobel's finest.

Batyshkov, whose real name was Stepan Khalturin, had recently been recruited into the People's Will, an underground terrorist organization. He had almost immediately been dispatched to be the central actor in a monthslong, deep-cover operation to assassinate the czar. Each morning, Khalturin left the palace grounds for a furtive meeting with his handler, the radical Alexandr Kvyatkovsky, who would slip him a stick or two of dynamite while Khalturin shared the latest intelligence gathered from inside the palace. Initially, Khalturin hid the explosives under his pillow, but before long the stash had grown too large to hide and his gray pallor and constant headaches made it clear that sleeping on top of a toxic substance like nitroglycerin for months on end was not a sustainable plan. As a cover, he devised the engagement and trousseau story to explain the locked trunk crammed into the corner of his room.

For the first month, the plan proceeded with few missteps. Inside the People's Will, a debate raged over the total amount of dynamite that would be required to blast through the guards' quarters and deliver a fatal blow to the occupants of the Yellow Dining Room. The group also weighed the moral burden of destroying the guardhouse as part of their ultimate attack on the czar. Khalturin calculated that the explosion would kill at least fifty of the sentries— a prediction that turned out to be too pessimistic in the end. In Khalturin's grim reasoning, that collateral body count meant one thing: the group should err on the side of stashing too much dynamite, to ensure, as he told his comrades, that the guards "did not die in vain."

And then one day, with no explanation, the handler Kvyatkovsky stopped showing up for the daily meeting.

CHAPTER 5

The Terrible Power
of the Powerless

The ease with which the carpenter Stepan Khalturin had managed to integrate himself into the Winter Palace—and to smuggle so many explosives into his quarters—gives a clear indication of the appallingly lax security that surrounded Alexander II. "Conditions at the palace," the historian Adam Bruno Ulam writes, "epitomized those of Russia itself: the outward splendor of the emperor's residence concealed utter chaos in its management: people wandered in and out, and imperial servants resplendent in livery were paid as little as fifteen rubles a month and were compelled to resort to pilfering." The poor security was particularly shocking because the czar had been the target of one of the most relentless campaigns to murder a world leader in history, a precursor to the long litany of assassination plots conjured up by the CIA to eliminate Fidel Castro almost a century later. If the events themselves had not shed so much actual blood, the procession of thwarted or incompetent attempts on the life of Alexander might seem to modern eyes like something out of a Road Runner cartoon, complete with the requisite boxes of TNT.

The first attempt on Alexander II's life came in 1866 when a well-born revolutionary named Dmitry Vladimirovich Karakozov fired a pistol at close range during one of the czar's regular walks in the Summer Garden alongside the Neva embankment. A sightseeing peasant standing next to Karakozov managed to jostle his elbow at the last second, causing the bullet to miss its mark. The next year, during a royal visit to Paris for the World's Fair, a Polish nationalist shot at the czar in the Bois de Bologne; but he had packed his double-barreled pistol with too much gunpowder, and the weapon exploded the moment he pulled the trigger. In April of 1879, a radical teacher named Alexander Soloviev shot five times at the czar during another walk this one on the Winter Palace grounds; somehow Alexander managed to avoid the bullets by running away from the killer serpentine style.

Eventually the revolutionaries gave up on gunfire and turned to what one historian called the "terrible power of the powerless": dynamite. In 1879, the People's Will orchestrated an elaborate three-pronged attack on the royal train as it returned from an excursion to Crimea. In part because there were two potential routes that the train could take, the revolutionaries went out of their way to build redundancy into their plans: explosives would be planted at three distinct points on the rail lines back to Saint Petersburg. One mine planned for Odessa was never laid because informants notified the radicals that the czar would be taking the alternate route; a second mine failed to detonate because it had been improperly wired. The third mine, planted in the suburbs of Moscow, did manage to explode as the train was passing over it, but mechanical problems had reversed the usual travel sequence for the imperial trains, and the explosion merely destroyed a carriage in the retinue train transporting fruit back from Crimea. No one was harmed in the incident, and the czar himself didn't even hear of the attack until he arrived in Moscow, where a minister of the court informed him that the "fourth car of the second train has been turned into marmalade."

Gallows humor aside, the sheer number of attempts on Alexander's life raises an inevitable question: Why were so many people so intent on killing him? When the czar had originally emancipated the serfs in 1861, the younger generation of students—many of them of aristocratic birth—had embraced the reforms as a preview of a new Russia that might transition to a constitutional democracy along the lines of its European neighbors to the west. "My feeling then," Peter Kropotkin later recalled, "was that if in my presence someone had made an attempt on the tsar's life, I would have shielded Alexander II with my chest." But the cohort of idealists who came of age in the early 1860s—Kropotkin, most famously—soon became disillusioned with the pace of reform that followed emancipation. With democratic revolutions sweeping across the neighboring countries of Europe, Russia remained trapped in its imperial past. While many on the left had assumed that the dissolution of serfdom would inevitably lead to more sweeping reforms, an entire decade passed with no real progress on a proper constitution.

As Kropotkin's generation grew increasingly frustrated by the standstill, Alexander II and the secret police of the notorious Third Department launched a sustained crackdown against the young radicals. (Formed a half century earlier, after the Decembrist revolt in 1825, the Third Department may have been the most powerful state surveillance agency in the world at the time, with undercover operatives tasked with infiltrating subversive groups that posed a threat to the czarist regime.) Kropotkin himself was arrested in 1874, imprisoned in the Peter and Paul Fortress, the star-shaped prison situated across the River Neva from the Winter Palace. He composed the final drafts of his seminal paper on European glaciers in his cell, before escaping in 1876 from a minimum-security prison to which he had been transferred while awaiting trial. Kropotkin's incarceration was part of a wave of mass arrests that put more than four thousand radicals behind bars, ultimately culminating in the Trial of the 193 in 1877, where almost two hundred alleged subversives—including thirty-nine women—were accused of a massive conspiracy to undermine the czarist state. The trial backfired; almost all of the radicals were acquitted, and the public attention it attracted gave the revolutionaries a megaphone far more powerful than any platform they could have erected on their own.

Inspired by Nikolai Chernyshevsky's radical novel *What Is to Be Done?* and enraged by the reactionary turn that Alexander II had taken in suppressing student activists, a new figure strode onto the geopolitical stage—one that would play a central role in world affairs for the next half century: the brooding, highly educated revolutionary, dedicated to the singular cause of smashing the state. "Nothing comparable existed before or after," wrote Sergei Kravchinsky, who assassinated the head of the Third Department in 1878, stabbing him to death in the streets of Saint Petersburg.

> It seemed as if some kind of revelation was at work. As if a mighty call coming out of nowhere had passed over the land. And everyone with a living soul responded and followed that call, imbued with longing and anger at their former lives. They left their home, wealth, honors, family, gave themselves up to the movement with the thrilled enthusiasm, with the fiery faith that knows no obstacles, measures no sacrifices, and for which suffering and doom are the most burning, insurmountable stimulus to action.

Some of those radicals called themselves Nihilists; some called themselves socialists. But over time the bomb planters and the assassins would largely be associated with the anarchist movement. A new mythology arose among the young radicals: "the propaganda of the deed," a phrase that Kropotkin began using after his release from prison. Mere words were not sufficient to incite revolutionary change. You needed an act of spectacular violence—also called an *attentat*—directed against a well-known target, a strike dramatic enough to be picked up and amplified by the global media networks of the day. It helped that those networks were now linked by telegraph: a dynamite mine exploding in a basement in Saint Petersburg could be front-page news in New York two days later.

The emergence of a class of radicals committed to "the propaganda of the deed" would have many consequences over the coming decades, but one of the most shocking would be the dramatic increase in mortality risk for heads of state all around the world. During the first sixty-five years of the nineteenth century, leading up to the initial attack on Alexander II, there were seventeen successful assassinations of world leaders, most of them in smaller countries outside of Europe or the Americas. Over the subsequent sixty-five years, the risk of assassination effectively tripled, with forty-eight heads of state killed in acts of political violence, many of them in industrialized European nations. The reign of terror would peak in the 1970s, a decade in which twenty-one leaders—and hundreds of other political dignitaries—were assassinated. Since then, the mortality risk in running a nation has dropped precipitously, almost back to the level it was before the first attack on Alexander II.

The carpenter Stepan Khalturin had no way of knowing it, but the reason his handler, Kvyatkovsky, had stopped showing up for the daily transfer of dynamite was because he had been arrested by the Third Department and was currently languishing in a detention cell while the secret police operatives ransacked his apartment. The investigation found copious evidence of the plot against the czar: a green glass filled with nitroglycerin and magnesium, along with fulminate of mercury, commonly used as a detonator. In the initial raid of the apartment, the police had found Kvyatkovsky desperately—but unsuccessfully—attempting to burn a piece of paper, which turned out to be a map of the Winter Palace with a conspicuous X hand-drawn over the location of the Yellow Dining Room.

The assembled evidence should have been sufficient to stop the assassination plot in its tracks. But amazingly, only a few rooms adjacent to the Yellow Dining Room on the third floor were examined; the Third Department interviewed a handful of employees inside the palace and set up a new security system to search laborers as they entered the property. But Stepan Khalturin was never interrogated, and his dynamite trousseau never discovered. Was this strange laxity a sign of incompetence or something more sinister? Alexander had enemies on all sides of the political spectrum, and Russia itself had a long tradition of rulers being deposed by their inner circle. To this day, many suspect that there were forces inside the secret police and the czar's security detail that were more than happy to allow the People's Will to bring Alexander II's reign to an end, given that the heir to the throne, Alexander III, was well known for having a more conservative worldview, closer ideologically to the law-and-order values characteristic of the members of the Third Department. But whether it was the product of malice or just ineptitude, the end result was that Stepan Khalturin was left alone in the Winter Palace cellar to continue his plot against the czar.

In late January, Khalturin managed to get access to the czar's agenda and learned that planning was under way for an official dinner in the Yellow Dining Room on February 5 to celebrate the arrival of the czar's beloved brother-in-law, Alexander of Hesse. Khalturin had not been able to assemble all 360 pounds of dynamite that he believed necessary to ensure the complete destruction of the dining room two floors above, but the longer the plot continued, the more likely it seemed that the palace security would find an occasion to search his trunk. And so, on the afternoon of February 5, as a winter storm settled in over Saint Petersburg, Khalturin attached a detonator to what the press later called a "system of clockwork," creating what is now considered to be one of the first time bombs ever built.

To spare the lives of the other carpenters he had been living with for the past few months—and ensure that his quarters were empty—

he invited his colleagues out for a dinner to celebrate his imminent marriage, leaving in the middle of the festivities with the promise that he would return momentarily with his fiancée. Instead, Khalturin slunk back to the palace cellar and set the timer on his infernal machine. Passing one of his co-conspirators among the snow drifts in Palace Square, he nodded quietly and said, "It's ready."

Seconds later, a pressure wave burst through the stone floor of the guardhouse. Instantly, the quarters of the Finnish sentries were transformed into a grotesque landscape of blood and rubble. A news report later described the scene: "Among the mounds in the smoke lay figures. It was impossible to walk—there were arms, legs, and other body parts strewn everywhere . . . The wretched guards were literally blown apart."

Eleven of them would die, far short of Khalturin's prediction of fifty. In the end, their deaths were not in vain—though they died in the service of a different cause from the one Khalturin had imagined. The guardhouse lived up to its name, functioning as a buffer zone that contained the blast and protected the Yellow Dining Room above, which was heavily damaged in the bombing, but not catastrophically.

Khalturin had been right about one thing: he needed more dynamite.

But even if Khalturin *had* managed to assemble the explosive force he wanted, the attack was still destined to fail. The blizzard had delayed the arrival of part of Alexander of Hesse's cohort, and so the royal dinner was running fifteen minutes behind schedule. For all of Khalturin's clockwork planning, the czar wasn't anywhere near the blast site when the time bomb went off.

The Winter Palace bombing—coming on the heels of the three-part railroad attack—sent an unambiguous signal, to Alexander II and to the world, that the radicals were capable of highly organized, systematic operations and were willing to sacrifice innocent bystanders to pull them off. Khalturin managed to escape without being caught—he would eventually be executed after assassinating a police general in Odessa two years later—but the scale of the blast made it clear that the palace had been infiltrated by revolutionaries who had enjoyed unfettered access to the grounds. The People's Will were laying dynamite mines a few dozen feet below where Alexander broke bread. Yes, the czar had once again narrowly avoided an attempt on his life. But for how long could he keep tempting fate?

The reprieve proved to be short-lived. Increasingly under the leadership of the steely twenty-seven-year-old Sofia Perovskaya, working in concert with her lover Andrei Zhelyabov, the People's Will decided to target the czar's transport network again, this time focusing on his movements around Saint Petersburg. A distant descendant of Peter the Great, Perovskaya had been encouraged by her father to attend university—an unusual choice for affluent young women at the time. Like so many other Russian students in that period, she had been swept up by the revolutionary movements and turned against her aristocratic bloodline. She initially worked with populist groups doing outreach to rural peasants, but by the second half of the 1870s she had broken with her family for good and joined the radical underground. With her intense blue eyes and selfless dedication to the cause, she was "probably the most likable personality among thousands and thousands of fighters against czarist autocracy," in the words of her biographer. She was also a preview of radical demographics to come: Women would play a disproportionately influential role in the anarchist movements over the coming decades, at least compared to other political factions at the time. And many of those future leaders—Emma Goldman most of all—would be directly inspired by Perovskaya's command of the People's Will.

Perovskaya initially planned to kill Alexander in Saint Petersburg by planting 250 pounds of dynamite under the Kamenny

Sofia Perovskaya

Bridge, hoping to destroy the czar's procession—and his armored carriage that had been a gift of Napoleon III—while it was en route to the train station. But the plan was comically foiled when the People's Will operative in charge of triggering the explosion overslept; Alexander and his guards traversed the bridge undisturbed, completely unaware of the trove of explosives lying beneath them.

Perovskaya and Zhelyabov shifted their focus to the czar's regular Sunday routine: traveling from the Winter Palace to Mikhailovsky Manège, where he would witness the changing of the guard, and then return home via one of two routes. He rode either down Malaya Sadovaya Street or along the embankment of the Catherine Canal. For weeks, Perovskaya surveyed the two itineraries, looking for vulnerabilities. Ultimately, she settled on a two-part plan. The People's Will rented a basement storage space underneath a cheese shop on Malaya Sadovaya Street and began digging a tunnel that would extend out to the center of the street, where another dynamite mine would be planted. On the Catherine Canal, Perovskaya had observed that the horses pulling the czar's carriage were forced to slow down to a walk as the entourage turned onto the embankment. "That's the best place," she told her co-conspirators in a meeting of the People's Will executive council in November of 1880. "A bomb can be thrown accurately at that moment."

For a time, the Third Department continued with its Keystone Kops routine. At one point, the police got wind that there was something suspicious happening in the cheese store on Malaya Sadovaya; the police inspector and two deputies were dispatched to search the premises but failed to look behind the flimsy wooden slats the radicals had nailed to the wall to conceal the tunnel entrance, and they somehow missed the barrel full of recently dug earth concealed beneath a few wheels of cheese. But in the first months of 1881, the newly appointed minister of the interior, Mikhail Loris-Melikov, created a small "special forces" security team working outside of the purview of the Third Department, in part because he suspected the secret police to be secretly collaborating with the czar's enemies. One by one, the key members of the People's Will were arrested in disciplined, targeted raids, culminating on February 27 with the arrest of Andrei Zhelyabov. From his prison cell he taunted the guards with the refrain: "If you kill us, there will be others . . . lots of people are being born these days."

Late in the morning of February 28, Alexander II made note in his diary of "three important arrests: including Zhelyabov." He reassured his minister of war that "the last conspirator has been captured . . . they will persecute me no more!"

The arrests were not quite as comprehensive as the czar imagined. Her lover might have been imprisoned, but Sofia Perovskaya herself was still at large.

There were warnings that the czar's life was in danger on the morning of March 1, but then again, there were always warnings. An anonymous communiqué had advised the czar not to make his customary Sunday visit to watch the changing of the guard, but Alexander had overruled his security forces and decided to keep to the original itinerary. He met with Loris-Melikov after breakfast, reviewing a draft of reforms designed to put Russia on a path toward a constitutional government. Shortly after noon, dressed in his military uniform, the czar entered the armored carriage, accompanied by six mounted Cossack guards. Three sleighs of gendarmes followed the royal carriage, one carrying the chief of police, Colonel Dvorzhitsky. Perhaps as a concession to his security team, the entourage stayed off the main boulevard of Malaya Sadovaya, and traveled via the side streets of the canal embankment.

At Mikhailovsky Manège, Alexander was greeting by two battalions of the Life Guards in formation. Observers later reported that the czar seemed to be in good spirits during the parade, trading jokes with the other dignitaries watching the proceedings. After the parade, he briefly stopped by the nearby Mikhailovsky Palace so that he could take tea with his cousin, the grand duchess. Just before two o'clock, the czar returned to the carriage, accompanied by his brother-in-law, and ordered the coachman to travel back to the Winter Palace, once again via the Catherine Canal. As the procession left the gates of the palace, a young woman appeared on a nearby sidewalk, pulled out a lace handkerchief, and blew her nose. It was Sofia Perovskaya, signaling to her comrades that the cheese shop detonation would not be necessary. It was up to the bomb throwers now.

It is just after two o'clock; the handful of pedestrians going about their business on the banks of the Catherine Canal have no idea that they are about to become participants in one of history's seismic shifts, one that will continue to reverberate well into the twentieth century. A young butcher's assistant carries a basket of meat through the snow on his way to make a delivery. Two men struggle to lug a couch across the cobblestones, while another leans idly against the iron railing that borders the canal. As the armored carriage turns onto the embankment, the coachman slows the gait of the horses to a walk, just as Perovskaya has predicted.

The People's Will had set in motion seven distinct plots to murder Alexander II using dynamite over the previous two years; all of them had been foiled—by bad wiring, faulty alarm clocks, snowstorms. But today, at long last, it seems their stars have aligned. As the bystanders gawk at the unusual sight of the czar and his entourage traveling along such a narrow passage, a blond man in a dark suit—his name is Nikolai Rysakov—strides confidently toward the procession, carrying a package wrapped in a white handkerchief.

Rysakov flings the package toward the czar's carriage, and with perfect timing, the nitroglycerin concealed inside it explodes, tearing a hole in the frozen street four feet deep and shattering the rear of the carriage. The blast kills one of the Cossack guards instantly, along with the butcher's assistant.

For a few seconds, there is nothing but white smoke and screaming. In the chaos, Rysakov darts away from the scene; bystanders pull him to the ground and remove the pistol and dagger he has stashed in his overcoat.

But then the dissipating smoke reveals a startling fact: the armor plating of Alexander's carriage has done its job. Other than a small wound above his eye, the czar is unharmed.

It is possible that Alexander's judgment was impaired somehow by the blast; perhaps the blow that cut his forehead also delivered a concussion that made him temporarily unable to process the danger he was in. Or perhaps the modern choreography of political assassinations that we now know so well from Kennedy at Dealey Plaza or Reagan at the Washington Hilton—the assassin strikes, and within seconds, the wounded leader is ushered away at top speed—simply hadn't yet become standard security protocol. A rapid transfer to the chief of police's sleigh, rushing the czar back behind the gates of the Winter Palace, would have once again thwarted the radicals' plans. But that is not what happens.

Whatever the explanation—delirium, incompetence, courage—after a few seconds, the carriage door swings open, and Alexander II

himself steps out to survey the scene. He stumbles across the cobblestones toward his would-be killer, shaking a finger at him and saying
contemptuously, "A fine one!" Colonel Dvorzhitsky implores the
czar to return to his sleigh, but for some reason, Alexander asks to
inspect the damage Rysakov has done with his nitroglycerin. As Alexander turns back toward the blast site, one of the royal guards, in
the confusion, fails to recognize the emperor and asks him if he
knows whether the czar has been injured in the blast. "Thank God,
I am fine," the czar replies, then gestures to the mangled bodies on
the ground, "but look . . ."

As he says the words, the man leaning against the canal railing
emerges out of the haze, a simple warning on his lips.

"It is too early to thank God," he says.

Ignaty Grinevitsky is twenty-five years old, a gifted student of
Polish birth who had joined the People's Will in 1879. Just a few
hours earlier, he had written a letter to be read after his death, only
fragments of which have survived:

> Alexander II must die . . . He will die, and with him, we, his en-
> emies, his executioners, shall die too. . . . Fate has doomed me to
> an early death, I shall not see our victory, I shall not live one day,
> one hour in the bright season of our triumph, but I believe that
> with my death I shall do all that it is my duty to do, and no one in
> the world can demand more of me.

For Grinevitsky, the mission at hand is too critical for him to
throw the dynamite from a safe distance, as Rysakov had done. Instead, the young Pole stands just three paces from Alexander II—
the patriarch of the House of Romanov, Emperor of Russia, King of
Poland, and Grand Duke of Finland—and drops a canister of dynamite at his feet.

The explosion comes close to severing the czar's legs from his upper body. The dazed police chief helps to lift Alexander into the sleigh, and in less than a minute the horses are off at a full gallop. With no time for an improvised tourniquet, the czar's blood leaves a visible trail in the snow all the way to the Winter Palace.

News reports later described the czar's last minutes, lying prostrate on the couch in his study, surrounded by physicians, clergy, and weeping relatives:

> Doctors prepared to amputate his legs, which were held to the body by the flesh alone. The bones of each limb were broken and the blood flowed so copiously that the sufferer fainted from its loss. India rubber bandages were applied, first to his right leg below the knee and then to the left, and the physicians as rapidly as possible caught up the ends of the arteries and tied.

According to one account, the czar regained consciousness just long enough to gesture weakly to the physician not to bother with the amputation. At 3:45, he drew his last breath.

In its headline copy two days later, *The New York Times* put it simply: "Nihilist Conspirators at Last Successful."

Ignaty Grinevitsky died from his own self-inflicted wounds just a few hours after the czar did. With that simple toss of a dynamite canister, he had become one of the most notorious political assassins of the nineteenth century. Only John Wilkes Booth's gunshot at Ford's Theatre had repercussions of comparable scale. But Grinevitsky's attentat on the Catherine Canal would also earn him a singular distinction in the annals of human violence: history's first suicide bomber.

The age of terror had begun.

CHAPTER 6

Dancing on the Surface of a Volcano

The crowds began gathering well before dawn on April 3, 1881, swarming the vast, unpaved parade grounds of Semenovsky Square with the hope of securing a front-row seat for the execution. In the days immediately after Alexander II's death, Nikolai Rysakov—the initial bomb thrower on the Catherine Canal—had turned on his comrades under interrogation, leading to the arrest of Sofia Perovskaya, and a quick trial of six conspirators: Perovskaya, her lover Zhelyabov, Rysakov, and three others. On the stand, the accused defiantly chronicled their plot to assassinate the czar. (An editorial in the *New York Herald* marveled at their willingness to openly confess to such grievous offenses, suggesting that there must be "some profound and radical difference between Russian nature and human nature generally as known in our part of the world.") All six were swiftly condemned to death, including the turncoat Rysakov, though one member of the group was found to be pregnant, and her sentence was ultimately commuted to a life of hard labor.

By the time the five remaining conspirators arrived in Semenovsky Square, just before nine o'clock, a hundred thousand Russians had assembled at the parade grounds to take in the spectacle. "A disdainful smile contorted Perovskaya's pinched, slightly flushed face," the historian Avrahm Yarmolinsky writes. "To at least one sympathetic eyewitness the condemned looked like victors riding in triumph." Strapped to their seats in a horse-drawn cart—and flanked on all sides by Cossack horsemen and priests—the condemned prisoners were led to the gallows wearing placards that announced their crime with a single, scandalous word: *regicide.*

By ten o'clock, all five had been hanged in front of the jeering crowd, their bodies carted off and buried in a common grave. Defiant to the end, Perovskaya had written a letter to her mother during her final hours in prison. "Believe me, dearest Mummy," she wrote, "my lot is not at all such a dark one. I have lived as my convictions have prompted me; I could not do otherwise; therefore I await what is in store for me with a clear conscience."

Measured by the immediate political objectives of its perpetrators, the assassination of Alexander II was an abject failure. The propaganda of the deed did not, in fact, trigger an upwelling of revolutionary spirit among Russia's vast peasantry. Instead, it ushered in one of those periods—not unlike the Bourbon Restoration in France seventy years earlier—where the arc of history appears to go backward. Under the conservative reign of Alexander III, a wave of pogroms and openly anti-Semitic decrees reversed the progress of the preceding decade. Roving mobs torched Jewish warehouses and stores; Jews were ultimately expelled from Kiev and Moscow and severely limited in their access to the educational system. The secret police took on new authority, cracking down on all suspected radicals. The constitutional reforms that Alexander II had been on the brink of signing into law were abandoned.

But if the Catherine Canal attack cooled, for a while at least, the embers of revolutionary activity inside Russia, it did manage to ignite a firestorm of terror that swept around the rest of the world—

much of it enabled by dynamite. The years after the assassination of Alexander II witnessed a terrifying surge of bombing attacks across Europe. Between 1881 and 1885, Irish republicans set off more than twenty infernal machines in England. On the Continent, dozens of financiers, industrial magnates, and political leaders were targeted by dynamite-wielding assassins.

Alfred Nobel had correctly forecast the asymmetric power his blasting powder would give industrial engineers, enabling a small group of workers to burrow a tunnel through a mountain with unprecedented ease. What he failed to anticipate was that those same powers would enable isolated bands of radicals to challenge some of the most powerful people and institutions in the world. And dynamite became more than just a force multiplier for the anarchists and other radicals; Nobel's invention was elevated to a symbol of the movement itself, a rallying cry. "The voice of dynamite is the voice of force, the only voice which tyranny has ever been able to understand," the American labor activist Lucy Parsons declared. "A girdle of dynamite encircles the world, not only the old but the new," the German American anarchist Johann Most wrote a few months after Alexander II's death. "The bloody band of tyrants are dancing on the surface of a volcano. There is dynamite in England, France, Germany, Russia, Italy, Spain, New York, and Canada." Almost every new technology that succeeds in finding a wide audience turns out to have unintended consequences in the long run, new uses or secondary effects that its creator never dreamed of. But the reinvention of dynamite as a terrorist weapon—indeed, as the very origin point of terrorism itself—ranks high in the canon of unanticipated uses of new innovations. Conceived as a tool for engineers intent on building a new industrial age, dynamite ultimately helped empower a movement intent on destroying the very institutions and social structures that made industrialization possible.

* * *

The Catherine Canal assassination shaped the future course of the anarchist movement in another crucial way, though this specific causal chain would take many years to become visible. Alexander II's relatively tolerant regime had allowed many Jewish families to migrate out of the Pale of Settlement—a region that stretched from the Baltic to the Black Sea, where Russian Jews had been forced to settle for more than a century. (The region includes modern-day Lithuania, Belarus, and parts of Poland and Ukraine.) In the 1870s, as part of that migration, two Jewish families had moved to Saint Petersburg in pursuit of a better life in the sprawling metropolis. The patriarch of one family was a prosperous leather merchant from Vilnius whose business quickly thrived in the capital city. The family soon acquired a country house in one of the suburbs of Saint Petersburg and hired private tutors to educate their children. The other family did not have it so easy. After an unsuccessful stint running a village inn in Lithuania, they moved to Saint Petersburg as well, where the father tried his hand at a series of failed businesses while the children worked in garment shops and other urban trades, in lieu of attending school.

Despite their economic differences, the two families had one crucial common denominator: they each had a precocious younger child—one a boy, the other a girl—who happened to be on the edge of adolescence in the spring of 1881, when Sofia Perovskaya's plot finally took the life of the Russian czar. Though the two children didn't know each other at the time, they were each captivated by the events and followed the trial of the five conspirators with a compulsive interest, pulled in by the drama of their martyrdom. Their parents rightly assessed that the death of the "liberator czar"—and the ascent of his reactionary son—would be bad news for Russian Jews. But for the children, there was something in the doomed conviction of the People's Will that stirred them. When the girl learned of the execution, she felt a "mysterious compassion" for the five radicals, and "wept bitterly over their fate."

The execution in Semenovsky Square marked the high-water point of a stretch of Russia's history when, as the girl would write many years later, "everything . . . was being torn from its old moorings, and the seeds for a new conception of human society—political, religious, moral, economic and social—were being planted." To be young in Saint Petersburg in the 1870s and early '80s was not unlike being a Beat poet in North Beach or a folk singer in Greenwich Village in the early 1960s. A generational movement was under way, a new vision of social change—but its icons were not musicians or poets but rather people who were willing to blow themselves up in the proximity of other, more powerful people. It was that radical spirit—the willingness to do anything for the cause of progress, even die for it—that initially captivated those two adolescents in Saint Petersburg. The propaganda of the deed had fallen on deaf ears among the agrarian poor of Russia's hinterlands. But the dynamite blast that killed the czar awakened something in young Alexander Berkman and Emma Goldman that would continue to animate them for the rest of their intertwined lives.

CHAPTER 7

The Reaper Works

When it was first constructed in the early 1870s, the McCormick Reaper Manufactory—an immense four-story structure sprawling over twenty acres along the south branch of the Chicago River—was heralded as one of the largest factories in the world. Approached from the farmland west of the city, the Reaper Works, as it was often called, loomed over the prairie like a mirage, a foreboding industrial behemoth improbably transported from Manchester or Birmingham and deposited amid the amber grain of the American heartland. The contrast was fitting, in a way: the original invention that generated the capital to build the factory had also helped generate the Midwest's agricultural economy. Three decades before construction began on the Reaper Works, an enterprising Virginia farmer named Cyrus McCormick had invented the mechanical reaper, an ingenious device that dramatically increased efficiency in cutting and threshing grain. Replacing human harvesters with McCormick's sled-like contraption, which housed a rotating blade and mechanical arms to gather the cut stalks, doubled the productivity of working farms. The prairies of the Great Plains were blessed with soil and climate well suited for the mass production of grain. But it was the mechanical reaper that made that production profitable.

Unlike most breakthrough innovations of the period, McCormick's reaper did not depend on fossil fuels as a source of energy, relying instead on old-fashioned horsepower. But *manufacturing* the devices—particularly after the demand for them surged during the westward expansion of the 1850s—required industrial-age processes and energy sources, all of which were on ample display at the Reaper Works, with its iron foundries and blast furnaces and engine rooms. In its early years, the McCormick plant operated as a kind of hybrid of industrial factory and craftsman's workshop, with little in the way of automated production or assembly lines. The iron molders who fabricated most of the harvester's essential parts were skilled workers, all of them members of a trade union, with years of experience working molten metal into precise shapes.

The conditions were straight out of Dickens's *Hard Times*: twelve-hour workdays, six-day workweeks, all conducted in a sweltering environment thick with pollutants. And the work was almost unimaginably dangerous. Because the new factories were entirely unregulated, we have very few accurate statistics on workplace safety in the late 1800s. Major fires or explosions would be reported in the local press, but the daily stream of accidental maimings—and even loss of life—would rarely make the news. But the indirect evidence suggests that the (grim) Reaper Works was aptly named. In the early 1900s, muckraker William Hard conducted an analysis of a Chicago steelworks not far from the McCormick factory. Based on public data released by the company, Hard estimated that the factory averaged almost four serious injuries or deaths *per day*. And that level of carnage was what remained after the passage of a number of occupational safety reforms in the late 1800s—the death rate at the McCormick factory in the 1870s might well have been higher. Hard published his findings in a fittingly incendiary essay called "Making Steel and Killing Men":

> Here, then, is the record of one American industrial establishment for one year! It is not an establishment that enjoys any pre-

eminence in heartlessness . . . The plant in South Chicago is just an American plant, conducted according to American ideals. Its officials are men whom one is glad to meet and proud to know. And yet in the course of one year in their plant, they had at least 1,200 accidents that resulted in the physical injury, the physical agony, of human beings. Must we continue to pay this price for the honor of leading the world in the cheap and rapid production of steel and iron . . . or could we strike a better bargain if we were shrewder and more careful?

Despite the long hours and the serious risk of death or dismemberment, the iron molders and other skilled craftsmen at least enjoyed relatively high wages in the early years of the Reaper Works, given how indispensable their skills were to the business. But after the death of Cyrus McCormick in 1884, control of the firm transferred to his twenty-five-year-old son, Cyrus, Jr., who made it his mission to replace the handcrafted labor of the molders with the new "American system" of manufacturing, built around single-purpose machines that output standardized parts, the forerunner of the assembly line systems that would become ubiquitous in the coming decades. The younger McCormick's reforms almost immediately bore fruit: productivity jumped 40 percent, and the firm's dependence on high-priced skilled labor dropped precipitously. Emboldened by his success, McCormick announced that he was cutting the wages of the iron molders, who promptly went on strike. There were only ninety of them in total—a small fraction of the thousands employed at the factory—but without their molds the entire production system ground to a halt.

Undeterred, McCormick built a small barracks inside the factory to house a cohort of nonunion laborers to run the foundries. And he hired the Pinkerton National Detective Agency to protect the new workers—at least from the strikers, if not from the furnaces.

* * *

The Pinkerton agency had itself gone through a generational transfer of power with the death of Allan Pinkerton in 1884; his two sons, Robert and William, who had been effectively running the business for several years before their father's death, had expanded the agency's role as hired guns for Big Capital. ("Since the death of the elder Pinkerton," one reporter noted, "the organization has increased in strength and efficiency until at present it is recognized as the great private resource by large corporations for the protection of lives and property in times of stress and storm.") At the Reaper Works, McCormick's initial deployment of the Pinkerton forces ended in abject chaos, as striking workers who had effectively laid siege to the factory surrounded a horse-drawn bus filled with Pinkertons, who briefly opened fire on the strikers before fleeing the property.

McCormick then shifted gears and decided to rely more on the Pinkerton expertise at undercover operations; working with other industrialists in the city, he recruited a handful of agents to infiltrate the thriving socialist and anarchist communities in Chicago, at that point the epicenter of America's increasingly vocal labor movement, which had recently begun to rally around the cause of the eight-hour workday. After another clash erupted between striking workers and Chicago police at the Reaper Works in May of 1886, anarchist groups organized a rally at the city's Haymarket Square as a memorial for the strikers killed by the police. Two thousand workers gathered to hear speeches by anarchist leaders August Spies and Albert Parsons. When the police moved in to break up the rally, an unseen assailant tossed a dynamite bomb at the officers, killing one immediately and maiming several others. Gunfire erupted; by the time the mêlée ended, seven officers were dead, along with at least four protestors. As many as a hundred others were injured in the riot.

The Haymarket Affair sparked an immediate crackdown against

the radical groups; Parsons and Spies were both arrested, along with
six others, and accused of being accessories to the murder of the officer killed by the bomb. During the trial, key evidence was supplied
by the lead Pinkerton undercover agent, Andrew C. Johnson, who
claimed firsthand knowledge of the anarchists' murderous plot. In
response, Albert Parsons denounced the Pinkertons as "a private
army . . . at the command and control of those who grind the faces of
the poor, who keep wages down to the starvation point." In the end,
the jury sided with Johnson, and all eight were condemned to death.
Four of them—including both Spies and Parsons—were executed,
despite the fact that no evidence ever directly connected them to the
infernal machine that had exploded during the rally. A fifth condemned prisoner committed suicide the night before the executions,
detonating a dynamite blasting cap with his teeth in his prison cell.

Two hundred miles east of Chicago, in Rochester, New York, a
teenage Emma Goldman devoured news of the Haymarket Affair
and its aftermath: the valiant struggle for an eight-hour workday;
the calumny of the Pinkerton men; the willingness of the state to
execute those who dared to challenge the brutality of the factory
system.

Goldman had arrived in America as part of the wave of Russian
Jews who departed after the assassination of Alexander II. The new
czar had tacitly encouraged the pogroms that swept across southern
Russia in the summer of 1881; the notorious May Laws of 1882
reinstated many of the occupational and education restrictions on
the Jewish population that Alexander II had lifted. After clashing
repeatedly with her conservative father, whose appalling track record as a businessman grew even worse with the new restraints placed
on Jewish commercial activity, the headstrong Goldman had immigrated to America in 1885, joining two of her sisters in the con-

servative manufacturing hub of Rochester, which had in recent decades developed a small but prosperous Jewish community—though mostly émigrés from Germany, not Russia.

Goldman floundered in the backwaters of Upstate New York, working as a seamstress and suffering through a loveless and short-lived marriage. Her first real intellectual escape from the dreary reality of Rochester lay in reading the news reports from Chicago in the spring of 1886, which reawakened the "mysterious compassion" she had felt as a young adolescent for the Perovskaya gang back in Saint Petersburg. Only, now, the feeling was closer to a righteous outrage. She surreptitiously read copies of Johann Most's *Freiheit*, the fiery anarchist newspaper published out of New York, to follow its coverage of the state's case against the radicals. "It seemed lava shooting forth flames of ridicule, scorn, and defiance," she wrote. "It breathed deep hatred of the powers that were preparing the crime in

Emma Goldman, 1886

Chicago." Furtively, Goldman consumed "every word about anarchism I could, every word about the men, their lives, their work . . . I saw a new world opening before me."

Looking back from the vantage point of the twenty-first century, imagining the horrors of those twelve-hour workdays in the Reaper Works, it is not hard to empathize with those "flames of ridicule, scorn, and defiance" that so moved young Emma Goldman. The forces unleashed by industrialization had been devastating, compelling massive numbers of human beings into intolerable working conditions; those who dared ask for an eight-hour workday were summarily fired, or shot down by the Pinkertons, or left hanging from a noose. Wherever industrialization put down roots, life expectancy declined, to say nothing of quality of life. And yet those same forces had, in just a few generations, allowed a handful of Gilded Age tycoons to amass an astonishing amount of wealth, rivaling the fortunes of today's Silicon Valley titans. Economic inequality was not a new phenomenon, of course; Goldman had seen plenty of it in czarist Russia. But there was something uniquely offensive about the wealth creation of the industrial era: the very conditions that made life in the Reaper Works so deadly were directly responsible for the wealth accumulating in the coffers of the McCormicks and the Vanderbilts and the Carnegies. Something about that system seemed monstrously unjust. While it was possible to imagine reforming that system incrementally—breaking up the trusts, passing labor laws, inventing new institutions to regulate workplace safety—it was also reasonable to look at the state of things and conclude that the system was fatally flawed, that it required radical reinvention.

Goldman's righteous sense that *something had to be done* to combat the violence and injustice of the factory system was shared by many. What exactly *was* to be done was a more vexing question. In 1886, as Goldman devoured the reports from Chicago and waited by the mailbox for her issues of the *Freiheit*, the answer wasn't yet entirely clear for the anarchist movement. (Some argue it never did become clear.) There was at least one point of consensus among the anarchists: whatever the utopia would turn out to be, it would not be oriented around a centralized government—or any top-down form of authority. But how a "society without a state," as Pierre Clastres would later call it in his seminal work of anthropology from the 1960s, would actually function was not exactly settled science. There were many open questions. Would there be private property? Would there be organizations at all? Artful deferrals abounded. "The economic change which will result from the Social Revolution will be so immense and so profound," Kropotkin wrote at one point, "it is impossible for one or any individual to elaborate the different social forms, which must spring up in the society of the future."

That kind of eloquent hedge would become a familiar line—Goldman and Berkman would deliver numerous variations of it over the course of their public lives—but the truth is that Kropotkin did more than anyone to put specifics on the anarchist proposal. He had seen the power of worker cooperatives among the indigenous people of Siberia. He had spent a fateful period of his life—the years leading up to the assassination of Alexander II—in the Jura mountains of Switzerland, living among arguably the most dynamic anarchist community in all of Europe: a cooperative of skilled watchmakers that had chosen to spread the vision of radical change not through "the propaganda of the deed" but rather through "the propaganda of work," demonstrating that a better life was possible through their productivity and the artistry of their creations.

In Jura, Kropotkin began compiling ideas that would eventually be published in 1892 in his book *The Conquest of Bread,* where he put forth a utopian vision of a world organized around small collectives of pooled expertise: a world run by local guilds, in a phrase. That you could sustain the basic needs of *Homo sapiens* through local collectives was self-evident; humans had survived in looser arrangements for millions of years. But what Kropotkin realized in Switzerland was that cooperatives could also produce the nicer things in life. Science, art, technology—all could thrive in a properly anarchist society. Only hierarchy would suffer.

It is conventional wisdom—in the United States, at least—to say that we live in an unusually polarized political climate today. But measured against the landscape Emma Goldman and Alexander Berkman encountered as young adults, even the much-lamented divisions of the Trump era look far less severe. The polar opposites might be *louder* now—thanks to the amplifiers of social media and cable news—but they sit on a much smaller globe of political possibility. Berkman and Goldman were living in a world where one side of the spectrum thought it was appropriate to execute people who objected to a seventy-two-hour week of life-threatening work—while the other side of the spectrum thought that we should abandon both governments and corporations and reinvent society along the lines of Swiss watchmaking collectives. Those were the distant poles of the debate. What we would now call the Overton window—the space of potentially valid political beliefs—was far wider than anything in American politics today.

Less than a year after the executions of the Haymarket protestors, Alexander Berkman made his own passage across the Atlantic from Russia. Berkman's father—the well-to-do merchant—had died in 1882, followed a few years later by his mother. Berkman, too, had begun reading widely in the anarchist tradition, devouring Proudhon and Bakunin, styling himself after Rakhmetov, the radical hero of *What Is to Be Done?* Orphaned at the age of sixteen, he moved in with a good-natured but excessively conciliatory uncle—"anxious to preserve order and avoid hassles"—who was gamely abiding by the deeply antisemitic restrictions of the new regime. Increasingly frustrated by his uncle's appeasement, Berkman sailed to the United States from Hamburg in 1888. He landed at Castle Garden at the tip of Manhattan—the entry point for immigrants that preceded Ellis Island—on February 17. "I did not know a single soul in the whole country," he would later recall, "but I looked upon the New World as the promised land of Liberty and Justice, and I was happy

Alexander Berkman, 1892

to have at last escaped from the tyranny of the Romanoffs."

Berkman found a room to let on Manhattan's Lower East Side, where so many new arrivals had washed ashore during the waves of nineteenth-century immigration. Despite his classical education and bourgeois upbringing, he had arrived in New York with almost no knowledge of English and sixty rubles to his name. He took on a series of odd jobs—cigar maker, printer, garment worker—comforting himself with the notion that his decline in economic status meant that he was at least enjoying "the full manhood conferred by the dignity of labor."

A few months after Berkman's entry into the United States at Castle Garden, Emma Goldman decided to give up on Rochester—and her family—for good, casting them off, as she wrote, "like a worn-out garment." She was twenty, just two years older than Berkman had been when he had first set foot in Manhattan. She, too, had made her way to the metropolis friendless, fortified only by "youth, good health, and a passionate ideal," as she put it.

Early in the morning of August 15, 1889, Goldman took the West Shore Railroad from Rochester, transferring to the Weehawken ferry to cross the Hudson just after dawn. In her possession she had five dollars, a sewing machine—and the address of Johann Most's newspaper, the *Freiheit*.

CHAPTER 8

Comrades

A line of thunderstorms had passed through the city overnight; the air was still cool and inviting as Goldman stepped off the Wee-hawken ferry at the far edges of West Forty-second Street. A hazy summer sun rose over Midtown's low-slung skyline. Although the massive influx of immigrants had made New York the second largest city in the world, with a population of roughly three million, the metropolis had not yet embraced the vertical drama that would come to define it in the next century. At 281 feet, Trinity Church, off Wall Street, was still Manhattan's tallest structure. Most of the Midtown buildings that sprawled in front of Goldman topped out at five or six stories, their growth stunted by the fact that mechanical elevators and steel-framed construction had only recently been invented.

Goldman's first stop was a photo gallery on the Bowery, run by an aunt and uncle she barely knew. Almost entirely ignorant of the city's basic geography, she blithely assumed that walking from West Midtown to the Lower East Side was a reasonable journey on an increasingly warm August day in Manhattan. (In fact, it was a fifty-block walk through some of the most densely populated neighbor-hoods on the planet.) Goldman herself offers the best description of what ensued in her memoirs:

> After receiving many directions and misdirections and making frequent stops at bewildering intersections, I landed in three

hours at the photographic gallery of my aunt and uncle. Tired and hot, I did not at first notice the consternation of my relatives at my unexpected arrival. They asked me to make myself at home, gave me breakfast, and then plied me with questions. Why did I come to New York? Had I definitely broken with my husband? Did I have money? What did I intend to do? I was told that I could, of course, stay with them. "Where else could you go, a young woman alone in New York?" Certainly, but I would have to look for a job immediately. Business was bad, and the cost of living high. I heard it all as if in a stupor.

Overwhelmed by the "prattling, chilling" tone of their questions, Goldman concocted a story about an old friend living on Henry Street who had invited her to stay, and abruptly walked out on the aghast aunt and uncle. In actuality, the old friend was more of a casual acquaintance, a twenty-five-year-old anarchist named Hillel Solotaroff who Goldman had briefly chatted with after attending one of his lectures in New Haven the year before. Solotaroff proved to be more welcoming than her relatives, offering up his room in the apartment he shared with his parents and brother, and promising her that'd she have no trouble finding a more permanent base in the city. And he claimed to know the perfect establishment to celebrate her new life in Lower Manhattan: Sachs's Café, a two-room establishment on Suffolk Street that served as the central hub of the Jewish anarchist movement.

For most of the nineteenth century, the stretch of Manhattan jutting out into the East River had been known as *Kleindeutschland*—or Little Germany—thanks to the large number of German immigrants that settled there. (For many years, only Berlin and Vienna had more German-speaking residents than New York.) But by the time Goldman arrived, more than two-thirds of the residents of the Tenth Ward, the handful of blocks east of the Bowery and north of

Canal Street, were Russian Jews—crammed into aging row houses that had been subdivided into tenement apartments with ghastly sanitary conditions. Most lacked indoor plumbing, relying instead on outdoor privies in the courtyards between buildings, often shared by hundreds of residents.

A few months after Goldman's arrival in the city, the muckraking journalist Jacob Riis would publish the first installments of his photographic essay *How the Other Half Lives*, documenting the squalor and misery of Manhattan's slums, ultimately triggering a reform movement that would greatly improve living conditions for the city's low-income immigrant residents. But in August of 1889, the reality of life on the Lower East Side was an almost intolerable crowding of human beings into an aging urban infrastructure barely able to support them. The *Times* described it in 1893 as "the eyesore of New York and perhaps the filthiest place on the Western Continent." In modern-day Manhattan, where residences can be efficiently stacked upward in vertical skyscrapers, the average population density is roughly one hundred people per acre. When Emma Goldman first strolled through the streets of the Tenth Ward, on her way to Sachs's Café, the low-rise buildings around her somehow accommodated a population density five times greater than that.

The new residents of the Lower East Side compensated for their cramped living quarters by pouring out onto the streets. Cars were still decades away, and trolleys only ran on central thoroughfares, which meant pedestrian traffic truly dominated the side streets above Canal. For Goldman, the most noticeable departure from Rochester's downtown blocks—beyond the sheer number of people swarming the streets—was the mêlée of activity around the portable wagons lining the sidewalks. The pushcarts—which would survive as an emblem of New York's street culture until Mayor Fiorello La Guardia finally banned them in 1938—were yet another legacy of czarist Russia: thanks to restrictions on Jews owning or renting property, street peddling had been a common practice in the old country. In Manhattan, the vendors set up shop on the sidewalk curb on each side of the street, leaving a narrow passageway down the center for horse-drawn carriages. Entirely unregulated by the city, the mobile entrepreneurs sold a staggering variety of goods, as Riis describes in *How the Other Half Lives*:

> There is scarcely anything else that can be hawked from a wagon that is not to be found, and at ridiculously low prices. Bandanas and tin cups at two cents, peaches at a cent a quart, "damaged" eggs for a song . . . The crowds that jostle each other at the wagons and about the sidewalk shops, where a gutter plank on two ash-barrels does the duty for a counter! Pushing, struggling, babbling, and shouting in foreign tongues, a veritable Babel of confusion.

The cacophony that greeted Goldman and Solotaroff when they finally entered Sachs's Café did not offer much relief from the tumult of the sidewalk. ("It was certainly not very soothing," she wrote.) Patrons were packed into every inch of the café's two rooms, all of them seemingly in a heated discussion with their companions, bouncing back and forth between Russian and Yiddish. Almost immediately, Solotaroff found two friends of his at a table, a pair of sisters by the name of Minkin, roughly Goldman's age—also recent immigrants from Russia. After a few minutes of friendly chatter and a little prompting from Solotaroff, the sisters invited Goldman to stay with them in the two-room apartment they shared with their father. Goldman could feel the anxiety and sensory overload of her Manhattan immersion begin to subside: "I had a roof over my head; I had found friends. The bedlam at Sachs's no longer mattered. I began to breathe freer, to feel less of an alien."

The bedlam continued, nonetheless. At one point, a nearby patron interrupted Goldman's conversation with her new roommates, bellowing to the staff: "Extra-large steak! Extra cup of coffee!"

"Who is that glutton?" Goldman asked Solotaroff derisively.

"That is Alexander Berkman," Solotaroff replied, laughing. "He can eat for three. But he rarely has enough money for much food. When he has, he eats Sachs out of his supplies. I'll introduce him to you." Within minutes, Berkman was seated at their table. "He was no more than a boy, hardly eighteen, but with the neck and chest of a giant," Goldman recalled. "His jaw was strong, made more pronounced by his thick lips. His face was almost severe, but for his high, studious forehead and intelligent eyes." Berkman, on his part, found Goldman "well-knit, with the ruddy vigor of youth," conveying "an atmosphere of strength and vitality."

They were two people on the edge of adulthood—one of them still a teenager—cast out of Russia by deep historical forces, stumbling into an encounter in a café on the other side of the planet, about to embark on a decades-long relationship that would ultimately bring them back to their homeland, in a different kind of exile. Goldman called Berkman "comrade," and the sound of the word on her lips thrilled him. "She is one of us," he thought.

Johann Most was speaking that night, just around the corner. Goldman had been planning on making her pilgrimage to Most's *Freiheit* offices in the coming days. But now, just hours after stepping off the Weehawken ferry, her new comrades were ushering her off to see Most in his true element: on stage, thundering against the order of things. Goldman would remember the moment for the rest of her days. It felt like "something wonderful was about to happen, something that would decide the whole course of my life."

They settled the bill at Sachs's and marched back out into the wild streets. Goldman lost her footing at one point; Berkman deftly grabbed her and prevented a fall.

"I have saved your life," Berkman joked.

"I hope I may be able to save yours someday," she replied.

Most was speaking in a meeting hall situated behind a saloon. The overwhelming majority of the attendees were Germans, like Most himself. Goldman could barely make out the stage through the haze of tobacco smoke; the room buzzed with intense conversation, only quieting after Most leapt onto the stage and began denouncing the corruption and brutality of the American capitalist system. "My first impression of him was one of revulsion," Goldman wrote. "He was of medium height, with a large head crowned with greyish bushy hair; but his face was twisted out of form by an apparent dislocation of the left jaw. Only his eyes were soothing; they were blue and sympathetic." Most turned his focus to the Haymarket Affair, and the executions that had transformed Goldman into a committed radical. Her initial revulsion dissipated as she listened. "He seemed transformed into some primitive power, radiating hatred and love, strength and inspiration," she wrote. "The rapid current of his speech, the music of his voice, and his sparkling wit, all combined to produce an effect almost overwhelming. He stirred me to my depths."

After the speech, Berkman brought Goldman to the edge of the dais and introduced her to Most. She found herself uncharacteristically bashful in the presence of such a legend, and merely mumbled a quiet hello and turned away. Her subsequent encounters with Johann Most onstage in Lower Manhattan would not be so mild mannered.

New arrivals in Gotham usually struggle for months to get their bearings. Emma Goldman had no such trouble. On her very first day in Manhattan, she had managed to meet both Berkman and

Most, arguably the two people—along with Peter Kropotkin—who would have the largest impact on her ideas and her actions over the subsequent decades.

By the end of her first week in the city, she had fallen into a thrilling routine. Berkman took her to the *Freiheit* offices, where Most offered her a part-time job handling the mailing list for the publication. After attending one of Solotaroff's lectures on Orchard Street, Berkman introduced her to his friend Modska Aronstam, who went by the nickname Fedya, who was a sensitive illustrator with delicate features and a "dreamy expression" in his eyes. Berkman teased him mercilessly about his penchant for aesthetic pleasures. ("If I'd let him, he'd spend all his money on useless things—'beautiful,' he calls them.") Later that week, Fedya took her to Central Park, strolling past the ornate mansions of the industrial magnates that had just begun to sprout along Fifth Avenue, many of them owned by the Vanderbilt clan: the gothic "petite château" built by William K. Vanderbilt, its stones imported from a quarry in France; the Triple Palace constructed by William's father for his daughters, which had required sixty European sculptors to design the building's façades and interior ornamentation.

Staring up at the stone-and-glass edifices of Millionaire's Row, Goldman pointed out the scandalous contrast between the Midtown mansions and the tenement squalor just a few dozen blocks to the south. "Yes, it is a crime that the few should have all, the many nothing," Fedya said, then added: "My main objection is that they have such bad taste—those buildings are ugly."

One night, after a long day in the harried, ramshackle offices of the *Freiheit*, Most invited Goldman out for dinner at a restaurant called the Terrace Garden. He ordered an expensive white wine from the Rheinhessen region in Germany, which prompted Goldman to confess that she'd never tasted wine before. Most burst into laughter and offered a toast to the "young, naïve lady"—and then proceeded to drain the bottle and order a second before Goldman had finished her initial glass. Under the influence, Most seemed to soften in Goldman's impression of him: "He was a gracious host, an attentive and sympathetic friend," she wrote. She told the story of her failed marriage in Rochester, and her conversion to the cause after the Haymarket tragedy.

"The path of anarchism is steep and painful," Most warned. "So many have attempted to climb it and have fallen back. The price is exacting. Few men are ready to pay it, most women not at all."

Goldman's mind flashed back to Sofia Perovskaya and the other prominent women in the Russian anarchist tradition. She asked Most if there was any equivalent in the American movement. Most shrugged dismissively—"None at all, only stupids"—but then offered the possibility that Goldman's Russian roots might make her the exception. "There is great need in our ranks of young, willing people—ardent ones, as you seem to be," he said, adding plaintively, "and I have need of ardent friendship."

When Berkman learned of the dinner the next day while paying a visit to Goldman at her flat, he erupted in what seemed almost like a fit of jealousy. "Most has no right to squander money, to go to expensive restaurants, drink expensive wines," he said, scowling. "He is spending the money contributed for the movement. He should be held to account." He stormed out without saying goodbye. For a week, she heard nothing from Berkman and assumed that she had traversed some unspoken line in dining with Most that had caused him to lose interest in her. And then he surfaced out of the blue—seemingly having forgotten about the Most dispute entirely—inviting her to a picnic in Brooklyn's Prospect Park, which Berkman favored over the formal esplanades and gardens of Central Park. It was, he explained, "less cultivated, more natural."

Strolling through the Long Meadow—the ribbon of greenway that runs alongside the western edge of the park—the conversation turned to matters of the heart; Goldman recounted the excruciating story of her ex-husband back in Rochester. In time, they found a private spot to eat in the shade of the old-growth oaks and sweet gums that bordered the meadow. Goldman confessed to Berkman—whom she had begun calling Sasha, the diminutive form of Alexander—that her failed marriage had left her jaded about the institution itself. "If ever I love a man again, I will give myself to him without being bound by the rabbi or the law," she vowed, "and when that love dies, I will leave without permission." They were scandalous values for a woman to hold in the late 1800s, much less give voice to, but Berkman received them approvingly. The genuine revolutionaries, he noted, had all rid themselves of the shackles of institutional marriage.

The talk of romantic love and the revolution brought the conversation back to their roots in Russia. Berkman recounted the story of Sofia Perovskaya's final days: with her lover, Zhelyabov, imprisoned after the assassination, she had chosen to surrender so that Zhelyabov would face the executioners with his true love at his side. Once again, the shadow of Alexander II's death loomed over the pair as they lay on the grass in a Brooklyn glade, five thousand miles from Saint Petersburg. For Berkman, Perovskaya's surrender was a cautionary tale. "Of course, it was wrong of her to be moved by personal sentiment," he explained. "Her love for the Cause should have urged her to live for other activities." Goldman fought back: to die alongside your partner in the name of revolution was beautiful, she said—even sublime.

Berkman teased that she was too sentimental for the cause. The task before them was hard, he said, and they must become hard.

For a time, though, life in Manhattan was anything but hard, despite the poverty and the crowds and the appalling sanitation. Most took on Goldman as a protégée, suggesting that she could become a powerful orator herself if she put her mind to it. Berkman worked as a typesetter for the *Freiheit,* while Goldman supplemented her labor at the magazine by doing piecework with her sewing machine, repairing shirtwaists and frocks. The two young immigrants began a passionate affair and moved uptown to a four-room flat on Forty-second Street with Aronstam and one of the Minkin sisters. There they lived what seems to have been a young bohemian's dream:

> From the very first we agreed to share everything, to live like real comrades. Helen [Minkin] continued to work in the corset factory, and I divided my time between sewing silk waists and keeping house. Fedya devoted himself to painting. The expense of his oils, canvases, and brushes often consumed more than we could afford, but it never occurred to any one of us to complain. From time to time he would sell a picture to some dealer for fifteen or twenty-five dollars, whereupon he would bring an armful of flowers or some present for me. Sasha would up braid him for it: the idea of spending money for such things, when the movement needed it so badly, was intolerable to him. His anger had no effect on Fedya. He would laugh it off, call him a fanatic, and say he had no sense of beauty.

Goldman began posing in the nude for Aronstam's sketches, and out of those encounters a sexual relationship blossomed between the two. Berkman did his best to resist his possessive urges, considering them to be an unnatural artifact of living in a culture dominated by the religion of private property. ("I believe in your freedom to love," Berkman told her.) In time, Goldman also found herself romantically entangled with Johann Most, twenty-three years her senior, who turned out to have the most traditional sexual values of the bunch, expressing his displeasure at Goldman's ongoing relationships with her roommates up on Forty-second Street and hinting that she should settle down and become his wife. (Unsurprisingly, Goldman bristled at both suggestions.) Despite the emotional conflicts, Most helped to arrange an eight-day speaking tour for Goldman—a remarkably ambitious career move for a twenty-year-old seamstress with a limited formal education. She traveled back to Rochester to deliver her first speech, on the emerging struggle for the eight-hour workday; onstage she found herself in a semi-hallucinatory state, the words flowing out with an unbridled intensity. ("The audience had vanished, the hall itself had disappeared, I was conscious only of my own words, of my ecstatic song.") The applause at the end thrilled her, until one audience member noted that in her rapture, she had forgotten to mention anything about the eight-hour workday campaign.

Eventually, though, the grind of New York City living caught up with the group. Berkman had a falling-out with Most over ideological matters and lost his job at the *Freiheit*; he struggled to find regular work and ended up sewing sweaters with Goldman to pay the bills, often working eighteen-hour days. Aronstam, too, had been having a difficult time covering his portion of the rent through his work as a freelance illustrator. In late 1891, he left the city to take a job at a photography studio in Springfield, Massachusetts; disenchanted with life in the big city, Berkman and Goldman soon followed. For a time, they slept together in a single room studio. Conditions became so grim that they contemplated returning to Russia. But after moving to the Jewish section of Worcester, about fifty miles east of Springfield, Berkman and Goldman leased a vacant storefront and, improbably enough, the two radicals decided to open a luncheonette and ice cream parlor.

Goldman prepared sandwiches and fried pancakes in the small kitchen; Berkman waited tables and worked the soda machine the two had purchased. The business flourished; before long, Aronstam had abandoned most of his photography and illustration work and joined them, waiting tables and helping Goldman at the grill.

The idyll in Worcester was by all accounts an untroubled, agreeable stretch for the three of them. They fell into the simple routines of the restaurant trade, attracting a regular set of patrons and easily covering the rent each month with the luncheonette's profits. It is possible, even, to imagine the three Russians putting down roots in Massachusetts, far from the metropolitan hub of New York, and living out the rest of their days selling soda pop and ice cream to the locals.

But that peaceful future minding the luncheonette did not come to pass, for a simple reason: Alexander Berkman decided he needed to assassinate one of the most powerful men in America.

PART TWO

Blasting Cap

1892–1913

The Pivot Around
Which the Story Is Written

Late in the evening of July 5, 1892, three hundred men armed with Winchester rifles boarded two barges anchored off of Davis Island, a few miles north of downtown Pittsburgh. Pulled by tugboats, the barges floated downriver under cover of darkness, stealthily making their way toward the Homestead Steel Works on the banks of the Monongahela River, which had been seized five days before by striking members of the Amalgamated Association of Iron and Steel Workers, after almost six months of contentious contract negotiations. Technically, the men huddled together in silence on the barges were in the employ of the Pinkerton National Detective Agency, but in actuality, they were working for Henry Clay Frick, the forty-two-year-old industrialist and chairman of the Carnegie Steel Company. While Andrew Carnegie liked to consider himself a friend to the working man, Frick was notorious for his anti-union attitudes. (He was equally notorious for having had a hand in the tragic Johnstown Flood of 1889, caused by failure of an earthen dam that had been improperly maintained by Frick's fishing club.) Enraged by the prolonged strike at Homestead, Frick had hired the Pinkertons and personally overseen the plans for the midnight assault.

The clash between the Pinkerton guards and the striking workers had been months in the making. Historically, wages at the

Homestead plant had operated on a sliding scale, rising and falling with the market price of steel itself. With its contract up for renegotiation, the union had asked for increased wages to reflect the enormous profits that Carnegie was making out of its near monopoly over the steel business. As Goldman described it many years later in her memoirs: "The philanthropic Andrew Carnegie conveniently retired to his castle in Scotland, and Frick took full charge of the situation. He declared that henceforth the sliding scale would be abolished. The company would make no more agreements with the Amalgamated Association; it would itself determine the wages to be paid. In fact, he would not recognize the union at all."

When the AA resisted those terms, the Homestead site quickly became the epicenter of the most closely followed labor dispute in the United States, with front-page stories running in papers around the country, recounting the latest twists in the negotiations. "Far away from the scene of the impending struggle, in our little ice-cream parlor in Worcester," Goldman wrote, "we eagerly followed developments. To us it sounded the awakening of the American worker, the long-awaited day of his resurrection."

In late June, contract negotiations collapsed, and Frick evicted the union workers from the steel plant, which he had fortified with a fence topped with barbed wire. Towers were built on the periphery of the factory to house snipers and searchlights. News of the eviction shook the three anarchists in Worcester out of their domestic reverie. "We must go to Homestead," Berkman announced. "The great moment has come at last."

While Goldman and Berkman packed up in Worcester and drafted pamphlets in support of the strikers, Frick put in motion his plans for a naval assault on the Homestead plant. The late-night barge journey had been executed with the aim of surprising the workers encamped at Homestead. ("We think absolute secrecy essential in the movement of these men," Frick had advised the agency's leader, Robert Pinkerton.) But a network of sentries organized by the strikers caught sight of the barges before they could make their landing. By two A.M., six thousand workers—and many of their family members—lined the banks on the river, peering through the dark for signs of the invading force. When the Pinkertons finally pulled up alongside the Carnegie plant, just as dawn was about to break over the Monongahela, the strikers were waiting for them with an arsenal they had been quietly assembling for weeks: rifles, double-barreled shotguns, pocket pistols, two mounted cannons that the town of Homestead had previously employed ceremonially for parades, and a trove of dynamite sticks that they flung across the river in an attempt to sink the invading vessels. The union workers had also commandeered barrels of oil from the steel plant; some loaded a railway car with garbage and oil and set it on fire, then rolled the car down the tracks to the water to prevent the Pinkertons from disembarking; others launched a burning raft toward the barges in a futile attempt to set them ablaze. "Three times during the morning, [the Pinkertons] tried to land, but each time they were repulsed," *The New York Times* reported the next morning. "The strikers had obtained complete possession of the mill, and from behind furnaces and piles of iron they could shoot at anything that appeared over the side of the barges without danger to themselves."

When the mêlée finally subsided nearly thirteen hours later, nine of the strikers were dead, including a young boy, along with seven of the Pinkerton men. It seemed at first to be a victory for the strikers, until a squadron of Pennsylvania militiamen arrived under the command of Major General George R. Snowden, who quickly made it clear which side of the dispute he was on. "I do not recognize your association," he told the strikers. "I recognize no one but the citizens of this city. We have come here to restore law and order and they are already restored."

*The Homestead riot / drawn
by W. P. Snyder*

The Homestead Riot, like the Haymarket Riot that had so transfixed young Emma Goldman six years before, would ultimately prove to be one of the most violent exchanges in American labor history. The riot was also, in the end, a colossal failure for the workers. "After five months out on strike, they were forced to accept the company's harshest terms, including a twelve-hour day and a wage cut of almost one-half," the historians Paul and Karen Avrich write. "Pinkerton spies were installed in the mill, grievance committees were done away with, and workers' meetings were banned. Total victory, as Frick had foreseen, lay with the company. He had proved that a modern corporation, combined with the authority of the state, could destroy the strongest union in America. Not until 1936 would another union emerge in the steel industry."

Stopping over in New York en route to Pittsburgh, Berkman and Goldman read reports of the Homestead defeat in the local papers. That the attack on the strikers had been led by the Pinkertons—the traitors behind the Haymarket Riot who had so outraged the two of them in their adolescent years—made the events even more enraging. After a few moments of shocked silence, Berkman was the first to speak. "Frick is the responsible factor in this crime," he announced. "He must be made to stand the consequences." The time for an attentat was now. Berkman would do to Frick what Sofia Perovskaya and the People's Will had done to Alexander II. "A blow aimed at Frick would re-echo in the poorest hovel, would call the attention of the whole world to the real cause behind the Homestead struggle," Goldman concluded. "It would strike terror in the enemy's ranks and make them realize that the proletariat of America had its avengers."

Naturally, Berkman's first choice of weapon was dynamite. The bookish twenty-one-year-old anarchist was entirely unversed in the craft of bomb-making, but he did have one expert close at hand: Emma's old lover, Johann Most.

Six years before the Homestead strike, Most had published the pamphlet that would remain a bête noire for law enforcement agencies well into the ensuing century. As with Most's oratorical style, there was nothing subtle about the work's title: *The Science of Revolutionary Warfare—A Manual of Instruction in the Use and Preparation of Nitroglycerine, Dynamite, Gun-Cotton, Fulminating Mercury, Bombs, Fuses, Poisons, Etc., Etc.* In addition to detailed descriptions of how to concoct all manner of deadly contraptions, *The Science of Revolutionary Warfare* extolled the virtues of dynamite in language that seemed almost to belong to a department store catalog: "[Dynamite] can be carried in the pocket without danger," he explained, going on to note that it was "a formidable weapon against any force of militia, police, or detectives that may want to stifle the cry for justice that goes forth from the plundered slaves."

As they plotted the attack on Frick, Goldman and Berkman squatted in a small apartment in the East Village with an Austrian anarchist named Frank Mollock who had two young children. Following the instructions in Most's handbook, Berkman acquired the materials to make two infernal machines, working on them in the cramped flat at night, after the children had gone to bed. Bomb assembly was exceptionally dangerous work; one false move and Berkman could have obliterated an entire floor of the tenement building. It tells us something about the radical mindset of that period that Mollock would allow his houseguests to experiment with timed explosives on the kitchen table with children sleeping just a few feet away. The moral burden of the risk weighed heavily on Goldman. "I lived in dread every moment for Sasha, for our friends in the flat, the children, and the rest of the tenants." Berkman, typically, entertained fewer doubts about the righteousness of their actions. "All means are justified in the war of humanity against its enemies," he declared. "Indeed, the more repugnant the means, the stronger the test of one's nobility and devotion."

Years later, at another turning point in Alexander Berkman's life, a homemade infernal machine would accidentally explode in a New York apartment, setting in motion a chain of events that would have momentous implications for both Berkman and his adopted country. But in 1892, preparing for his attentat against Henry Clay Frick, Berkman faced a different kind of problem. He took his two bombs to a remote forest on Staten Island and attempted to detonate one of them, with no success. The test run convinced him that he could not rely on the explosive device as a weapon, thus ending his short career as a bomb manufacturer. For the rest of his life, Berkman's incendiary production was limited to words, not actual devices.

Berkman took one last trip up to Worcester, depositing most of the remaining dynamite with Aronstam. Furtively, without telling either of his comrades, he retained a small capsule of mercury fulminate for another purpose.

On the night of July 13, after a farewell dinner with a few friends, Goldman and Berkman traveled to the Baltimore and Ohio Station, where Berkman would board a night train bound for Pittsburgh. As the conductors announced the train's departure, the two young radicals embraced on the car's steps, steam swirling around them in the night air. Just two years earlier they had been strolling under the elms of Prospect Park, arguing over the conflict between romantic love and revolutionary sacrifice, rhapsodizing about Sofia Perovskaya's brave stand at the gallows in Semenovksy Square. Now they were living that drama themselves. It seemed probable that they would never see each other again. "My sailor girl, comrade," Berkman whispered, "you will be with me to the last." In the final seconds, as the train began to rumble out of the station, Goldman leapt back onto the platform. "I stood glued," she later wrote, "my arms outstretched for the precious life that was being snatched away from me."

Almost forty years later, long after Goldman and Berkman had left their adopted country behind, an American publisher interested in a biographical manuscript Goldman had submitted wrote to the now world-famous anarchist with a plea that she delete the section that addressed the events of July 1892. The acts described in Goldman's draft would scandalize readers, he warned, and would threaten her ongoing case to be readmitted to the United States. Goldman wasted no time in posting her reply:

> Dear Arthur, I appreciate deeply your interest in my autobiography and in my chances of a possible return to the States. But it will be out of the question to consider your suggestion of eliminating the story . . . There are numbers of reasons why I could not possibly do that. The principal being that my connection with Berkman's act and our relationship is the leitmotif of my forty years of life [since]. As a matter of fact it is the pivot around which my story is written. You are mistaken if you think that it was only "the humane promptings of a girlish heart" which impelled my desperate act contained in the story. It was my religiously devout belief that the end justifies all means. The end, then, was my ideal of human brotherhood. If I

have undergone any change it is not in my ideal. It is more in the
realization that a great end does not justify all means.

What were the means in question? Settled in Pittsburgh, room-
ing with a few German anarchist comrades, Berkman cased the
twenty-three-room Italianate mansion where Frick lived in the tony
suburb of Homewood but ultimately decided that the security
around the home would be too formidable for him to penetrate. He
turned his focus to the Chronicle Telegraph Building in downtown
Pittsburgh, where Carnegie Steel had its offices. Back in Manhattan, Goldman attempted unsuccessfully to raise funds from like-
minded radicals to support Berkman's mission. In a moment of
desperation, she decided to try her hand at prostitution, modeling
herself on a character from *Crime and Punishment* who walks the
streets in order to put food on the table for her impoverished brothers and sisters. "Sasha is giving his life," Goldman admonished herself, "and you shrink from giving your body, miserable coward." She
took stock of her physical assets in a mirror. "I looked tired, but my
complexion was good. I should need no make-up. My curly blond
hair showed off well with my blue eyes. Too large in the hips for my
age, I thought; I was just twenty-three. [But] I would wear a corset."
   Goldman's brief tenure as a prostitute proved to be roughly as
successful as Berkman's experiments in bomb-making. Three days
after Berkman's departure, she made her way to the red-light district around Fourteenth Street. "I felt no nervousness at first," she
recalled, "but when I looked at the passing men and saw their vul-
gar glances and their manner of approaching the women, my heart
sank." Eventually, she accepted the invitation of a well-dressed older
man with white hair and a ruddy complexion; they retired to a
nearby saloon for a beer.
   Sensing her unease, he asked: "You're a novice at this business,
aren't you?"

"Yes, this is my first time," Goldman admitted. "But how did you know?"

Goldman's "client" explained that he'd observed her hesitation on the sidewalk, and suspected that some other motivation had drawn her to the streets beyond mere "looseness or a love of excitement," as he put it.

Goldman snapped back: "Thousands of girls are driven by economic necessity!"

Seemingly unprepared for a discussion of the systemic links between sex work and urban poverty, the man slid a ten-dollar bill—roughly three hundred dollars today—across the table and told Emma that she "didn't have the knack" for prostitution. "Take this and go home," he said. "You're an awfully nice kid, but you're silly, inexperienced, childish."

Goldman bristled at the condescension but also found something appealing in her companion's demeanor. They continued their banter at the saloon. "The simplicity of his manner pleased me," she wrote in her autobiography, "I asked for his name and address so as to be able to return his ten dollars some day. But he refused to give them to me. He loved mysteries, he said." They wandered back out into the tumult of Union Square. On the lamplit sidewalk, as the carriages and trams rumbled past them, they held hands for a moment and then parted ways.

Her career as a streetwalker finished, Emma resorted to the less adventurous approach of sending a plea for fifteen dollars to her sister Helena back in Rochester, concocting a story about being ill. Helena's funds gave her a total take of twenty-five dollars (the equivalent of just under a thousand dollars today). She deducted five to cover the wardrobe expenses of playacting as a prostitute for a night and sent the remaining twenty dollars to support the cause in Pittsburgh.

It was enough for Berkman to make three crucial purchases: a new suit at the J. Kaufmann and Brother department store; a printed business card; and a Bulldog .38-caliber revolver.

Posing as an employment agent from New York, Berkman made two unsuccessful attempts to enter Frick's inner sanctum at the Chronicle Telegraph Building. But early in the afternoon of July 23, after lurking outside the building for much of the morning, Berkman caught sight of Frick returning to work after lunch. Gathering his courage, Berkman strode through the lobby a few minutes later, the revolver and a homemade dagger concealed in Kaufmann's fine apparel, and took the lift to the second floor, where Frick's offices were located. As the elevator operator cranked open the door, Berkman found himself face-to-face with his nemesis, who just happened to be walking through the hallway at that moment, headed to a meeting with Carnegie vice-chairman John Leishman. Too startled by the encounter to make his attack, Berkman hesitated for a few seconds, then quietly trailed behind Frick as he made his way toward his quarters.

There was no security visible in the reception area outside Frick's office, only an assistant whom Berkman had already encountered during one of his earlier visits. Berkman pressed his business card into the man's hand and informed him that he had returned to discuss some important business matters with Mr. Frick. As the assistant swung open the door to the office, Berkman caught another glimpse of his target, "a black-bearded, well-knit figure at a table at the back of his room."

In a matter of seconds, the assistant returned with the predictable news that Mr. Frick was engaged and could not be disturbed. Berkman made a brief feint as though leaving the executive suite, and then pivoted abruptly, charging past the man into Frick's private quarters.

* * *

The room is bathed in sunlight; for a moment, emerging out of the lamplit gloom of the reception area, Berkman is blinded. As his eyes adjust, he makes out the figures of the two men silhouetted against the midday sun streaming through the grand bow windows overlooking Fifth Avenue. Frick stands abruptly from his seat on the right side of the elegant oak table. Berkman calls out the name of his would-be victim. "The look of terror on his face strikes me speechless," Berkman will write, many years later. "It is the dread of the conscious presence of death. 'He understands,' it flashes through my mind. With a quick motion I draw the revolver."

Assuming that Frick might be wearing an armored vest, Berkman takes aim at the industrialist's head, at a twenty-foot range, and fires.

> There is a flash, and the high-ceilinged room reverberates as with the booming of cannon. I hear a sharp, piercing cry, and see Frick on his knees, his head against the arm of the chair. I feel calm and possessed, intent upon every movement of the man. He is lying head and shoulders under the large armchair, without sound or motion. "Dead?" I wonder. I must make sure.

As Berkman strides toward Frick's body, Leishman tackles him. The two men wrestle at the center of the office for a second before Berkman hears the cry "Murder! Help" coming from the suddenly not-so-lifeless body of Henry Frick. The bullet has sliced through the lobe of Frick's left ear, dug a path through his neck, and ultimately buried itself in his right shoulder. Frick is bloodied, but still alive.

Berkman fires two more shots in rapid succession. The first burrows through Frick's neck again, landing in the other shoulder. The second shot misfires. Before he can pull the trigger again, a carpenter's hammer slams into his cranium, disrupting his motor control so dramatically that he drops to the floor.

Confused voices ring in my ears. Painfully I strive to rise. The
weight of many bodies is pressing on me. Now—it's Frick's voice!
Not dead? . . . I crawl in the direction of the sound, dragging the
struggling men with me. I must get the dagger from my pocket—
I have it! Repeatedly I strike with it at the legs of the man near the
window. I hear Frick cry out in pain—there is much shouting and
stamping—my arms are pulled and twisted, and I am lifted bodily
from the floor.

Two office boys and a police officer who happened to be in front
of the Chronicle Telegraph Building when the initial shots rang out
restrain Berkman. As the would-be assassin struggles to release
himself, the officer presses his pistol against the back of Berkman's
head. Frick, bleeding profusely from both the gunshot and dagger
wounds, commands the officer to put down his weapon: "Don't kill
him. We have got him all right. Leave him to the law."

As doctors arrived to attend to Frick's injuries, an agitated crowd
drawn by the sound of gunfire gathered underneath the office's bow
window on Fifth Avenue, surging against the building's imposing
granite walls. When Berkman emerged under police custody, his
suit stained with Frick's blood, he was greeted with jeers. Frick was
taken to a back room and laid out on a sofa serving as an improvised
surgical table, where the physicians labored to extract the bullets.
While the doctors stitched his wounds, he dictated a private correspondence to Carnegie back in Scotland, assuring him that he
would survive the attack and that business would proceed as usual.
He refused to be taken to the ambulance until he had composed a
public statement as well, a message targeted directly at the strikers
back at Homestead: "This incident will not change the attitude of
the Carnegie Steel Company toward the Amalgamated Associa-

tion. I do not think I shall die, but whether I do or not, the Company will pursue the same policy and it will win."

Berkman was brought by paddy wagon to the central police station, where he was interrogated by senior members of the Pittsburgh police force. Asked to explain his motives, Berkman answered tersely: "Frick is an enemy of the working man and had to die." When asked to name his accomplices, he said simply, in slightly broken English: "I come of myself."

After the initial interrogation ended, officers ushered Berkman to the police gymnasium, where a makeshift photography studio had been set up for the then-novel practice of taking mug shots. As the photographer prepared his plates, Berkman sat on a bench in front of the camera, folding his arms with an indifferent look. One of the detectives noticed "an odd twitching of his mouth," as if he were chewing an unusually stiff wad of tobacco. Later, during a physical examination conducted by the police surgeon, the twitching grew more pronounced. A quick probe revealed that Berkman had been chewing on the one remaining piece of his bomb-making experiments: a capsule of mercury fulminate, the primary detonator used to trigger nitroglycerin explosions. In the words of one reporter's account: "the desperate wretch had deliberately attempted to add another thrilling chapter to the tragedy, by blowing off his own head while in front of the camera."

News of the attack dominated headlines around the country. "Henry Clay Frick, the executive head of the Carnegie firms, lies at his home, twice shot and twice stabbed by a Russian Hebrew Nihilist named Alexander Berkmann [*sic*], now a resident of New York," *The Pittsburgh Dispatch* announced, devoting seven of eight columns on its front page to the crime. Berkman languished in jail for two months, waiting for his trial, while Goldman suffered alone back in

New York. The *attentat* divided the radical community. Peter Kropotkin, now living in exile in London after five years in prison in France, took Berkman's side, despite his many misgivings about political violence. Berkman's act, Kropotkin wrote, had demonstrated to the world that there were "men capable of being revolted by the crimes of capitalism to the point of giving their life to put an end to these crimes." But many of the labor organizers on the ground in Pennsylvania felt that Berkman's attack had turned public sympathy toward Frick and ultimately hurt the union's cause. ("The bullet from Berkman's pistol, failing in its foul attempt," one wrote, "went straight through the heart of the Homestead strike.") Perhaps because he feared being arrested as an accomplice, Johann Most renounced Berkman's act in the pages of the *Freiheit* and in a series of newspaper interviews. Outraged by Most's lack of support, Goldman stormed onstage during one of his speeches and lashed at his face with a horsewhip. "It was painful enough to be called vile names by the man who had once loved me," she wrote, "but it was beyond endurance to have Sasha slandered and maligned."

The buildup to Berkman's trial in September was reported by the national press with a fervor that matched the coverage of the initial attack. But the trial itself lasted only four hours. Charged with felonious attempts on the lives of Frick and Leishman, along with the additional offenses of unlawful entry and unlawful possession of a concealed weapon, Berkman was convicted on all counts and sentenced to twenty-two years in prison.

There was a coda to the events of 1892 whose long-term significance was not perceptible at the time. While Frick's statement from the makeshift operating table ("the Company's policy will continue, and it will win") proved correct, the brutality of the Pinkerton attack on the Homestead encampment—the sight of a private company effectively hiring a mercenary army to settle a labor dispute—turned popular opinion against the Pinkertons. "There was a time, in the days of sturdy old Allen [sic] Pinkerton, when the Pinkerton agency was useful and reputable," journalist Myron Stowell wrote after the Homestead assault, but now "another wing [has been] attached to this bird of prey, whose function consisted of spreading death throughout the ranks of laborers having misunderstandings with their employers." Since the formation of the Department of Justice in the early 1870s, the Pinkertons had served as an informal investigative arm of the United States government, building on the espionage work the firm had done for Lincoln during the Civil War. But Homestead changed all that. The Department of Justice recognized that continuing to outsource work to Pinkerton men would ensure public wrath. Thanks to Homestead, the feds were forced out of the detective business altogether. The government could still arrest you if you committed federal crimes. But it lacked anyone on payroll or under contract to figure out whether you were committing those crimes in the first place.

This, then, was the ultimate tally of Homestead: the labor movement lost one of the most decisive battles in its history; that loss set off the dark swarm of motivations that led one person to try to kill another person in the name of a greater cause. ("The first terrorist act in America," Berkman himself called it, not inappropriately.) And that act—"the pivot around which the story is written," in Goldman's words—coincided with the United States government losing its investigative agents, an absence that would endure for almost thirty years.

There is an ironic symmetry to that story. The very same crisis that compelled Berkman and Goldman to import terrorism to American shores also cost the federal government its detectives. Three decades later, Goldman and Berkman would play an instrumental role in bringing those detectives back.

CHAPTER 10

Western Penitentiary

The hulking ruins of the Western Penitentiary lie on the banks of the Ohio River, just a mile downstream from where the Pinkerton men boarded the barges on their way to Homestead. Surrounded by forty-foot-high stone walls, built in the neo-Romanesque style popular in the late 1800s, the twenty-four-acre complex had a reputation for being one of the most inhumane prisons in the United States—the site of numerous prisoner riots and protests—before it was finally abandoned in 2017. Thousands of criminals lived within those walls over the century and a half that the prison was in operation: serial killers, sex cult leaders, Mafia assassins. But the most notorious inmate in the facility's history was also one of its first: Alexander Berkman.

In his initial months as an inmate at the Western Penitentiary, confined to a damp, subterranean cell, Berkman remained committed to the project of ending his own life. He first attempted to hone a metal spoon into a blade sharp enough to slash his throat, then contemplated bashing his skull against the cell bars. Eventually he learned of a clandestine postal system that the prisoners had engineered to correspond privately with the outside world. He wrote to Goldman imploring her to smuggle a dynamite capsule into the prison so that he could complete the job he had initiated in front of the police photographer back in Pittsburgh.

Posing as his Polish sister "Sonya Niedermann," Goldman traveled to Pittsburgh after Berkman had secured permission for a meeting. On Thanksgiving morning, she was ushered into the fortress of the Western Penitentiary and escorted through a maze of corridors before finally making her way to an airless room in the bowels of the prison. When Berkman arrived, under the watchful eye of a warden, he could see without so much as a word passing between them that Goldman would not be delivering the dynamite capsule. "A glance at your face," Berkman wrote to her several days later, "and I knew my doom to terrible life."

Goldman found herself uncharacteristically at a loss for words. "For weeks I had been looking forward eagerly, anxiously to this visit," she wrote. "A thousand times I had gone over in my mind all I would say to him of my love and undying devotion, of the struggle I was making for his release, but all I could do was to press his hand and look into his eyes." Berkman looked pale and haggard after three months behind bars. At first they spoke in Russian. "My appearance frightens you," Berkman said, noting that American prisons were more "crude and brutal" than even the notorious prisons of their native country. Goldman spoke of the latest news from Europe: an anarchist named Émile Henry had planted a bomb at the Paris Opera; it had been discovered and removed from the venue but then detonated at a police station, killing five officers.

Perhaps sensing that the two were conveying seditious ideas in their native language, the warden intervened, demanding that they keep their conversation to English. The two of them reverted to silence under his "lynx-like" scrutiny, gazing into each other's eyes, Berkman quietly playing with Goldman's watch chain "like a drowning man holding onto a straw." After twenty minutes the warden announced that their time was up.

A second meeting had been arranged for the following day, but in the interim Goldman's cover was blown, and she was forced to leave Pittsburgh before getting in trouble with the law herself. Her misery was only magnified by the bleak industrial landscape that enveloped her as she walked to the station.

> The night was black as I walked . . . to the station to take the train for New York. The steel-foundries belched huge flames that reflected the Allegheny hills blood-red and filled the air with soot and smoke. We made our way past the sheds where human beings, half man, half beast, were working like the galley-slaves of an era long past. Their naked bodies, covered only with small trunks, shone like copper in the glare of the red-hot chunks of iron they were snatching from the mouths of the flaming monsters. From time to time the steam rising from the water thrown on the hot metal would completely envelop the men; then they would emerge again like shadows. "The children of hell," I said, "damned to the everlasting inferno of heat and noise."

Berkman and Goldman would not see each other again for nine years.

CHAPTER 11

Le Département
d'Anthropométrie

Sometime in the late morning of February 13, 1894, an armed officer escorted a twenty-one-year-old mechanic and accused murderer out of a holding cell in the crypts beneath the Palais de Justice, on the Île de la Cité in Paris. The suspect—who had identified himself as Leon Breton to the authorities—was well dressed for a tradesman, though his dark suit and overcoat were rumpled from sleeping in them overnight. The young man squinted in the morning sun as he walked across a small courtyard to the imposing beaux-arts grandeur of the préfecture de police. Slowly, the two men trudged up four flights of stairs to the building's top floor, where they passed through a door marked DÉPARTEMENT D'ANTHROPOMÉTRIE.

Behind the door they found a bustling, double-height studio, illuminated by skylights built into slanted ceilings. Clerks shuffled between towering filing cabinets. The officer deposited the suspect in a small photography studio that had been erected in one particularly well-lit corner of the department. It was there that "Leon Breton" found himself face-to-face with Alphonse Bertillon, the former clerk and now head of the Department of Anthropometry, and the man who had, more than anyone, invented the science of forensics over the preceding decade.

Bertillon had reason to be interested in the suspect seated before him. His real name was Émile Henry—the anarchist whose attempted bombing of the Paris Opera two years earlier had been the headline news Goldman had relayed to Berkman during their aborted conversation in the Western Penitentiary. Just twelve hours before his meeting with Bertillon, Henry had strolled into the bustling Café Terminus in the Eighth Arrondissement and taken a seat at a table near the glass windows looking out onto the Rue Saint-Lazare. After smoking a cigar, drinking two beers, and listening to the house orchestra play a short set of classical pieces and polkas, Henry had paid the bill and casually walked out toward the street. Before reaching the doorway, he had pulled a heavy workman's lunchbox out from the inside of his overcoat, pressed his still-lit cigar against a wax-coated fuse extending from the contraption, and hurled it toward the chandelier suspended above the café patrons.

The explosion that followed—triggered by a deadly mix of dynamite, buckshot, and mercury fulminate—killed one and left twenty others seriously wounded. It was a scene not unlike the mass shooter tragedies that would become so terrifyingly familiar a century later: the pale young man in a trench coat, intent on sowing destruction. But Henry was in the service of what he considered a higher cause, beyond the demented rush of mass murder. He was a student of Proudhon and Prince Kropotkin. Like Sofia Perovskaya and the many other members of the Dynamite Club before him, Émile Henry was blowing people up to make a political point.

But Émile Henry's attack on the Café Terminus offered a new twist in the long history of human violence: the first instance of a terrorist attack deliberately targeting ordinary citizens instead of political leaders or industrial magnates like Alexander II or Henry Clay Frick. In time, the tactic that Henry devised would become the default modus operandi of terrorist groups around the world. Henry's victims were just a handful of customers enjoying their meal in a café and not thousands of office workers stacked in a pair of skyscrapers, but a direct conceptual line connects the bombing of the Café Terminus with the attacks of 9/11: the tactic of advancing a political cause by disrupting everyday life with shocking, sudden violence.

Under the skylights in the Departement of Anthropometry, Bertillon took detailed measurements of Henry's body parts including the length and breadth of his head, the length of his middle figure, the length of his index finger, the span of his outstretched arms, and the length and breadth of his ear. He photographed Henry in both portrait and profile views—images that would be subsequently annotated with Henry's measurements, in a format that had come to be called the *portrait parlé*: a talking picture. (Even today, almost a century and a half after he first developed the format, the portrait parlé lives on in police mug shots around the world.) In the photograph, Henry looks composed, well groomed; his hair has been recently cut and swept back above his forehead. He looks like an earnest law student, not a mass killer.

In the years that had passed since his tenure as clerk measuring inmates at La Santé, Bertillon had developed an entire identification system that had transformed the way that the French police dealt with newly admitted criminals like Henry. (In the age before driver's licenses and other forms of state-authorized identification, any suspect under custody could easily supply a fake name, as Émile Henry had done in calling himself Leon Breton.) Bertillon's system was attempting to do for law enforcement what

Émile Henry, photographed by Alphonse Bertillon, 1894

statisticians and epidemiologists had done for public health a generation or two before: using standardized datasets of information to solve
crucial societal problems. Where public health officials had reduced
the burden of epidemic disease by systematically mapping the reported cases and deaths, Bertillon aimed to reduce the burden of
crime—in Henry's case, political violence—by mapping the biology
of suspected criminals: not to reveal some latent criminality that was
somehow expressed through their physical being, but rather to create
a unique identifier that would enable the police to determine almost
instantaneously whether a detainee had a criminal record.

Because photography was still a new medium in the late nineteenth century, much of the public's interest in Bertillon at the time
focused on the physical object of the portrait parlé itself. But the
true brilliance of the bertillonage system was not in the mug shots
themselves but in the file cabinets where they were stored. Bertillon
had realized early in his research that photography—as powerful as
it could be in establishing identity—would not suffice on its own in
a metropolitan police department. It was one thing to sift through
a few hundred mug shots when a new suspect was booked, eyeball-
ing each one for a match. But in 1894, the population of Paris alone
was more than two million people; cities of that size could easily
amass more than ten thousand images of detained suspects. Today,
of course, data science has advanced to the point where facial recognition software running on our phones could pick out a match with
a database of photos of that size in a split second. But in Bertillon's
time, only humans could perform that kind of visual identification,
at a laborious pace. Admitting just ten prisoners a day would require
weeks of sifting through the archives establishing whether the new
arrivals had criminal records.

Bertillon's innovation can be thought of as a low-tech version of
what we would now call a search algorithm. The system increased
the speed almost a hundredfold with which a new inmate could be

matched with a photo. Bertillon organized his file cabinets into nested categories: Each new entry was grouped into one of three categories—small, medium, large—based on the length of the head. Those groups were then subdivided into another three categories based on the width of the head. The final subdivision was organized around the length of the left middle finger. Those subdivisions created eighty-one distinct categories. Bertillon employed his training as a statistician to ensure that the definitions of small, medium, and large for each body part were established in such a way as to create a balanced distribution in each category. An officer could take three measurements of a new detainee, and if it turned out the suspect had a long but narrow head and a short middle finger, he could ignore eighty of the eighty-one file cabinets filled with portrait parlés when looking for a match. Bertillon's system transformed the process of identifying potential criminals in large cities from a laborious, near-hopeless search to something closer to flipping through a photo album. Identifications that would have otherwise taken days could be made in a matter of minutes.

As word spread across Europe of Bertillon's new "scientific" approach to crime fighting, officials from other law enforcement agencies began making pilgrimages to the Departement of Anthropometry. First, there was a procession of well-respected Italians, all followers of Lombroso, the then-influential phrenologist. Scotland Yard integrated elements of Bertillon's system into their own crime fighting approach. Francis Galton also paid a visit to Bertillon's offices, making the case that a similar classificatory system could be designed for fingerprints. In time, the bertillonage system would be expanded to incorporate fingerprint data as well, for one primary reason: criminals often inadvertently left traces of their fingerprints at the scene of a crime. But they rarely had the courtesy to leave behind exact measurements of their middle finger.

✳   ✳   ✳

The encounter between Bertillon and Henry at the Department of Anthropometry had none of the terrible drama of the Café Terminus bombing; to an outsider, it might have been mistaken for an annual physical at a doctor's office. But the meeting had historical implications: it was one of the first direct encounters between two rival ideologies that would, over the subsequent three decades, play a pivotal role in global affairs. Henry represented the vision of the world that had captivated Goldman and Berkman back in America: the dream of a stateless society, radically egalitarian, free of the oppressive institutions that had come to define the industrial and imperial age. Bertillon, on the other hand, was the vanguard of a different kind of society, one that would ultimately triumph over the anarchist's dream: the surveillance state, where individual identity is measured, recorded, and archived by vast and often invisible institutions, using the latest science and technology to contain potential subversion.

Bertillon—and his contemporaries at Scotland Yard—had no shortage of subversion to contain. Two days after Henry's attack, across the Channel in London, a French anarchist accidentally blew himself up while plotting an attack on the Royal Observatory in Greenwich, later inspiring a crucial plot point in Joseph Conrad's novel *The Secret Agent*. (The *Times* reported in the opening paragraph of its account: "One arm had been blown from his body, and he had been almost completely disemboweled.") In the weeks that followed, a dynamite bomb exploded in Lyon, and another was discovered before it could detonate in the town of Saint-Étienne. Back in Paris, another unexploded infernal machine was found in a railway station. In early April, a bomb planted by an anarchist literary critic—directly inspired by Henry's act—exploded at a hotel restaurant across from the Luxembourg Palace. A few days later, the Special Branch of

Scotland Yard—which had initially been created to combat a bombing campaign led by Irish revolutionaries in the previous decade—arrested two Italian anarchists who had been plotting an attack on the London Underground. In early June, the French president Sadi Carnot was assassinated by a knife-wielding anarchist in Lyon. Over the ensuing six years, he would be joined by the Spanish prime minister Cánovas del Castillo, Queen Elisabeth of Austria, and King Umberto I of Italy: all victims of anarchist attentats.

"A girdle of dynamite encircles the world," Johann Most had warned more than a decade earlier, after the assassination of Alexander II. "The bloody band of tyrants are dancing on the surface of a volcano." Even if Most had softened his rhetoric in the wake of Berkman's attack on Frick, that earlier warning had grown increasingly prophetic. Only now it seemed as though all the citizens of Europe—not just the "tyrants"—were in the blast zone.

"My dynamite will sooner lead to peace than a thousand world conventions," Alfred Nobel had once boasted, during his early years as an industrial magnate. "As soon as men will find that in one instant, whole armies can be utterly destroyed, they surely will abide by golden peace." Now in his early sixties, living what would prove to be his final years in an Italian villa outside the town of San Remo, Nobel followed the headlines during the spring and summer of 1894 with a grim sense of resignation. Several years before, his brother Ludvig had passed away, and a few papers in France mistakenly assumed that it was Alfred himself who had died, giving Nobel the unusual opportunity to read his own obituaries. All his achievements, he discovered to his dismay, were only a footnote to the carnage he had inadvertently unleashed on the world. "The Merchant of Death Is Dead," one headline announced. The opening lines that followed continued in a similar vein: "Dr. Alfred

Nobel, who became rich by finding ways to kill more people faster than ever before, died yesterday." Now, reading the papers in his garden above the Mediterranean in the early summer of 1894, as the infernal machines erupted across the Continent, it was all too apparent that world events, left to their own incendiary devices, were unlikely to improve his legacy.

Facing that bleak future, Nobel returned to an idea that had first been planted in his mind several years earlier through his conversations with the Austrian peace activist Bertha von Suttner. Nobel had spent a passionate, though sexually unconsummated, weekend with von Suttner in Paris in 1876, after she had applied for a job as Nobel's assistant. Even then, as a young woman with no experience in the fledgling peace movement, she had challenged his easy assumptions about dynamite leading to a decline in violence, and since their aborted, though by all accounts good-natured, romantic encounter, they had developed a profound intellectual kinship that was sustained almost entirely through letters. Von Suttner had urged him through their later correspondence to use his fortune to support the peace cause. If Nobel was destined to be eulogized as a "merchant of death," perhaps there was a way to give his reputation at least the chance of an afterlife.

On November 27, 1895, at the Swedish-Norwegian Club in Paris, Nobel signed his third and final will—this one with a striking proviso at its core, news of which was withheld from Nobel's descendants until after his death. Almost the entirety of Nobel's fortune would be dedicated to supporting an annual series of five prizes, honoring "those who have conferred the greatest benefit to humankind." Advances in chemistry would of course be honored with one prize—a fitting choice given Nobel's personal history—alongside achievements in physics, medicine, and literature. But the fifth prize was the most striking one, an implicit gesture of atonement for the carnage dynamite had inflicted on the world: a prize for "the person who has done the most or best to advance fellowship among nations, the abolition or reduction of standing armies, and the establishment and promotion of peace congresses."

To a certain extent, the Peace Prize, as it came to be known, succeeded in rehabilitating Nobel's reputation. After a long legal battle with his heirs over the legitimacy of the third will, the first prizes were awarded in 1901, five years after Nobel's death. His name is now more commonly associated with the awards he endowed than it is with the explosives that made that endowment possible, and the Peace Prize itself arguably carries more prestige than any other honor in the world today. (Appropriately enough, Bertha von Suttner would be awarded the prize in 1905.) But for the fin-de-siècle law enforcement agencies on the front lines of the battle against the new specter of terrorism, gold medals were hardly sufficient to contain the threat.

In December of 1898, after the assassination of Queen Elisabeth, representatives from twenty-one European nations gathered in Rome for the International Conference for the Social Defense Against Anarchists. The conference marked the origin point of Interpol, the first truly international crime-fighting organization in history. The sessions in Rome, which lasted almost a month, produced a wide range of agreements about a common strategy to fight the anarchist threat. But the most significant one was this: all the represented countries agreed to adopt the portrait parlé system that Alphonse Bertillon had invented almost two decades before. Sending actual mug shots electronically across international borders was an impossibility in 1898, of course. But Bertillon *measurements* could be transmitted almost instantly over telegraph wires. An arrest in Paris could send police clerks combing through card catalogs all across Europe, looking for a potential match. That was a genuinely new idea, with momentous implications. If the "girdle of dynamite" was indeed threatening to incinerate the world, as Johann

Most had put it, maybe information science was the best tool to extinguish it.

There was a noticeable absence among the twenty-one nations represented at the Rome conference in 1898: the United States of America. The lack of an American presence reflected more than just the geographical separation between the two continents. The notion of a trained detective versed in statistics and anthropometry serving as an agent of the law was simply a foreign idea to most Americans. Beyond Allan Pinkerton, the most famous detective in the United States during the closing decades of the 1800s had been Thomas Byrnes, who had helped establish the NYPD Detective Bureau in the 1880s, and served as one of the police commissioners from 1890 to 1895. To his credit, Byrnes did bring some organizational structure to the city's crime investigations: detectives were instructed to keep detailed journals documenting their cases, and Byrnes invested in a photography lab that maintained photos of accused criminals, though the files—popularly known as "the rogues' gallery"—were not organized using the Bertillon method. But Byrnes was better known for roughing up his suspects in brutal interrogations than he was for actual investigative work. (The slang phrase "give him the third degree" comes from Byrnes's tenure at the NYPD.) The idea of a police officer conducting a forensic *investigation*—solving a crime rather than simply beating a confession out of a suspect—would have seemed preposterous. Partly this was due to the retrograde attitudes of the notoriously corrupt police forces of the day. (By the time he left the force, Byrnes had somehow accumulated a net worth of $350,000—roughly $10 million in today's dollars—despite an official annual salary of $5,000.) But even after reform-minded Teddy Roosevelt joined the Police Commissioners Board in 1896—forcing Byrnes out and spearheading an initiative to recruit more intellectually sophisticated detectives to the force—the department failed to catch up to its European equivalents. The corruption was too endemic, and the forensic sciences had not yet traveled across the Atlantic. Roosevelt only lasted two years on the board, ultimately leaving the post to serve as assistant secretary of the navy in the McKinley administration, where he would soon ascend to the vice presidency.

Bertillon's ideas did eventually make their way to the NYPD headquarters, partly as a response to a wave of bombings even more terrifying than the ones that swept across Europe in the 1890s. But if the modernization of the NYPD was still a decade or two away, there were a few hints of the new roles that would become necessary in the coming century.

At some point in 1896, a witless beat cop brought a suspicious package back to his precinct and gamely handed it to a superior, who immediately recognized it as a live infernal machine, likely planted by an Italian mobster. Somehow, the device didn't explode in the police station, but the near tragedy made it apparent that the NYPD and the fire department could use the services of an explosives expert capable of dismantling these devices safely. A few days later, the NYPD placed a classified ad that opened with the line: "Wanted—a man with nerve enough to open bombs."

Unsurprisingly, the position remained unfilled for more than a month, until one day a middle-aged Irish fireman named Owen Eagan applied for the position and was quickly hired. Something about the job just seemed to suit him. He would go on to serve as the primary bomb defuser for the city for twenty-four years. It was, as the *Times* later reported, "the only city job for which there was never any keen competition."

Over that time Owen Eagan would successfully defuse seven thousand infernal machines. Only twice would anything go wrong.

CHAPTER 12

A Little Joan of Arc

As Berkman languished in the Western Penitentiary, Goldman became a fixture on the dais at rallies and lecture halls around the city. The papers dubbed her "the queen of the anarchists," recounting her fiery speeches with a mix of prurient intrigue and contempt. After the economic collapse of 1893, which triggered a massive spike in unemployment in a nation that lacked anything resembling a modern social safety net, Goldman began instructing her audiences to take the law into their own hands. "If you are hungry and need bread," she announced, "go and get it. The shops are plentiful and the doors are open." The open calls for shoplifting attracted the ire of Thomas Byrnes; he sent police stenographers to Goldman's public appearances, where they furtively transcribed the speeches to document her seditious statements. In August of 1893, a little more than a year after Berkman's attentat, Goldman was arrested and charged with incitement to riot after a rally in Manhattan's Union Square.

Predictably enough, the arrest only brought more attention to the twenty-three-year-old agitator. In September, the New York *World* dispatched their star reporter Nellie Bly to interview Goldman, then awaiting trial in the Manhattan Detention Complex—commonly known as the Tombs—in the Five Points district. (One measure of Goldman's growing celebrity: *The World* teased the upcoming interview in a banner headline running at the top of each edition of the paper for an entire week.) Bly's portrait of the imprisoned radical was an object lesson in reframing the reader's expectations. She began by parroting the language of the tabloid press: "You have read of her as a property-destroying, capitalist-killing, riot-promoting agitator. You see her in your mind a great raw-boned creature with short hair and bloomers, a red flag in one hand, a burning torch in the other; both feet constantly off the ground and murder continually upon her lips." But instead, the Emma Goldman that Bly encountered in the Tombs was dressed in a "modest blue serge Eton suit," less the "Queen of the Anarchists" and more a kind of militant pixie: "Goldman is a little bit of a girl, just 5 feet high . . . not showing her 120 pounds; with a saucy, turned up nose and very expressive blue-gray eyes that gazed inquiringly at me through shell-rimmed glasses."

While Goldman had never been officially charged in the attack on Frick, Berkman's attentat hovered over the conversation. Bly asked point-blank: "Do you think murder is going to help your cause?" Goldman contemplated the question for a few seconds, and then replied:

> That is a long subject to discuss. I don't believe that through murder we shall gain, but by war, labor against capital, masses against classes, which will not come in 20 or 25 years. But some day, I firmly believe we shall gain and until then I am satisfied to agitate, to teach, and I only ask justice and freedom of speech.

The ambiguity expressed in the statement—*I do not believe in murder, but I do believe in war*—would become a constant refrain over the course of Goldman's future as a public figure. Asked about that future, Goldman told Bly: "I cannot say. I shall live to agitate to promote our ideas. I am willing to give my liberty and my life, if necessary, to further my cause. It is my mission and I shall not falter."

A few weeks after the interview, Goldman was convicted of one count of incitement to riot and sentenced to a year in prison. She was transported to Blackwell's Island, at that point one of the most desolate tracts in greater New York, a sliver of land in the East River—now called Roosevelt Island—where the city deposited its undesirables: the site of a lunatic asylum, a smallpox hospital, a poorhouse, alongside the woman's prison that would be Goldman's home for most of 1894.

Despite the bleak environs, by all accounts Goldman managed to use her time on Blackwell's Island productively. She read widely—mostly in English, improving her confidence in the language as she expanded her intellectual horizons. The prison library contained novels by George Eliot and George Sand, both pioneers in the Free Love movement that would become a central component of Goldman's worldview. She read deeply in the American libertarian tradition: Emerson, Hawthorne, Thoreau. She took up work as an orderly in the prison hospital, cultivating a growing interest in the practice of medicine, which would ultimately inspire her to learn the trade of midwifery. She later wrote that her prison experience enabled her to "see life through my own eyes"—and not through the lens of Berkman or Johann Most.

Goldman was released on August 17. Two days later, an event was held at the Thalia Theatre on the Bowery to celebrate her emancipation. A long list of luminaries from the anarchist community were invited; the organizers even promised, as a sign of solidarity, a reunion with her adversary Johann Most, whom Goldman had never forgiven for denouncing Berkman's attack on Frick.

"The theater was crowded from top to bottom," the *Times* reported. "Men, women and children kept trooping in. Every seat was taken, and the aisles were being filled until the fireman and police objected . . . The crowd was made up of various nationalities: Germans . . . Italians, Russian Jews, Hungarians, Frenchman, Cubans, and Spaniards. If there were any native Americans there, they were so few as not to be noticeable." An interminable succession of opening acts preceded Goldman's appearance onstage: an anarchist singing society, followed by a panel led by the French radical Voltairine de Cleyre, followed by three rambling speeches. Eventually, though, the nearly three thousand people crammed into the Thalia were treated to the main attraction, as Emma Goldman herself strode onto the stage, greeted by more than a minute of "howls, screeches, handclapping, and thumping of feet," according to the *Times* report, before Goldman finally convinced the crowd to return to their seats.

"Here I am again," she announced triumphantly, "and as you see, I am alive. You know it is impossible to kill a woman . . . I have come back to you after having served ten months in prison for talking. If the representatives of your government intend to prosecute women for talking, they will have to begin with their mothers, wives, sisters and sweethearts, for they will never stop women from talking."

As she had done in her interview with Nellie Bly, Goldman flirted with endorsing political violence on the stage, alluding to the Italian anarchist Sante Caserio, who had stabbed the French president Sadi Carnot to death earlier that summer. "It was not Emma Goldman who was prosecuted," she told the crowd. "It was the thoughts of Emma Goldman, the principles of Anarchy, that were prosecuted; the views held by thousands of brave men and women who have died and who are ready to die as did Sante. It was the right of free speech that was prosecuted in the Court of General Sessions, and not little Emma Goldman."

From the wings, Johann Most watched his former protégée bask in the adulation of the crowd. Perhaps sensing that the baton had been passed to a new generation, he skulked out of the theater. The promised reunion never happened.

✳ ✳ ✳

The following year, Goldman sailed to Europe, intending to get a degree in midwifery from the Allgemeines Krankenhaus in Vienna. Since her time on Blackwell's Island, Goldman's fame had spread across the Atlantic, enabling her to organize a lecture tour across England, speaking at multiple events in London, Leeds, Edinburgh, and Glasgow. She fell in easily with the intelligentsia of Europe, discussing Nietzsche in cafés, attending performances of Wagner's Ring Cycle, even sitting in on lectures by a neurologist with a burgeoning reputation named Sigmund Freud. (His frank discussion of human sexuality, she wrote, "gave one the feeling of being led out of a dark cellar into broad daylight.") But her most cherished encounter took place in the quiet London suburb of Bromley, where her long-distance mentor Peter Kropotkin had settled, after a second stint in prison in France during the 1880s.

Riding the train out of the city into London's sprawling commuter neighborhoods, Goldman found herself on edge at the prospect of finally meeting her "great teacher." "I feared I should find Peter difficult of approach," she wrote, "too absorbed in his work for ordinary social intercourse." Her fears proved to be unwarranted. Her hero—one of Europe's most dangerous thinkers—turned out to be a "kindly and gracious" man, living with his wife in what seemed like the middle-class suburban dream, in a two-story semi-detached townhouse at 6 Crescent Road, with a small garden in the back. Kropotkin offered to make his guest tea and brought her to his study, which doubled as a carpentry workshop.

> He pointed with great pride to a table, a bench, and some shelves he had fashioned. They were very simple things, but he gloried in them; they represented labour and he had always stressed the need of combining mental activity with manual effort. Now he

could demonstrate how well the two can be blended. No artisan ever looked more lovingly and with greater reverence on the things created by his hands than did Peter Kropotkin, the scientist and philosopher.

Over tea, they discussed the American and British labor situation; Kropotkin voiced his skepticism about true revolutionary struggle ever being possible in a "nation of shopkeepers" like England. He asked probing questions about Berkman's condition at the Western Penitentiary, and the possibility of his release. The meeting would be the beginning of a lifelong friendship between the two, establishing an intellectual kinship that was challenged only by Goldman's increasing focus on sexual liberation. That dispute would come to a head in a subsequent meeting at Bromley, during which Kropotkin complimented Goldman on her publications, saying that she was doing "splendid work," but then noting that her writing might be more effective "if it did not waste so much space discussing sex."

Goldman flared up against Kropotkin's condescending tone and snapped back that sexual liberty had to be central to the anarchist platform, alongside economic liberation. As Kropotkin's wife quietly sewed a dress for their daughter, the two began pacing around the study in intense disagreement. Eventually, as Goldman remembered it, she brought the debate to a close by playing the generational card:

> "All right, dear comrade, when I have reached your age, the sex question may no longer be of importance to me. But it is now, and it is a tremendous factor for thousands, millions even, of young people." Peter stopped short, an amused smile lighting up his kindly face. "Fancy, I didn't think of that," he replied. "Perhaps you are right, after all." He beamed affectionately upon me, with a humorous twinkle in his eye.

* * *

As Goldman noted, Kropotkin's eagerness to show off the "simple things" he had crafted at his carpenter's bench was itself an expression of his broader political philosophy. Kropotkin was, at that moment, at the end of a five-year stretch of furious research and writing, publishing the essays that would appear in book form seven years later in his magnum opus, *Mutual Aid*. The original spark had been his disagreement with Spencer and Huxley's social Darwinism, to this day one of the most influential—though oft-criticized—translations of scientific ideas into political philosophy. Spencer and Huxley had reformulated Darwin's concept of the "struggle for existence"—a category that left ample room for cooperative alliances between organisms—as the "survival of the fittest," which remains a shorthand description for both evolutionary and market competition, almost 140 years after the phrase first began to circulate. (Darwin famously never used the phrase "survival of the fittest" in the original edition of *The Origin of Species*, though it is now commonly associated with his ideas.) Given the provocation, Kroptokin sensibly began his counterattack against the social Darwinians with a close look at the biological record: the insect colonies, the deer, and the seabirds of Siberia. But by the time Goldman showed up for tea in Bromley, Kropotkin had moved on to sociology.

The closing essays in *Mutual Aid* offered an extended paean to the triumph of the "free cities" of the medieval era, which were to Kropotkin the pinnacle of human social organization. Kropotkin considered the emergence of these communities as "a natural growth, in the full sense of the world," the human equivalent of the spontaneous collaborative networks of the ant colonies that he had studied:

The movement spread from spot to spot, involving every town on the surface of Europe . . . free cities had been called into existence on the coasts of the Mediterranean, the North Sea, the Baltic, the Atlantic Ocean, down to the fjords of Scandinavia; at the feet of the Apennines, the Alps, the Black Forest . . . in the plains of Russia, Hungary, France and Spain. Everywhere the same revolt took place, with the same features, passing through the same phases, leading to the same results . . . their "co-jurations," their "fraternities," their "friendships," united in one common idea, and boldly marching toward a new life of mutual support and liberty. And they succeeded so well that in three or four hundred years they had changed the very face of Europe.

The fundamental economic unit of the free cities was not the industrial corporation or the feudal estate; instead, the defining unit was the artisanal guild, the elective associations of craftsmen: carpenters, weavers, painters, jewelers, musicians, scholars. Grounded in useful labor and expertise, sustained through shared resources, the guilds and the free cities that contained them offered a golden ratio of individual liberty and communal belonging that echoed the ancestral hunter-gatherer communities, only now updated with technological wonders and achievements in art and architecture. That was the natural equilibrium that the hydra of state capitalism had demolished, with its vast hierarchies and deadening, robotic labor, now justified by Huxley's pseudoscience of "survival of the fittest." "Whole populations are periodically reduced to misery or starvation," Kropotkin wrote. "The very springs of life are crushed out of millions of men, reduced to city pauperism; the understanding and the feelings of the millions are vitiated by teachings worked out in the interest of the few. All this is certainly a part of our existence."

The fixation with the guilds and associations of the medieval town is a quality of the anarchist movement that is little remembered today. What lives on is the image of the bomb-throwing terrorist, willing to kill innocent civilians in the name of some imagined revolution to come. But there was also a strangely quaint, nostalgic quality to the movement—most apparent in Kropotkin himself— a longing for a simpler, more pleasant form of life. It is true that on some level Kropotkin wanted to smash the state, using whatever means necessary. But it is also true that, at his core, he wanted everyone to get to live in a modernized version of, say, fifteenth-century Siena.

That vision was not quite as implausible—or naïve—as it might seem at first glance. Even today, medieval and Renaissance villages that have preserved their original settlement plans and architecture—if not their guilds—are enormously popular tourist destinations. One could argue that people make pilgrimages to San Gimignano, or Fez, or the hill towns of Andalucía not just because of the natural beauty on display in those places, or the luxury hotels, but rather because the scale and shared spaces of each of those towns are intoxicating, because it *suits* us as social animals in some deeper way. In 1895, England was still teeming with villages that lived by those ancient customs more than with the modern ways. (Even Bromley might have had a hint of it.) When Goldman sat down for tea in his carpenter's workshop, Kropotkin was in the middle of documenting just how much of that old order had survived.

"Europe is up to this date covered with *living* survivals of the village communities," he wrote, "and European country life is permeated with customs and habits dating from the community period." The final essays in *Mutual Aid* document dozens of examples of extant communities, still abiding by those older practices, untouched by the "war of each against all" raging in Manchester and

Pittsburgh and other industrial centers. Kropotkin the sociologist had been collecting them for years, the way Darwin had curated his beetles and mollusks: the self-governed villages of Switzerland, ringed by the communal land of Alpine meadows and forests, the shared grazing lands and fields in France, tilled by members of the new *syndicats agricoles*, the common gardens of Westphalia, the collective ownership of threshing machines in peasant collectives in Russia, the Arab *djema'a* and the Afghan *purra*, the encampments of the semi-nomads of Central Asia.

At that moment in time, a return to a social system organized around autonomous free cities still seemed eminently viable, as a possible future. Part of the viability derived from the fact that the old cities, as Kropotkin went to such lengths to document, were not all that old. There were "living survivals" of the free city way of life out there, in large numbers.

But the other reason a return to the communal model was a viable future was the rhetorical strength of the anarchist movement itself. If you pause the film right there in Kropotkin's workshop in 1895 and ask who was most likely, at that specific juncture in history, to end up as the faces of revolutionary left-wing politics in the twentieth century, it might well have been the two new acquaintances sharing a cup of tea in Bromley, and not Karl Marx, resting a few miles north in his grave at Highgate. Anarchism was certainly seen as a more dangerous movement by the establishment at the time. Imagine a twentieth century where multinational capitalism is challenged not by a totalitarian, militaristic Soviet Union but instead by a sustained mass return to the guilds and small-scale industries of free cities. That may seem preposterous to us now, but it might well have been within reach, back in 1895.

The sheer magnitude of the stakes at that moment—the possibility that you could play a central role in steering human society away from the abyss of industrial hegemony, and back to a more communal way of life—helps explain why even "kindly and gracious" Peter Kropotkin could find it in himself, at points, to tolerate the use of violence in the name of the anarchist cause. The body count from the infernal machines was a footnote compared to the violence of the factory system, after all. Recall "the everlasting inferno of heat and noise" that Goldman had experienced on her dismal last day in Pittsburgh. That apocalyptic landscape was not just an affront to the senses; it was killing and maiming workers at an accelerating rate. A few years after Goldman's meeting with Kropotkin, a systematic survey was conducted to account for all workplace accidents in greater Pittsburgh in one twelve-month period. The study found that 526 people had been killed outright on the job in Allegheny County alone, and another five hundred had been seriously injured. An inventory of some of those injuries gives a sense of the enormous physical peril that industrialization had created:

> Seven men lost a leg, sixteen men were hopelessly crippled in one or both legs, one lost a foot, two lost half a foot, five lost an arm, three lost a hand, ten lost two or more fingers, two left with crippled left arms, three with crippled right arms, and two with two useless arms. Eleven lost an eye, and three others had the sight of both eyes damaged. Two men have crippled backs, two received internal injuries, one is partially paralyzed . . .

From the anarchist's perspective, the true infernal machine that had been unleashed on the world was not Alfred Nobel's invention; it was James Watt's steam engine. The industrialists had been blowing people up or dismembering them long before Émile Henry walked into the Café Terminus. It was the capitalists who had armed the Pinkerton men and sent them up the river; it was the state that dispatched the militia to break up the Homestead strike. Terrible violence was already ubiquitous in the day-to-day operations of the steel mills and coal mines and railroads. Yes, the 526 dead in Allegheny County had each, individually, been the victim of an accident, not deliberate murder in the mode of Berkman's attentat. But the fact that hundreds would die horrifying deaths on the job in a calendar year was no accident; it was the cost of doing business.

And that "everlasting inferno of heat and noise" was still *new* in 1895. Society had not yet had time to become inured to industrialism's terrible destructive power, or to implement reforms that would make those workplaces less deadly. When Kropotkin was communing with the watchmakers in the free cities of Switzerland in the 1870s, the southern banks of the Monongahela River where Carnegie would eventually build the Homestead Steel Works were still lined with family farms. The lived reality of that community had been radically transformed in just a generation: from cattle grazing in pastures to open-hearth furnaces heating molten iron to three thousand degrees. Who was to say it couldn't be transformed yet again?

The contrast between those two ways of life helps explain why Peter Kropotkin never veered from his public support for Berkman's act of violence against Frick, even as he grew increasingly wary of terrorism as a political strategy in his old age. During one of his lecture tours in the United States, the Russian anarchist had received an unlikely invitation from Andrew Carnegie for a meeting at his Fifth Avenue mansion in New York. Carnegie styled himself something of a free thinker, willing to entertain a wide range of perspectives. Kropotkin would have none of it. "Because of your power and influence," he responded, "my comrade Alexander Berkman was given twenty-two years in prison for an act which in the State of Pennsylvania calls for seven years as the highest penalty. I cannot accept the hospitality of a man who has helped to doom a human being to twenty-two years of misery."

Later, en route to Chicago for a speech, Kropotkin stopped over in Pittsburgh to make a pilgrimage to the Western Penitentiary, with the hope of meeting his comrade face-to-face. But the visit turned out to be poorly timed. Berkman had been recently sent to solitary confinement after an attempted escape, at one point being put in a straitjacket for more than a week. ("They bound my body in canvas, strapped my arms to the bed, and chained my feet to the posts," he wrote. "I was kept that way eight days, unable to move, rotting in my own excrement.") Rebuffed by the warden, Kropotkin wrote to his imprisoned comrade several days later. He addressed the envelope with wording deliberately designed to draw the ire of the authorities at the Western Penitentiary:

Alexander Berkman, Political Prisoner.

CHAPTER 13

September 6, 1901

The crowds began gathering outside the Temple of Music hours before the president's entourage was scheduled to arrive. As they waited in the sweltering afternoon heat, the visitors—who had traveled to Buffalo from around the country for the Pan-American Exposition of 1901—gazed in awe at the 410-foot-tall Electric Tower looming over the sprawling exhibition. The genius inventor Nikola Tesla himself had wired the quarter-million light bulbs that illuminated the so-called rainbow city, powered by state-of-the-art AC electricity generated by nearby Niagara Falls. Most of the visitors milling about at the entrance of the Temple of Music had enjoyed the expo's many attractions in what was, effectively, a pop-up Disney World: the scenic railway, the Trip to the Moon ride, canal tours of a simulated Venice.

One figure in the assembled crowd, though, had a different mission in mind. Twenty-four-year-old Leon Czolgosz, dressed in a gray suit, stood quietly near the front of the line, offering only curt replies to the friendly banter of an African American man standing next to him. His coat pocket held a folded newspaper article, a report on the recent assassination of the Italian king Umberto I, shot to death by the Italian American anarchist Gaetano Bresci. Umberto I had been killed with a silver-plated Iver Johnson .32-caliber revolver—the very same model that Czolgosz clutched in his right coat pocket.

A few minutes before four P.M., President William McKinley—

newly reelected to a second term, boosted by an economy finally recovering from the crisis of the mid-1890s—was ushered via a separate entrance into the Temple of Music. A photographer captured him dressed in a top hat and morning coat, grinning broadly as he entered the building. Inside, he was brought to the dais, surrounded by potted trees and backed by an oversize American flag. His private secretary, George Cortelyou, stood beside him, along with John Milburn, the president of the exposition. At McKinley's command, the doors were flung open, and an organist commenced playing a Bach sonata to welcome the crowd. One by one, the president greeted the guests, shaking hands heartily with each of them. It is not exactly clear why Leon Czolgosz, with his right hand obstinately stuck in his coat pocket, did not attract the attention of the Secret Service men protecting the president. One account has it that Czolgosz happened to be standing behind a dark-skinned Italian American who fit the stereotype of a Bresci-style assassin more than Czolgosz, an ashen Pole from Chicago.

President McKinley ascending the steps of the Temple of Music, 1901.

Whatever the explanation, the salient fact remains: At 4:11 in the afternoon, Leon Czolgosz strode onto the dais in the Temple of Music, pressed his .32-caliber revolver into the expansive midsection of William McKinley, and fired twice.

* * *

Chaos enveloped the stage. McKinley tumbled backward, but was caught by Milburn and Cortelyou before he could fall. A swarm of attendees and Secret Service tackled Czolgosz. Minutes later, the fifty-eight-year-old president, his white waistcoat turned a shocking shade of crimson, was whisked away in an electric ambulance to a medical facility on the exhibition grounds. In a scene echoing the one that had transpired outside of Frick's office almost a decade before, a mob of enraged exhibition attendees followed Czolgosz as he was escorted from the Temple of Music to the local police headquarters, shouting out demands for vengeance. *The New York Times* reported the following day:

> In a few minutes the crowd had grown from tens to hundreds and these in turn quickly swelled to thousands, until the street was completely blocked by a surging mass of eager humanity. It was at this juncture that some one raised the cry of "Lynch him!" Like a flash the cry was taken up, and the whole crowd re-echoed the cry. "Lynch him!" "Hang him!" Closer the crowd surged forward . . .

Before the scene outside the police headquarters could descend into a full-blown riot, a phalanx of officers, guns drawn, emerged from the station and drove the crowd back. Inside, the police took Czolgosz to a cramped interrogation room, where he provided a short, semi-grammatical written confession: "I killed President McKinley because I done my duty. I didn't believe one man should have so much service and another man should have none." When the Erie County district attorney probed further, Czolgosz offered a justification for his act that would be plastered on newspapers across the country the next day.

"I am an anarchist," he said solemnly, "a disciple of Emma Goldman. Her words set me on fire."

Emma Goldman herself was in St. Louis when McKinley was shot, visiting an old friend named Carl Nold who had housed Berkman in Pittsburgh in the days leading up to the attentat on Frick. She was still recovering from a harrowing encounter days earlier with Berkman at the Western Penitentiary, their first meeting in nine years. Newly released from a year in solitary confinement, Berkman was hollowed out and frail, barely able to speak. But there had been encouraging news: his sentence had been shortened, and he faced only four additional years in prison.

Goldman first heard word of the assassination attempt on a crowded streetcar; when she returned to Nold's apartment, he shared the latest developments: the assassin had been a young man known as Leon Czolgosz, a name that was unfamiliar to either of them.

"It is fortunate that you are here and not in Buffalo," Nold remarked. "As usual, the papers will connect you with this act."

Goldman dismissed the idea out of hand—"Nonsense"—and for roughly twelve hours remained blithely unaware that she had overnight become the most wanted alleged criminal in the United States. While Goldman dined with Nold and slept through the night, police raids all across the country rounded up anarchist groups. Dozens of Goldman's allies in Chicago were arrested and charged with conspiracy to kill the president. In New York, two hundred detectives were assigned to the task of locating "Red Emma," clearly the mastermind behind the plot on the president's life. Rochester police surveilled her family. "A wrinkled ugly Russian woman," the New York *World* wrote, "inspired McKinley's assassination, working in secret with slayers who are singled out from her body of anarchists." Alluding not so subtly to the Frick attack, the paper added, "She has been in more than one plot to kill."

Late in the morning of September 7, Goldman wandered out to run a few errands. At a stationery store, her eyes happened to alight on a newspaper headline: "ASSASSIN OF PRESIDENT MCKINLEY AN-ARCHIST. CONFESSES TO HAVING BEEN INCITED BY EMMA GOLD-MAN. WOMAN ANARCHIST WANTED." Stunned, she bought a stack of papers and retreated to a nearby restaurant to read through the coverage. One of them included a photograph of Czolgosz. Her stomach sank at the image. Four months earlier, after a lecture in Cleveland, Goldman had chatted with a nervous young man who introduced himself as Fred Nieman as he browsed through pamphlets for sale near the lectern. He had soulful blue eyes and "a most sensitive face," Goldman wrote. Now, sitting in a restaurant in St. Louis, that same face stared out at her from the front page of the local paper.

Nieman had paid Goldman a visit several days after their encounter at the lecture, and the two had struck up an amiable rapport. He followed her to Chicago, where she introduced him to a few other anarchist comrades, most of whom found the young Pole more than a little creepy. "There is a fellow here from Cleveland who asks very peculiar questions," one of them noted. Rumors spread that he had called on multiple anarchists around Chicago, probing them inexplicably for information about "the password." The concerns about Nieman grew so severe that the September issue of *Free Society*—the Chicago-based anarchist journal—included a warning about him:

> The attention of the comrades is called to another spy. He is well dressed, of medium height, rather narrow shouldered, blond, and about twenty-five years of age. Up to the present he has made his appearance in Chicago and Cleveland. In the former place he re-

mained but a short time, while in Cleveland he disappeared when the comrades had confirmed themselves of his identity, and were on the point of exposing him. His demeanor is of the usual sort, pretending to be greatly interested in the cause, asking for names or soliciting aid for acts of contemplated violence. If this same individual makes his appearance elsewhere, the comrades are warned in advance, and can act accordingly.

Reading through the papers with a growing sense of dread, Goldman learned that the police had swept up many of her allies in Chicago and charged them with conspiracy to kill the president, and they had raided the offices of *Free Society* itself, while back in New York the authorities had arrested her nemesis Johann Most— all part of the national dragnet for "Red Emma." Before she settled the bill in the restaurant, Goldman made up her mind. "It was plainly my duty to surrender myself," she wrote. "I knew there was neither reason nor the least proof to connect me with the shooting. I would go to Chicago."

Goldman took the train to Chicago, thinly disguised in a sailor hat with a blue veil that concealed her features. As an additional precautionary measure, she removed her trademark pince-nez glasses for the voyage. Arriving in the city, she flagged down her old friend and former lover Max Baginski on the sidewalk, but he pretended not to recognize her, whispering furtively, "Walk toward the next street. I'll do the same." Once they had verified that neither of them were under surveillance, Baginski told her that she had been insane to come to Chicago. The atmosphere in the city was like the aftermath of the Haymarket Riot all over again. "It's your blood they want," he warned her.

Goldman was undeterred. Baginski set her up with mutual

friends—a preacher's son named Charles Norris and his wife—who were outside the anarchist circle, living in a fashionable neighborhood near Lincoln Park where police surveillance would be light. (In her memoirs, Goldman discreetly referred to them only as "Mr. and Mrs. N.") Goldman spent her first hours in her temporary safe house tearing up old correspondence that might incriminate her comrades once she turned herself in. Through Norris, she learned that the *Chicago Tribune* was offering five thousand dollars for an exclusive interview. Overriding Baginski's objections—"If you go to the police, you will never come out alive"—Goldman decided on a plan: she would grant the interview to the *Tribune,* giving her sufficient funds to pay for legal support during the inevitable trial to come, and then turn herself into the authorities.

Somehow the interaction with the *Tribune* tipped the local detectives off to Goldman's sanctuary in Lincoln Park. The morning after she arrived at the Norrises', she took a bath and began dressing for her clandestine meeting with the newspaper. From her bedroom, she heard the sound of glass breaking; within a few seconds, Goldman, dressed only in a kimono, found herself surrounded by a dozen police officers.

At first she pretended to be a Swedish servant with limited English skills. The ruse initially succeeded. In an exchange that bordered on slapstick, one of the officers held up a picture of Goldman, demanding: "We want this woman. Where is she?"

"This woman I not see here," the diminutive Goldman protested. "This woman big."

After searching the apartment, the officers were on the brink of leaving when one of them stumbled across a fountain pen engraved with Goldman's name. Even that clue was not sufficient for the cops to realize that the very suspect they were seeking was standing right in front of them. "By golly, that's a find!" the lead detective declared. "She must have been here and she may come back."

Exasperated, Goldman finally turned to the detective and ended the charade. "I am Emma Goldman."

"Well, I'll be damned," he uttered in shock. "You're the shrewdest crook I ever met."

At nine A.M. the next morning, Goldman was brought from her holding cell to the Harrison Street Police Court and arraigned on charges of conspiracy to murder the president. She was defiant, as always. The *New-York Tribune* described her entry into the courtroom:

> Emma Goldman's blue eyes flashed angrily at the crowd that pressed upon her, and when she swept her straw hat from her head and ran her fingers through her blond hair it was plain that restlessness and movement were among her characteristics. Two deep lines were between her eyes, and her irregular mouth was shut in a hard line. She leaned in a corner, obscured by the six-foot policemen around her. When she spoke in her throaty authoritative voice, touched with a Russian accent, she seemed to force herself into the most prominent place of all.

"The police are fools," she told the courtroom. "They can prove nothing against me."

The prognosis for the wounded president was initially upbeat. "Strong hopes entertained for the president's recovery," *The Washington Times* reported three days after the assassination attempt. "There was life and hopefulness in the atmosphere of Buffalo today. The cheering news from the President's sick room seemed to spread all over the city like a general inspiration." But quietly, beneath the perception of McKinley's doctors, a more ominous development was unfolding in the president's internal organs. The second bullet Czolgosz fired had sliced through McKinley's abdomen, crossed into and out of his stomach, and embedded in his pancreas. After a few days of promising vigor, the president began to fade in and out of consciousness. Gangrene had attacked the lining of his stomach, and now its agents were in his bloodstream. In the end, he lived for eight days after that fateful visit to the Temple of Music. The wound itself was not life-threatening; the infection was. Like many gunshot victims in the age before penicillin, William McKinley was ultimately killed by bacteria, not bullets.

Early in the evening of September 14, after paying his respects to the fallen president, Theodore Roosevelt took the oath of office in a private home in the suburbs of Buffalo. From an actuarial point of view, the job promotion was not a promising one. Three of the previous seven men to occupy the White House had been murdered on the job.

Despite intense pressure from the prosecutors, Czolgosz refused to name Goldman—or anyone else, for that matter—as an accomplice in the attack on McKinley. His trial lasted less than two days. At his sentencing, asked for the final time to give up the names of his co-conspirators, he said, in a voice so soft and faltering that his lawyer found it necessary to repeat each sentence to the courtroom: "There was no one else but me. No one else told me to do it, and no one paid me to do it. I was not told anything about the crime and I never thought anything about murder until a couple of days before I committed the crime."

The sentence surprised no one. He was to be executed the week of October 28, just one month later.

* * *

The anarchist community—those who weren't behind bars, that is—largely renounced Czolgosz. The editor of one prominent anarchist rag proclaimed, "If I thought that anarchy led to assassination, I would not be an anarchist." Another leading figure in the movement dismissed Czolgosz as "an insane man," his attentat a "stupid, idiotic crime." Even Berkman disapproved, writing to Emma from the Western Penitentiary:

> In Russia, where political oppression is popularly felt, such a deed would be of great value. But the scheme of political subjection is more subtle in America. And though McKinley was the chief representative of our modern slavery, he could not be considered in the light of a direct and immediate enemy of the people; while in an absolutism, the autocrat is visible and tangible. The real despotism of republican institutions is far deeper, more insidious, because it rests on the popular delusion of self-government and independence. That is the subtle source of democratic tyranny, and, as such, it cannot be reached with a bullet.

Goldman herself was never willing to distance herself from Czolgosz, other than continuing to claim—truthfully, it would appear—that she had no part in any plot to kill the president, beyond the indirect means of setting young Czolgosz's mind on fire. As Czolgosz sat on death row in New York's Auburn Prison, Goldman published an editorial in the October 6 issue of *Free Society*. The president's killer was a "soul in pain, a soul that could find no abode in this cruel world of ours, a soul 'impractical,' inexpedient, lacking in caution . . . but daring just the same, and I cannot help but bow in reverenced silence before the power of such a soul, that has broken the narrow walls of its prison, and taken a daring leap into the unknown." For the most part, she stuck with that story for the rest of her life.

Almost two decades later, the defense of Czolgosz would be used against her in a pivotal legal hearing, and it remains an important datapoint in gauging the true nature of Goldman's attitude toward political violence. With the attack on Frick, her personal connection to Berkman might have skewed her judgment. But she had no such attachment to Czolgosz. She was in her midthirties, a worldly, independent thinker who had learned to "see life through my own eyes"—no longer the impressionable young woman under the sway of Berkman or Most. She could have easily disavowed Czolgosz's act. Her inner circle wanted her to; it would have helped her legal case. A man shot the president of the United States at point-blank range and said to the world that he was a disciple of Emma Goldman. If there were ever a violent act you might find it reasonable to wash your hands of, that would be the one. And yet Goldman stood by him.

On October 29, Czolgosz was transferred from his cell in New York's Auburn Prison to the execution chamber, where the world's first electric chair had been installed just a few years earlier. Strapped into the wooden device, he spoke to the witnesses assembled before him in a trembling voice. "I killed the president because he was an enemy of the good people—of the working people," he said. "I am not sorry for my crime." As the guards tightened the leather mask around his face and attached the electric cables, he struggled to say one last pitiful sentence: "I am awfully sorry I could not see my father."

At 7:11 in the morning, the warden gave the signal, and the executioner flipped a switch that directed 1,700 volts of AC current through the prisoner's writhing body. After three applications of the current, an attending physician announced that he could no longer detect a pulse. Czolgosz's body was removed to an autopsy room, where surgeons sawed off the top of his skull and dissected his brain. "It was the unanimous agreement of the microscopical examination that the brain was normal or slightly above normal," the *Times* reported. "This demonstrated to the satisfaction of the physicians that in no way was Czolgosz's mental condition, except as it might have been perverted, responsible for the crime." They placed the corpse in a black pine coffin and lowered it into a grave on the prison grounds. Before the authorities sealed the casket, they poured sulfuric acid over the assassin's remains.

By the time the sun set over Auburn Prison, all traces of Leon Czolgosz had vanished from the earth.

In early December, Theodore Roosevelt took a carriage to Capitol Hill to deliver his first address to a joint session of Congress as president. After an opening eulogy for his predecessor—"It is not too much to say that at the time of President McKinley's death he was the most widely loved man in all the United States"—Roosevelt turned his focus to the grave threat facing the United States. He did not mention Emma Goldman by name, but the subtext was clear:

> When we turn from the man to the Nation, the harm done is so great as to excite our gravest apprehensions and to demand our wisest and most resolute action. This criminal was a professed anarchist, inflamed by the teachings of professed anarchists, and probably also by the reckless utterances of those who, on the stump and in the public press, appeal to the dark and evil spirits of malice and greed, envy and sullen hatred. The wind is sowed by the men who preach such doctrines, and they cannot escape their share of responsibility for the whirlwind that is reaped. This applies alike to the deliberate demagogue, to the exploiter of sensa-

tionalism, and to the crude and foolish visionary who, for whatever reason, apologizes for crime or excites aimless discontent.

Roosevelt used the speech to advocate for immigration reform that would keep anarchists from entering the United States—and potentially expel those who were already here. "I earnestly recommend to the Congress that in the exercise of its wise discretion it should take into consideration the coming to this country of anarchists or persons professing principles hostile to all government," he argued. "They and those like them should be kept out of this country; and if found here they should be promptly deported to the country whence they came."

A little more than a year later, Congress delivered on Roosevelt's appeal, passing the Immigration Act of 1903, commonly known as the Anarchist Exclusion Act. For the first time since the dark days of the Alien and Sedition Acts of 1798, immigration officials were authorized to interrogate immigrants about their political beliefs. In this initial form, the act would only have a minimal impact on the existing anarchist communities; only a dozen or so anarchists were deported under its provisions. But it would have one significant consequence. Thanks to the Anarchist Exclusion Act, Peter Kropotkin never set foot on American soil again.

Surprisingly, the case against Goldman quickly lost steam, and she was released within a few days of Czolgosz's indictment. Baginski's dire predictions had been wrong; not only did she come out alive after surrendering to the Chicago police, she was never even brought to trial. One might have thought, given the general corruption still rampant in big-city police precincts, that prosecutors would have been able to mount some kind of case against Red Emma, even if based on circumstantial evidence. The country was hungry for vengeance, after all, and she did seem awfully determined to defend her protégé. But for some reason they never even tried to indict her.

At least one simple explanation exists for her release: there wasn't an FBI to make the case against her. Whatever alleged crimes Emma Goldman had committed were subtle transgressions, with no clear jurisdiction. There would be no literal smoking gun—just *words* that set people's minds on fire. Most municipal law enforcement agencies couldn't perform the investigative work required to pursue that manner of crime, even if the crime in question had definitively happened in their backyard. If Goldman was breaking the law, the case against her had to be made with information-age tools. You couldn't make it with the third degree.

Teddy Roosevelt had firsthand experience with the limited investigative resources of urban police departments. He recognized, almost immediately, that the looming menace of anarchism was going to require new federal powers. In his December address to Congress, Roosevelt had used the bully pulpit to argue for additional reforms to contain the threat:

> Anarchy is a crime against the whole human race; and all mankind should band against the anarchist. His crime should be made an offense against the law of nations, like piracy and that form of man-stealing known as the slave trade; for it is of far blacker infamy than either. It should be declared by treaties among all civilized powers. Such treaties would give to the Federal Government the power of dealing with the crime.

The Europeans had used similar language in drafting the Rome agreement three years before. McKinley's death had made it clear that the United States needed a comparable approach to address the "black infamy" of anarchism: modern forensic science and surveillance, a unified national system for identifying criminals, detectives on the federal payroll. Throughout his two terms, Roosevelt would petition endlessly for the creation of a proper national detective force, an American Interpol. Each time, Congress would rebuff him, wary of consolidating too much power in the federal government. Lawmakers argued that "spying on men and prying into what would ordinarily be considered their private affairs" went against the "American ideas of government." Others maintained that a "central police or spy system in the federal government" would be "a great blow to freedom and free institutions."

Near the end of his presidency, Roosevelt did manage to persuade his attorney general to bypass congressional approval and create a small force of thirty-four special agents, in a new division of the Justice Department called the Bureau of Investigation. But the BOI remained chronically underfunded and understaffed.

For the next decade, it would be up to a distributed alliance of metropolitan police departments—and not federal investigators—to wage war against the anarchists. Fittingly, it would be some of Teddy Roosevelt's former colleagues from the NYPD who would lead the charge.

CHAPTER 14

The Black Hand

A careful reader of the February 5, 1906, edition of the *New-York Tribune* might have noticed a small item on page twelve of the paper, wedged between an ad for Dr. Sheffield's anti-septic tooth powder and a story about mice devouring the receipts of a local business. "Detective Sent to Study Systems Says English Now Depend on Fingerprints," the headline read.

> Detective Sergeant Joseph A. Faurot, who for ten years has been in charge of the identification bureau at Police Headquarters, came in yesterday on the Cunarder Carmania. He has been in London and Paris, where he was sent by Police Commissioner McAdoo to make a study of identification systems.

Detective Joseph Faurot was thirty-six, the grandson of French immigrants, raised north of the city in Cornwall-on-Hudson. In lieu of college, Faurot had attended a vocational business school, learning bookkeeping and stenography, before enlisting in the army for two years. In his early twenties, he moved to Manhattan and took a job managing the accounts of the Spalding sporting goods store in Times Square. There he befriended a burly shipping clerk who dreamed of becoming a cop and had hired a tutor to help him pass the police exam. Faurot was interested in the line of work, but thought himself too small for the job, given the emphasis on brawn over brains that had historically been dominant in the NYPD. But his interest in joining the force happened to coincide with Teddy Roosevelt's brief tenure on the Police Commissioners Board, and the department was beginning to show an interest in its recruits' intellectual aptitude. The shipping clerk ended up giving up on his police ambitions, but the tutor was impressed by Faurot's intelligence and persuaded him to take the exam himself. By 1896, Faurot was walking the streets of the Tenderloin as a patrol cop.

With his slight build and professional mien, Faurot did not look the part of a New York City police officer, a trait that he ultimately learned to use to his advantage when interrogating accused criminals. He had slate-blue eyes that would lock into an uninterrupted gaze with his suspects as he quietly probed their stories, with no suggestion of physical force, just an intense focus. Years later, after he had

Joseph Faurot, circa 1914

become one of the most famous detectives in America, a magazine profile described his unlikely demeanor:

> His suave, pleasing way has deceived many crooks . . . Instead of the typical third-degrees manner they had been used to, they found themselves engaged in amicable conversation with a prosperous-looking man of that type that is cast in moving pictures as a bank president. It was easy to lie to such a man, they felt when the talk began. But before long even the most obtuse of them noticed that his eyes contradicted the smiling face. The face

looked amiable, trustful and confiding. The eyes were looking into the criminal's soul finding out the truth.

Faurot did not last long as a beat cop. Within a few months of joining the force, his training brought him into the NYPD headquarters as a stenographer. It was there that he first encountered the fledgling identification division, with its disorderly rogues' gallery of photographs. Something about the project of classifying all those images captured Faurot's imagination; before long he was running the division itself, almost as a one-man shop.

For nearly a decade Faurot labored in the identification division, quietly arguing for more modern forensic techniques with little success. But the rise of the anarchist threat—and the news stories traveling by wire from the Continent about Scotland Yard and Bertillon's Département d'Anthropométrie—made it increasingly clear that the NYPD needed to embrace the new science. In late 1905, the reform-minded commissioner William McAdoo decided to send an emissary from the department to study the European methods. (The three-member Commissioners Board from the Byrnes/Roosevelt era had since been consolidated into a single position.) Thanks to his longtime affiliation with the Identification Bureau—and his fluency in French—Faurot landed the assignment.

Entertaining reporters at his apartment in Washington Heights the night after his return, Faurot said that he had been "royally treated" while overseas. His studies had only enhanced his belief that fingerprints were the future of criminal identification systems. "The London police have so much confidence in the finger print system that they have discontinued the use of a photographic reproduction of the features of criminals," he told the journalists. "There is considerable foundation for this confidence, too. I heard of a number of instances where convictions had been obtained in celebrated cases almost solely through impressions of the fingerprints of suspected persons, and this too after the system had been in use only a few years." He even offered the reporters a bit of mangled history: "Professor Dalton [*sic*], a cousin of Darwin, the famous scientist, is the originator of the finger print system."

The *Tribune* story noted that Faurot was scheduled to deliver a report to the police commissioner on his European findings the next day. The problem, for Faurot, was that the commissioner who had dispatched him on his mission just two months before was no longer in office. On January 1, just as Faurot was settling in at the Department of Anthropometry, Commissioner McAdoo had been replaced by Thomas Bingham, an unapologetic nativist who believed the solution to New York's crime problem lay in shutting down our borders and not importing so-called scientific approaches to fighting crime. Speaking to reporters from the Mulberry Street headquarters, Bingham blamed the crime wave on "foreigners, not American citizens . . . It is the wave of immigration that lands here hundreds and thousands of criminals and fellows who don't know what liberty means and don't care, don't know our customs and cannot speak the English language, and are the scum of Europe mostly." Bingham dismissed Faurot's plan for integrating fingerprint science into the Identification Bureau. "It's a fad," he jeered, "and a London fad at that."

Rebuffed from above, Faurot waited patiently for an opportunity to prove the value of his new method. One arrived a few months after his return from Europe, when a suspicious Englishman was apprehended wandering the halls of the glamorous Waldorf-Astoria hotel, claiming to be looking for a friend whose name he couldn't quite seem to recall. Faurot took a gamble and fingerprinted the suspect, then sent the prints on the next steamer, back to his friends at Scotland Yard, without any additional description of the suspect. Two weeks later, a matching set of prints arrived from London, belonging to an inveterate thief with an extensive criminal record named James Jones. Scotland Yard even included a photograph of the man, a dead ringer for the mysterious Brit at the Waldorf.

Cracking the Waldorf case earned Faurot the begrudging approval to launch a makeshift fingerprint division inside the Identification Bureau. He bought a table with a copper slab, a bottle of printer's ink, and a hand roller. Anyone convicted of a crime would be photographed, portrait parlé style, and then brought to Faurot's fingerprinting studio. "Fresh ink was spread on the slab with the roller and his fingers were rubbed on the ink and then on a piece of paper ruled and marked for each finger of each hand," the *Times* reported. "The man then received a bottle of benzine and some soap and was invited to wash up. Meanwhile, the prints were examined under microscope, classified, and filed."

To an outside observer, Joseph Faurot's copper slab and hand roller wouldn't have looked like much, and indeed, for many years Faurot would continue to be seen as an eccentric inside the department. But those systematically organized ink prints accumulating in the file cabinets were a sign of what was coming for the NYPD.

In March of 1906, Emma Goldman published the first edition of a new monthly publication, which she called *Mother Earth*. It would become one of the central intellectual hubs of the anarchist movement over the next ten years, covering a constellation of topics that reflected the range of Goldman's intellect. (As if to underscore the passing of the baton to a new generation of anarchist thinkers, Johann Most died within a few days of the first issue's release.) *Mother Earth* featured many accounts of labor struggles, of course, but also essays on the birth control movement and political philosophy. The inaugural issue featured a poem by Maxim Gorky, a Kropotkin-influenced tribute to the "free unions" called "Without Government," and a dispatch from England on the latest parliamentary elections. Goldman herself co-wrote an opening statement announcing her vision for the publication:

> Mother Earth will endeavor to attract and appeal to all those who oppose encroachment on public and individual life. It will appeal to those who strive for something higher, weary of the commonplace . . . Quacks of history speak only of "great men" like Bonapartes, Bismarcks, Deweys, or Rough Riders as leaders of the people, while the latter serve as a setting, a chorus, howling the praise of the heroes, and also furnishing their blood money for the whims and extravagances of their masters . . . Our aim is to teach a different conception of historical events. To define them as an ever-recurring struggle for Freedom against every form of Might. A struggle resultant from an innate yearning for self-expression, and the recognition of one's own possibilities and their attitude toward other human beings.

On May 18, Alexander Berkman was released from the Allegheny County Workhouse in Pennsylvania, where he had completed the final ten months of his sentence. Goldman was not there to greet him; Berkman had written several weeks before to say that he could not bear to see her again "in the presence of detectives, reporters, and a curious mob." More than fourteen years after the attentat—thirteen of them spent in the Western Penitentiary— Berkman was a free man. A group of reporters waited at the gates of the workhouse, along with several local police officers, who urged him to leave the region as quickly as possible. Berkman told the reporters that he planned to travel by train to St. Louis, and that he had no definite plans beyond that. "There is one thing I want to deny, and that is that I am to become the leader of the anarchists in this country and take Herr Most's place," he added. "There is nothing in that. I am going to lead a quiet life and try to make an honest living, and I have no doubt that I can do so."

Changing trains in Pittsburgh, Berkman was overwhelmed by the chaos of the modern city, after so many years behind bars. "I am afraid to cross the street; the flying monsters pursue me on every side," he wrote in the final pages of his prison memoirs. "A horseless carriage whizzes close to me; I turn to look at the first automobile I have ever seen." Perhaps with the aim of throwing off the detectives on his tail, he skipped the train to St. Louis and boarded one bound for Detroit, where Carl Nold was now living with his girlfriend. When he arrived at the Detroit station, Goldman was waiting for him, roses in hand. Once again, she was shocked by his appearance. "His face deathly white, eyes covered with large, ungainly glasses; his hat too big for him, too deep over his head—he looked pathetic, forlorn," she wrote. "I was seized by terror and pity, an irresistible desire upon me to strain him to my heart."

Exactly one month after Berkman's release, a crowd of almost three thousand people gathered at the Grand Central Palace—the enormous exhibition space straddling the rail lines running north of Grand Central Terminal—to welcome Alexander Berkman back to his adopted home city. Goldman introduced him to thunderous applause as a "graduate of the University of the Western Penitentiary." The *Times* reported that Berkman appeared "nervous and ill at ease" as he delivered his remarks. But his words made it clear that his comments outside the workhouse gates—"I am going to lead a quiet life"—did not reflect his true ambitions. "As it appears to me, society has not changed since I was imprisoned," he told the crowd. "I propose to devote all of my energies and whatever abilities I may possess to that noblest of all causes, the freeing and regenerating of humanity."

✳　✳　✳

Despite his claim to the contrary, society *had* changed since Berkman first entered the Western Penitentiary—and New York City had changed most of all. The city had been the most populous in the United States since the 1790s—and the country's financial center since the building of the Erie Canal—but the merging of the five boroughs in 1898 had turned it into a true metropolis, rivaled only by Paris and London on the world stage. The skyline was unrecognizable to Berkman, who had been imprisoned before steel-framed construction and mechanical elevators became standard practice in Manhattan. (In fact, the word *skyline* itself would have been unfamiliar to him, having been coined in 1896 to describe the dramatic new vistas conjured by high-rise urban living.) As Berkman addressed the crowd at Grand Central Palace, construction was under way to build the Singer Building on Broadway, soon to be the tallest building in the world at more than six hundred feet. The transformation of the city was most evident after sundown. When Berkman entered prison in 1892, only a small stretch of Fifth Avenue had been fully electrified; now almost all commercial districts in the city had access to Edison's miraculous source of power. Electric trolleys and elevated railway lines connected the outer boroughs. Beneath the noise of the crowd gathered to welcome him home, Berkman might have heard the rumble of the newly opened IRT—New York's first subway—hurtling through tunnels carved into bedrock and schist using Alfred Nobel's explosives.

There was another crucial change in the city, more a matter of demography than infrastructure. The two decades that overlapped with Berkman's time in the Western Penitentiary witnessed one of the United States' most dramatic waves of immigration, with more than two million Italians entering the country through Ellis Island. In 1891, there were fewer than one hundred thousand Italians living in New York. Now their numbers were approaching four hundred thousand—making them the city's largest immigrant population.

When Berkman and Goldman first met at Sachs's Café on the Lower East Side, the neighborhood was dominated by Russian and German Jews. Now, in the first years of the twentieth century, the streets just north of Sachs's had been endowed with a new name that would persist to the present day: Little Italy. This was the world famously captured in the flashback scenes from *The Godfather Part II*: the girls on tenement stoops crocheting lacework; the limonati stands; the pushcart vendors hawking produce, cheese, books; the endless soundtrack of organ-grinders playing "Torna a Surriento" and "Santa Lucia."

Yet the bustling urban tableau evident on the streets of Little Italy was shadowed by a new threat that loomed over the community, one that also relied heavily on Alfred Nobel's dynamite as a show of force: the loose affiliation of criminals and extortionists known as the Black Hand. "Every New Yorker had read of or knew someone who had opened a letter with no return address, only to find it covered inside with primitive drawings of black crosses, daggers, and skulls, all dripping with black ink meant to look like dripping blood," the historian Brad Ricca writes. "There would usually be a simple, ungrammatical message asking for money—or sometimes worse: a note claiming the abduction of one's son or daughter. These letters were almost always signed the same way: with the ink-bloody imprint of a black hand."

One typical letter from the period read: "You dog, spy, informer. If you do not do what we say, we have a shot gun prepared for you. What a fine feast for the rats your fat carcass will make. Do what we say, it will be better for your skin." Almost unheard of in 1891, the Black Hand had become New York's public enemy number one by the time Berkman returned to private life in 1906.

For Police Commissioner Bingham, the Black Hand was a persistent bête noire. While his aversion to immigrant communities was wide-ranging—he once described the city as being besieged by "predatory criminals of all nations: the Armenian Hunchakist, the

Neapolitan Camorra, the Sicilian Mafia, the Chinese Tongs"—he reserved a special animus for "the Italian malefactor . . . by far the greater menace to law and order." Faurot might not have convinced him that the—suspiciously European—methods of forensic science could be central to the fight against the Black Hand. But Bingham *did* want to import one law enforcement practice from overseas: undercover operatives—then known as a "secret service"—styled after the Italian Carabinieri, or the British Special Branch. "The crowning absurdity of the entire tragic situation in New York," he wrote in a briefing for the mayor, "lies in the circumstance that the Police Department is without a secret service." The only way to break up a decentralized underground organization like the Black Hand was to infiltrate their ranks.

But the need for a "secret service" put Bingham in a difficult bind. To infiltrate a group like the Black Hand you needed operatives who could pass for Italian—and certainly speak Italian fluently. But demographically, the police department was still trapped in 1850, the Gangs of New York era, when the Irish ruled the Lower East Side. In 1906, in a city with nearly half a million Italian-born residents, only nine Italian speakers were on the payroll of the NYPD.

This was Bingham's dilemma. He loathed Italian immigrants. And he couldn't do his job without them.

In early September, a Brooklyn tailor named Fransesco Messina began receiving threatening messages marked with the signature skulls and daggers of the Black Hand. Messina lived with his wife and three young children in an apartment above his small shop at 280 Bushwick Avenue in Williamsburg. Ten other Italian families lived in the three-story structure, which also contained a frame store on the ground floor next to Messina's shop. At first, the anonymous notes demanded that the tailor hand over $1,500 if he wanted to ensure the safety of his business and his family. After Messina ignored the first few threats, the number dwindled down to $400. Perhaps sensing desperation on the part of his would-be extortionists, Messina continued to brush off the warnings—neither paying up nor alerting the authorities. At times, he would look up from work and see suspicious men lingering across the street, staring into the shop with a vaguely menacing expression. Messina did his best to ignore them—until at two A.M. on the morning of Sunday, November 5, when someone threw a dynamite bomb through the window of his shop.

The blast blew out the entire front of 280 Bushwick, along with that of the adjoining building. Dozens of windows on the block were shattered. The explosion rattled the NYPD precinct five blocks away. When officers arrived at the scene, they found "hundreds of people, among them women and children who were screaming, swarming out into the street" among the rubble, the *Sun* reported the next morning. An ambulance was immediately dispatched to the scene, but miraculously no one was hurt in the blast. The *Sun* noted that the Messina bombing marked the third time in just two months the Black Hand had detonated a bomb in that neighborhood alone.

A few weeks after the Bushwick bombing, forty men gathered in the assembly hall at the United Charities Building just north of Gramercy Park for a public discussion of the city's crime problem, headlined by former commissioner McAdoo. After some opening grumbling that the turnout for the event had not lived up to expectations, and a spell of bureaucratic throat clearing about passing bylaws and appointing chairmen to the committee, McAdoo delivered some extended thoughts on his tenure at the NYPD, and his vision for the future of the department. Corruption, as usual, was a primary complaint. McAdoo boasted that he could have shut down all the gambling houses and brothels in town if he had been able to

find "twenty-five absolutely honest men for the vice squad." The solution, he argued, was to extract the police department from the
city's political machine. "The public indictment of the police force
of the city may be summed up in two words—politics and graft," he
argued. "You will never accomplish anything if you don't put your
axe to the very root of that police cancer—political influence." To
fight the growing menace of anarchist subversives and the Black
Hand extortion racket, McAdoo made the case for a radical overhaul of the Detective Bureau, creating a staff of men to act as "[the
Commissioner's] eyes and his ears and his arm—the strong arm of
the law." No doubt recalling the mission he had sent Joseph Faurot
on almost a year earlier, McAdoo argued for the Detective Bureau
to be modeled after Scotland Yard.

McAdoo's comments were echoed in the remarks of the other
main speaker at the event, thirty-six-year-old Arthur Hale Woods,
who had recently compiled a pamphlet entitled "The Police Problem
in New York City." Woods's comments on the state of the Detective
Bureau were scathing:

> The detective force is as bad as it can be. We could hardly imagine
> that being a member of the police force is about the only qualifi-
> cation needed to put a man in line for promotion to the Detective
> Bureau. We all know that a good policeman is not necessarily a
> good detective. No discriminating judgment is shown in appoint-
> ing detectives, and it entirely a matter of luck if we get any that are
> fit for the position. The detective force in this city, as a matter of
> fact, does not do any detective work in the real sense of that word.
> The members do not depend on their own shrewdness in doing
> their work.

In their reports on the meeting the next day, both the *Times* and
the *Sun* identified Woods as an "instructor at the Groton School."

Neither article seemed to raise an eyebrow at the rather unexpected sight of a high school teacher penning a pamphlet on police reform and sharing center stage on a panel with the former NYPD commissioner himself.

Who was this mysterious Arthur Woods? The broad facts of his upbringing are a matter of record. He was born in 1870 to an affluent Boston family, with a Kennedy-esque enthusiasm for the new sport of football. His father had been a prominent businessman and a devout Episcopalian, for many years the senior warden at St. Paul's Church in Brookline. Woods's teenage journals, now preserved in a special collection at the Library of Congress, do not suggest much of the cerebral reformer Woods would become. (They largely contain accounts of football scrimmages and extended sessions at the local gymnasium.) He received his degree from Harvard in 1892 and did some graduate work at the University of Berlin's pioneering sociology program, an intellectual itinerary W. E. B. Du Bois would follow several years later. For almost ten years he was a beloved teacher and coach at the elite Massachusetts boarding school Groton. Technically, Woods taught English, but he had a habit of leaving the novelists and poets behind and launching into an inspiring oration about municipal reform. After mending an injured pitcher's arm in the middle of a crucial baseball game, he earned the sobriquet "Doc" Woods. "He is the most sympathetic and congenial person in the world," one of his former students told a reporter, many years later. "At Groton, when a boy was in trouble, he would always go to Doc Woods and tell him about it and get his help."

But by the time Arthur Hale Woods rose to speak at the police reform panel, he had left his teaching days behind. For several years he had dabbled in journalism, traveling to Europe and Asia. He spent long hours at the Harvard Club in Manhattan, extolling the possibilities of "social betterment" among his less progressive-minded former classmates. "You will see him there at the center of

the group, expounding his ideas," one Harvard Club member recalled. "And after it is over you will see the men he has been talking
to sitting around and pounding the table and telling each other, 'By
George, we've got to take our coats off and do something for this
uplift business.'" According to later society accounts, he was widely
considered to be a confirmed bachelor, too driven by his intellectual
and political pursuits to have time for romantic affiliations.

Woods was so committed to his newfound interest in police reform that at some point—either leading up to the November 1906
reform meeting or shortly after—he made the pilgrimage to visit
Bertillon and Scotland Yard, just as Faurot had; it is possible that
the two men did the exploratory mission together.

None of that history, though, quite explains how a Groton School
teacher drifted into the orbit of
crime fighting. The conventional explanation—one that
appears in several profiles written about Woods in his later
years—is this: In his first days
as a junior reporter at the *Evening Sun,* he had been assigned
to write the daily police blotter
for the paper. Documenting
the day-to-day activities of the
NYPD had planted the idea
that his longstanding interest

Arthur Hale Woods, circa 1915

in municipal reform could be productively directed toward the city's
police force. But that alone doesn't account for how swiftly Woods
seems to have ascended through the ranks, from cub reporter to
headlining a panel with the former commissioner in a matter of
months.

Another, more intriguing explanation for Woods's meteoric rise begins with a handwritten letter, penned in the fall of 1903, that Woods wrote to a Groton parent, advising them on the question of whether their son should try out for varsity football. "There is no doubt in my mind but that he should play on the lower team," Woods explained. "The only possible objection would be the feeling of disappointment to him personally." After a long review of the athletics situation, he closed with these upbeat words: "Ted is doing very well. He is studying hard, playing hard and intelligently, and is on very good terms with the boys. He is a different boy from the Ted of last winter's troubles."

A few days after sending the note, he received a typewritten response from the boy's father, dated October 10, 1903.

My Dear Mr. Woods.

Mrs. Roosevelt has said all along that she thought your judgment would be best about Ted. I am delighted with your letter and have written Ted accordingly at once.

Sincerely yours,

The grateful parent had added a handwritten "with hearty thanks" to the final lines of the letter, and signed it: Theodore Roosevelt.

These letters are the earliest surviving documents from a correspondence between the two men that would continue through Roosevelt's presidency and beyond. Woods seems to have ingratiated himself to the Roosevelts' inner circle initially as a trusted counsel, largely focused on their children's education. In subsequent letters, Woods helped the First Family sort out issues with their son Kermit's course schedule at Harvard. (Woods had also taught a young Franklin Delano Roosevelt in his tenure at Groton.) By 1905, the president was writing letters of introduction for Woods to various New York luminaries, describing him as a personal friend. It strains credulity to assume that, just by coincidence, a former high school English teacher and junior reporter would find himself on a panel of dignitaries pitching a police reform plan if the sitting president hadn't given Woods some kind of encouragement or support—particularly given how closely the reform plan resembled the one Teddy Roosevelt had been arguing for all along. Perhaps Roosevelt saw in Woods a version of his younger self that had taken on the challenge of the NYPD back in the 1890s—a charming, moneyed Harvard grad with progressive values and an appetite for new ideas. As president, Roosevelt had neither the authority nor the spare time to reorganize the detective bureau of a city police department. But perhaps his protégé Arthur Hale Woods could do it for him.

Whatever chain of events actually led Woods into the world of law enforcement, the pamphlet and the panel remarks made an impression. In early 1907, Commissioner Bingham created a new position specifically for Woods: the fourth deputy police commissioner, giving him oversight of the Detective Bureau.

His first two assignments were hardly the sort of thing that one would normally hand off to an English tutor with no police experience; but then again, Arthur Woods seemed to be playing by different rules. His mandate was this: assist Joseph Faurot in modernizing the rogues' gallery archive of criminal photographs—and develop an undercover team to destroy the Black Hand.

CHAPTER 15

Palermo

It took Alexander Berkman almost two years to return to some measure of normalcy after his time in the Western Penitentiary. He had spent the overwhelming majority of his adult life behind bars, much of it in excruciating conditions, including months at a time in solitary confinement. Now a free man in his midthirties, he battled depression and struggled to settle into a productive work regimen. Suicidal thoughts haunted him. Goldman did her best to nurse Berkman back to mental health. The two lived together platonically at Goldman's apartment on East Thirteenth Street, and Berkman spent long stretches upstate at a cottage Goldman had purchased in Ossining, a hamlet on the banks of the Hudson River.

Life at the cottage brought the two old compatriots back to that brief stretch of small-town harmony that they had enjoyed running the luncheonette in Worcester before the Homestead Riot had turned their lives upside down. Eventually, Berkman began taking notes on his experiences in the Western Penitentiary. For the first time since his release, he began to feel a sense of purpose, as the notes slowly transformed into the manuscript pages of a prison memoir. "While Sasha pored over his manuscript and enjoyed the open space and quiet," the historian Paul Avrich writes, "Emma cooked, read books, wrote letters, and tended to the garden, growing potatoes, cucumbers, beets, lettuce, beans, and radishes." For Berkman, the fog of depression slowly gave way to a fierce hunger.

"Having been starved for so many years, he now ate ravenously," Goldman wrote later of this period. "It was extraordinary what an amount of food he could absorb. . . . It was nothing at all for him to follow up a substantial meal with a dozen blintzes . . . or a huge apple pie."

Goldman fell into a passionate—and sometimes turbulent— romance with a ruggedly handsome American physician named Ben Reitman, who had spent several years of his early adulthood as a drifter before somehow finding his way to medical school. "His eyes were brown, large, and dreamy," Goldman wrote of her first encounter with Reitman.

> His lips, disclosing beautiful teeth when he smiled, were full and passionate. He looked a handsome brute. His hands, narrow and white, exerted a peculiar fascination. His finger-nails, like his hair, seemed to be on strike against soap and brush. I could not take my eyes off his hands. A strange charm seemed to emanate from them, caressing and stirring.

While Goldman held on to her free-love principles in theory, Reitman had an unwelcome habit of enjoying those liberties to excess, a practice that would cause much stress in the relationship over the years.

Goldman's account of her tumultuous romance with Reitman points to a central part of her public persona that may be lost to a modern audience that knows her only through the way she chose to photograph herself, with her stern look and pince-nez. (In Warren Beatty's wonderful film *Reds*, Maureen Stapleton played her in a similarly matronly mode.) But there were few female intellectuals in that period who were more comfortable discussing their sexual appetites in public. (Much to Peter Kropotkin's dismay, of course.) In her autobiography, Goldman tells a story about being reprimanded

by one of Berkman's younger cousins for dancing. "It was undigni-
fied for one who was on the way to become a force in the anarchist
movement," the comrade informed her solemnly. "[Her] frivolity
would only hurt the Cause." Goldman would have none of it. "I
grew furious at the impudent interference of the boy. I told him to
mind his own business, I was tired of having the Cause constantly
thrown into my face. I did not believe that a Cause which stood for
a beautiful ideal, for anarchism, for release and freedom from conventions and prejudice, should demand the denial of life and joy. I
insisted that our Cause could not expect me to become a nun and
that the movement should not be turned into a cloister. If it meant
that, I did not want it."

Berkman, meanwhile, entered into a more troubling sexual relationship with a new member of the anarchist set: a rowdy fifteen-
year-old Latvian named Becky Edelsohn. Even in the libertine
culture of the radical underworld, the age difference between the
two was alarming. (With the age of consent in New York set at
sixteen, the affair was also, legally, statutory rape.) Goldman did her
best to construct a justification for Berkman's behavior, attributing
it to the years he had lost at the Western Penitentiary:

> For fourteen years he had been starved for what youth and love
> could give. Now it had come to him from Becky, ardent and wor-
> shipful as only an eager girl of fifteen can be. Sasha was two years
> younger than I, thirty-six, but he had not lived for fourteen years,
> and in regard to women he had remained as young and naïve as he
> had been at twenty-one. It was natural that he should be attracted
> to Becky rather than to a woman of thirty-eight who had lived
> more intensely and variedly than other women double her age. I
> saw it all clearly enough, yet at the same time I felt sad that he
> should seek in a child what maturity and experience could give a
> hundredfold.

✳   ✳   ✳

For the rank and file of the NYPD—many of whom were working-class Irish Catholics with little education beyond grade school—it was not unusual to see a patrician figure like Arthur Woods setting up shop in a comfortable office at the Mulberry Street headquarters. The department had a long tradition of appointing blue bloods to prominent roles, though not often ones that hailed from the tony suburbs of Boston. Woods certainly looked the part: Well dressed and clean-shaven, he had an easy authority that was interrupted only by a "cackling little laugh," as one profile put it. But most such highbrow appointees were there for show, dabbling in city government as a hobby between society parties and long weekends in Oyster Bay. From his first days as deputy commissioner, Woods struck a markedly different posture, throwing himself into the task of re-inventing the Detective Bureau.

Woods lived alone in a suite at the Harvard Club, regularly forgoing the society high life to accompany detectives out into the field. (He would later observe, "You cannot do detective work in high hat and kid gloves.") He introduced a new structure for the bureau, modeled after the Europeans, with branch offices distributed across the city to give the investigators a better neighborhood-level vantage point to do their work. Recognizing the vast geographic territory the department now protected in the five boroughs, Woods had city maps plastered across his office walls, with pushpins marking the locations of recent crimes, color coded to designate the type of crime committed—a low-tech version of the CompStat system that played such a prominent role in reducing crime in New York during the 1990s. Still shaped by the regular gymnasium sessions he had written about in his teenage diaries, Woods championed physical fitness on the force, a notable change from the beer-bellied stereotype of the old-school NYPD.

And yet, despite his ample intelligence and charm, Arthur Woods's initial foray into law enforcement proved to be something of a disaster. Shortly after assuming his new office, Woods began working closely with the charismatic detective Joseph Petrosino, head of the NYPD's newly formed "Italian Squad." With Bingham's blessing, Petrosino had managed to corral a handful of native Italian speakers to form an ad hoc undercover unit dedicated to infiltrating the Black Hand. To keep the team members' identities separate from those of the uniformed men, the Italian Squad worked out of a claustrophobic office on Elm Street, around the corner from the Mulberry Street headquarters. The room was packed with mug shots and a small museum display of stilettos they had confiscated from Black Handers.

The Italian Squad was underfunded and understaffed, but Petrosino had a commanding presence and a fearlessness that won him fans both inside the department and in the press. Calabrian by birth, he was a stocky man in his late thirties, with a "strong and determined jaw . . . and lips set in a straight line, suggesting purpose rather than severity," according to a profile that ran in the *Times*. (One might reasonably question the wisdom of allowing a reporter to publish such nuanced physical descriptions of an officer engaged in undercover work.) The headline of the *Times* profile called him "a detective and a sociologist." He had the sharp-eyed cunning of a gifted undercover agent. But he was also capable of the wide-angle view. "The Italians who keep Little Italy in fear and trembling are generally from Sicily and Southern Italy. They are transplanted rustic brigands," he opined in the *Times* profile. "Their work is surprisingly crude. No New York highwayman would think of holding up a man in the streets of New York and cutting his face with a pencil sharpener to frighten him into turning over his money. Nor would a New York crook dare to threaten to dynamite the place of business of a man if he did not appear at a certain time with a certain amount of money. The crimes committed here among the Italians are the same that are committed by country brigands in Italy and Sicily."

They made a strange trio: Woods, Petrosino, and Bingham—the dashing English teacher, the Calabrian sleuth, and the bigoted commissioner. Nonetheless, their fates were linked through the Italian Squad.

Not all the explosions during Woods's first tenure at the NYPD were the work of Black Handers. For several weeks in March of 1908, a socialist organization had been petitioning the city to hold a rally in support of the unemployed; reflecting Bingham's zero-tolerance policy for protest, the request had been repeatedly denied. But on March 28, seven thousand supporters—a mix of socialists, anarchists, and out-of-work laborers—descended on Union Square in defiance of the city officials. Bingham ordered his officers to clear the rally. As a cavalry of mounted officers rode through the surging crowd, swinging sticks to disperse them, an anarchist named Selig Silverstein lifted his right hand to toss something toward the advancing police: a nitroglycerin bomb he had constructed using the brass top of a bedpost, supplemented with broken nails. But the sudden movement of his arm caused the device to detonate in his grasp. When the smoke cleared, the police found Silverstein prone on the sidewalk, a bloodied stump where his hand had been a few seconds before.

As Silverstein lay dying in a Manhattan hospital, the police raided his apartment in Williamsburg, where they found a membership card for an "Anarchist Federation of America," stamped with the signature of Alexander Berkman, Treasurer. Berkman was promptly arrested and brought down to headquarters, where Faurot's men added his portrait to the rogues' gallery and recorded his fingerprints. (Berkman later referred to it as being "Bertillioned.")

But they were unable to make any connection between Silverstein and Berkman beyond the membership card, and the charges were soon dropped.

Never one to avoid endorsing an act of political violence, Berkman penned an essay for Goldman's *Mother Earth* in response to the Union Square bombing called "Violence and Anarchism." In the essay, Berkman laid out perhaps his most concise justification of the prominence that deadly attentats had taken in the movement:

> "You can't regenerate society by violence, by a Union Square bomb," the well-meaning people argue. Indeed, full well we know we cannot. Be fair; give ear. Do not confound the philosophy of a better, freer, and happier life with an act resulting from the very evils which that philosophy seeks to abolish. . . . The bomb is the echo of your cannon, trained upon our starving brothers; it is the cry of the wounded striker; 'tis the voice of hungry women and children; the shriek of those maimed and torn in your industrial slaughterhouses; it is the dull thud of the policeman's club upon a defenseless head . . . The bomb is the ghost of your past crimes.

Observing the chaos of the Union Square protests, Woods began developing his own vision of how the city should handle the radical threat: Not by suppressing rallies and marches but through other, less visible means: Keeping tabs on radical groups using modern intelligence operations. Shutting down protests only amplified the rage of the protestors and normalized the idea that the city's streets and squares were spaces for violent confrontation. Better to let the anarchists and the socialists sing full-throated renditions of "La Marseillaise" in Union Square, and do the real work of law enforcement outside the public view.

In this sense, the Italian Squad was the first test of Woods's larger project. Despite the fact that its undercover operations showed a promising success rate, for most of the squad's first two years of existence, Woods struggled to secure enough funding to support the effort.

And then, out of nowhere, in early 1909, the Italian Squad found itself flush with cash. "Police Commissioner Bingham has a secret service of his own at last," the *Times* reported.

> It is a secret in every sense of the word, for no one at 300 Mulberry Street, with the exception of Lieut. Petrosino and, perhaps, Deputy Commissioner Woods, knows its personnel. Ample funds for the maintenance of the secret service have come to the hands of the Police Commissioner. This much he admits. As to the source from which it came he will not talk, further than to say that it did not come from the city.

Bingham intimated to reporters off the record that prosperous merchants in Little Italy had pooled the funds together, in an effort to reduce crime in the neighborhood—arguably one of the first examples of public-private partnership in the city's history. But the *Times* also noted rumors that two patrons from uptown had also subsidized the Italian Squad endowment: Andrew Carnegie and John D. Rockefeller.

There is a compelling symmetry to the rumored identity of the two anonymous donors. Carnegie, of course, had played an indirect role in disbanding the federal detective force, thanks to the ruthless strikebreaking at the Homestead Steel Works. Several years after making his alleged contribution to the Italian Squad, Rockefeller would go on to initiate his own brutal assault on striking workers, setting off a chain reaction that would ultimately resurrect those detectives—and create a national system of inves-

tigation far more omniscient than anything that had existed in the
Pinkerton era.

While Bingham kept mum on the sources behind the Italian
Squad's new funding, he was less discreet when reporters probed
him for more information on the whereabouts of Petrosino, who
was last seen meeting with Woods several days earlier. Perhaps carried away with excitement over the scope of his new operation,
Bingham chortled at the reporter's question, replying: "Why, he
may be on the ocean, bound for Europe, for all I know."

Bingham's remark—even in its jocular, hypothetical form—
proved appallingly reckless. Lieutenant Petrosino was, in fact, on
board a ship bound for Italy, where he planned to meet secretly
with authorities to compile a list of Italian *desperados* now living in
New York who were wanted for crimes back in their homeland. (In
another interview, Bingham let it slip that Petrosino was headed
for both the mainland of Italy and Sicily.) Woods had helped arrange the voyage, writing to an old friend in the State Department
in early 1909: "We do not want to make this a formal visit. We
want to send Lt. Petrosino over rather on the quiet in order to get
information which takes forever if we ask for it officially, and which
we find great difficulty in getting at all when we try through private agents."

Somehow—perhaps because an overly talkative police commissioner back in Manhattan had decided to mention his mission on
the record to a *New York Times* reporter—Petrosino's cover was
blown. While registering at the Hotel d'Inghilterra in Rome with
an old family friend at his side, Petrosino noticed a familiar face
from back home lurking in the lobby. "I cannot recall his name, but
he is from New York," he told his friend. "His being here means no
good to me." Petrosino pulled his obliging friend into an impromptu
surveillance operation and followed the suspect through the streets
of Rome. "He headed directly for a telegraph office, frequently

looking back," the friend later told the *Times*. "He caught sight of us just as he was entering the door, and, wheeling on his heel, walked rapidly in another direction." Eventually they tracked him to a second telegraph office, where they learned the suspect had sent a wire to the town of Noto, in Sicily. "That man has notified his friends in Sicily that I am here," Petrosino observed solemnly.

Despite warnings from the Italian ambassador that he was a known target to "perhaps a thousand criminals" in Sicily, Petrosino continued his mission, traveling by ferry to Palermo. On the night of March 12, he went to meet an informant in a darkened corner of the Piazza Marina, where two assassins shot him point-blank in the face. The American consul in Palermo wired the State Department the next morning: "Petrosino shot, instantly killed, near his hotel early this evening. Assassins unknown. Dies martyr . . . protecting peaceful Italian[s] in America."

Bingham had been in Washington when the cable arrived. He immediately returned to his Manhattan apartment, bypassing the

Telegram announcing the murder of Detective Petrosino

throngs of reporters gathering at Mulberry Street. It was left to Woods to release an official statement to the press:

> It is hoped that the assassination of this faithful servant of New York City may bring home to people some idea of the seriousness of the Black Hand situation. Although the number of Black Hand crimes has been decreased about 50 per cent in the last few months, it is impossible to make any radical move against these outlaws unless the Police Department can have the use of a secret service fund provided by the city.

When asked by reporters to verify a rumor that Petrosino had been compelled to make the trip to Italy against his will, Woods snapped back, "You can say as hard as you want to, officially, that Petrosino was very enthusiastic about going and hot on the job."

Later that morning, another flock of reporters gathered outside a home on West Thirty-first Street, where Teddy Roosevelt—newly out of office—was visiting his aunt. "I cannot say anything about anybody or thing," the former president said with a smile and a wave to the press when he first emerged. But when the reporters began peppering him with questions about Petrosino's death, he stopped short, jolted by the news.

"I can't say anything except to express my deepest regrets. Petrosino was a great man and a good man," Roosevelt told them. "I knew him for years, and he did not know the name of fear."

Arthur Woods never revealed to the press any of his personal misgivings or grief over the death of Petrosino, though it must have weighed heavily on him in the months that followed. The most troubling element was not just the fact that he had dispatched Petrosino on the mission that ended his life; it was also that Woods himself had been a far better candidate to make the voyage. As police historian Thomas Reppetto observed, the Italian officials were sensitive to social standing, and took offense at the Americans sending what they saw as a "simple peasant" to represent the United States in such delicate circumstances. "The investigation should have been carried out by the U.S. State Department in consultation with a European-educated police official like the patrician Deputy Commissioner Woods," Reppetto notes. "If Woods had come over, the Italian police would have taken steps to ensure that a Harvard gentleman and an intimate of Pres. Theodore Roosevelt was not murdered on their soil."

Woods channeled his remorse into writing a long essay that expanded on the reform ideas he had alluded to in the official statement on Petrosino's death. Published in *McClure's,* the influential muckraking periodical regularly home to reformers like Lincoln Steffens and Ida Tarbell, the essay was titled "The Problem of the Black Hand."

At its core, "The Problem of the Black Hand" was a continuation of Roosevelt's "black infamy" speech after McKinley's assassination, only with a different European immigrant as the villain: mobster extortionists instead of the philosophizing bomb throwers of the anarchist set. But the solutions were the same. Woods called it "beyond a question" that an adequate secret service force would have delivered a "hard blow" to the Black Hand. But that level of undercover activity posed an enormous risk if you tried to carry it out on the precinct level. "Secrecy is impossible for the police detectives. There are so few of them, and they work so constantly in the Italian colonies, that their faces are as well known as those of old friends," he noted, before making his only reference to his fallen compatriot. "Lieutenant Petrosino, in spite of his devotion to duty, his long experience, and his great detective skill, was unable to overcome the handicap of publicity."

While Petrosino had framed the Black Hand crisis as a clash between "rustic brigands" from the old country and one of the world's "most civilized" cities, Woods offered a different explanation. The Black Handers were drawn to America not because its burgeoning wealth made it an appealing target. They were drawn to America because its mode of law enforcement—particularly the way it gathered and stored information—was so *backward* compared to the modern Italian approach. "There is every reason why America should attract the Italian criminal. He certainly has a hard enough time in Italy," Woods argued in *McClure's*.

One thing that annoys him there is the seeming impossibility of escaping the watchfulness of the government. The registry system is so comprehensive and is carried out so carefully that no matter how much a man may move about in the kingdom, he can always be traced. If he goes from his home town to another place and puts up in a lodging-house or a hotel, the police are at once notified. If he takes a house, the tax assessors register him with the police; and, if occasion arises, his whole history can be found in the place of his birth. The records are centralized in this way: From wherever a man moves to, information is sent to the town of his birth, where his complete record is kept. If he gives a false name he can be prosecuted for fraud, and he could not long pose under an assumed name, since a record would be made of anything that he did and he would be looked up in his home town. Anything wrong in his report would be easily detected. The absence of this kind of surveillance in the United States appears attractive to a person who does not care to have his doings made a matter of record. In Italy it seems to him impossible to escape the government; in the United States he goes practically unnoticed by the government.

The lesson to be drawn from the Italians was clear: The United States required a federal secret service, modeled after the institutions that had proved so successful in Italy and the rest of Europe. "The carbineers are a fine body of police. Being under federal control, local influences do not affect them. They cover the whole of Italy," Woods explained. Whereas in the United States, "the police are local, and although the police forces of different cities cooperate, they do so spasmodically and only as occasion arises; there is no comprehensive system. If a man gains a bad reputation in one city, he can be fairly certain of leaving it behind him and starting all over again if he goes to another city. We have no national police force."

Bingham and Woods soldiered on for a few months, their ambitious plans for an undercover division foiled by the tragedy in Palermo. Soon thereafter, they became embroiled in a civil liberties controversy revolving around the rogues' gallery. A nineteen-year-old milkman named George Duffy had been picked up on suspicion of participating in a robbery. The arrest appears to have been a simple case of mistaken identity; Duffy was quickly acquitted and released—but not before the NYPD added his portrait parlé to the newly modernized file cabinets of the Identification Department, standard operating procedure for all suspects put under arrest.

Now a free man, acquitted of all charges, Duffy nonetheless found himself the constant target of police harassment thanks to his familiar face. It was the kind of persecution regularly experienced by the denizens of the Lower East Side, but Duffy happened to come from a more affluent, well-connected family. His father petitioned a New York State Supreme Court justice to have the photograph removed from the gallery, arguing—quite reasonably—that the police should not retain biometric information about innocent

civilians. Bingham and Woods opted to fight back, leaking scurri-
lous information to the press suggesting that Duffy was some kind
of "degenerate" whose visage belonged in the Identification Department. "While reporters interviewed his parents, employers, and
even former teachers—all of whom confirmed the milkman's good
character—the police attempted to link him to prostitution and
fraud," the historian Thai Jones writes. "The cover-up drifted over
toward intimidation."

The combination of Palermo and the "Duffy Boy scandal" made
it clear that the already controversial Bingham was more trouble
than he was worth. He was relieved of his duty on July 1; Woods
resigned on the same day. Within two weeks of their departure, the
doors were shut on what remained of the Italian Squad as well. It
was the end of Thomas Bingham's short and ill-fated career as a
police reformer.

Arthur Woods, though, was just getting started. Five years later,
he would have another opportunity to implement the European
model—only then it would be the anarchists, not the Black Handers, that necessitated undercover surveillance and a European-style
identification system. But that was all in the distant future. In the
short term, it would be left to Detective Joseph Faurot to make the
case for the new science.

CHAPTER 16

The People Versus
Charles Crispi

On the morning of February 23, 1911, Detective James Fitzpatrick arrived at 171 Wooster Street in SoHo—just a few blocks west of the NYPD headquarters—to investigate a potential burglary at a garment factory operating under the name M. M. Bernstein and Brother. A quick survey of the crime scene made it clear to Fitzpatrick that the break-in had been the work of a professional. The thief had clearly managed to case the premises beforehand: He had entered through an abandoned third-floor loft, and then used carpenter's tools to cut a hole through the ceiling, giving him access to the sweatshop above where the Bernstein brothers produced muslin underwear. To exit the crime scene, the thief had disabled an alarm wired to the entrance by methodically removing a pane of glass set in the doorframe with his tools. He had escaped unseen with $350 worth of corsets and embroideries.

At first, the sweatshop break-in appeared to be the perfect crime—until Fitzgerald examined the glass pane that the burglar had left propped against the wall and noticed several greasy fingerprints visible on the surface of the glass. Fitzgerald confiscated the windowpane as evidence and immediately brought it back to the Identification Bureau at 300 Mulberry. There Joseph Faurot commenced the protocol he had learned five years before at Scotland Yard. He dusted powder on the print with a camel's-hair brush to make it more visible, and then photographed it. He retreated into the Identification Bureau's darkroom, where he developed the image, then enlarged it four times over. He placed the final photograph on his desk and carefully documented the fingerprint's signature characteristics: the whorls and loops and deltas and arches that made it unique. Once those characteristics had been defined, using a variation of the nested-search algorithm that Bertillon had invented thirty years before, he explored the sixty-five thousand fingerprints in the NYPD's file cabinets.

Before long, he had a match: a man named Charles Crispi, whose fingerprints Faurot had taken four years earlier. Tellingly, in that original booking, Crispi had been brought in on charges of breaking into a SoHo loft.

Joseph Faurot had little in his personal life to distract him from the cause of modernizing the detective bureau. He had married a young woman named Nellie Riley shortly after joining the force, but she had died tragically of a pulmonary edema—likely from pneumonia—only three years later, at the age of twenty-four. By 1911, he was living the middle-class version of Arthur Woods's bachelor lifestyle at the Harvard Club—in Faurot's case, sleeping in a spare bedroom in his brother's apartment on 148th Street. But Faurot's reputation at the Mulberry Street headquarters had grown steadily over the years since his return from Europe in 1906. In part, he was riding a wave of interest in forensic science that was rolling across the United States. In Chicago, a freelance detective named Mary Holland—who also dabbled as a true-crime writer—became one of the first certified fingerprint analysts in the country. She served as an expert witness at a murder trial in 1910, the first appellate case in United States history where fingerprints were accepted as a legitimate form of evidence. But the Crispi case would prove to be a milestone as well—in part because Faurot was not just an earnest student of forensic science but also something of a showman.

Opening arguments in *The People of the State of New York v. Charles Crispi* began on May 11, in the courtroom of Judge Otto Rosalsky. Assistant district attorney Isidore Wasservogel led the state's case. Because Crispi had executed the crime with such precision—other than the print left behind on the glass pane—Wasservogel was forced to build almost his entire argument around the science of fingerprint identification, an utterly novel discipline for the twelve members of the jury. After eliciting a quick survey of the crime-scene layout from Detective Fitzpatrick, and after a brief interview with the officer who had arrested Crispi, Wasservogel called Faurot to the stand, where he would testify for two days as the only other witness for the prosecution.

Wasservogel opted to have Faurot begin with a general overview of how the police used fingerprints to identify suspects. After noting that he had studied the fingerprint method "at Scotland Yard and in Paris, France, under Mr. Alphonse Bertillon," Faurot launched immediately into a technical description of the craft. It did not go well.

> Situated upon the palm or surface of the hands are elevations and depressions in the skin surface. These elevations constitute ridges, and when they come in contact with ink frayed out to a smooth surface upon a slab and the finger rolled upon the ink, these elevations pick up the ink, and when the finger is rolled upon paper it transfers the ink to the paper, causing a fingerprint. . . . [The shapes] are divided into four types: loop, arch, whorl, and composite. Those are different patterns. We get our primary classification from the numerical additions of the sum totals of relative weights allowed these different patterns. The whorl is the only one that is given numerical weight, the arch and loop being cast aside, and the impressions are divided—the ten impressions are divided into five pairs.

Perhaps sensing some confusion emanating from Judge Rosalsky, Faurot paused there, before Rosalsky nudged him along: "Go on, for the present."

"The whorl occurring in the first pair is given a weight of sixteen," Faurot continued, no doubt confounding his audience further with each additional detail. "The second pair eight; the third pair four, the fourth pair two, and the fifth pair one. Now, a whorl occurring in any of these pairs is given the relative weight in which it falls—"

Perplexed by the barrage of numbers and technical terms, Rosalsky interrupted from the bench: "Not so rapidly. The whirl, you say?"

"The whorl: w-h-o-r-l," Faurot explained.

The spelling lesson turned out to be less helpful than Faurot had hoped. "What do you mean by *whorl*?" Rosalsky asked.

After an even more in-depth discussion that parsed the distinctions between whorls, loops, deltas, ridge tracing, and inner terminals, which must have left the jury baffled, Wasservogel opted to shift gears away from the technicalities.

"Do you know of any institutions in this country that have adopted this method of identification?" he asked. After heated objections from the defense, Faurot was finally allowed to answer the question:

"The War Department, the Navy Department, the English government, the banks here in North America and in South America and in Europe. Railroads use it; public businesses use it; municipal civil service of this city uses it," Faurot declared. "Lawyers use it in signing wills. The Chinese have used it for centuries on their passports."

After more protests from the defense attorney, Wasservogel turned to Exhibit 1: the pane of glass recovered from Bernstein's loft. Unnerved by the mixed reaction to his opening statements, Faurot confused the date he had first received it, placing it in early

March and not late February. Eventually, though, Wasservogel got around to the core question:

"From your experience, as a fingerprint expert, after the comparison made by you as you have testified to, what conclusion did you come to?"

"The prints were left by the same person. The identification of the prints is the identification of the person."

What followed that declarative sentence was another hour of arcane forensic science. In one extraordinary stretch of the transcript, Faurot speaks almost uninterrupted for *nine* pages—somewhere on the order of fifteen minutes in the courtroom—identifying each shared characteristic between the three sets of prints.

> FAUROT: Number 4, a bifurcation of ridges, two ridge lines running up and over, running on into one, curving down. Number 4, the core of the whorl. What I mean by the core is the center circle which occurs in both prints. Number 6, termination of ridge, ridge running up and abruptly ending to the right of core. Number 7 is the termination of ridge, next line to number 6 line running in the same direction up and abruptly ending slightly below number 6.

Perhaps the strategy was to overwhelm the jury with the sheer, mind-numbing magnitude of the evidence. Or perhaps Faurot's droning litany was meant to set the stage for what was to follow. Or perhaps Wasservogel and Faurot began to realize that they'd miscalculated with the jargon and the math, and decided to change it up at the last minute. All we know for certain from the transcript is this: The second Faurot relayed the final shared characteristic, Wasservogel asked the judge for an immediate recess. And by the time they returned, they had swapped the hard science for magic tricks.

* * *

What exactly transpired during that recess has long been lost to history. Did Faurot and Wasservogel dream up the stunt that followed, or had it always been their game plan? Either way, they seem to have prepared the judge for the stunt beforehand, for reasons we will see. If in fact the DA and the detective realized they were overloading the jury with technical minutiae and needed to take a different tack, they still would have had time to both dream up the scheme *and* brief the judge before the recess ended. If so, it was one of the all-time greatest legal improvisations: real-world courtroom hijinks straight out of *Perry Mason*.

When the court resumed session, Wasservogel began by asking Faurot if he had successfully identified other criminals using the fingerprint method. Faurot recounted the story of the mysterious guest at the Waldorf-Astoria and reflected briefly on his time at Scotland Yard. Then Wasservogel turned to the main event.

"Lieutenant," he asked Faurot, "if impressions were taken of a dozen or more persons in this courtroom upon pieces of glass and marked with their names, and then you were to leave this courtroom, and one of the persons who had made the original impression were to make another impression, could you upon returning to the courtroom pick out the person who made the two impressions?"

Crispi's attorney leapt up immediately to protest: "I object to that as incompetent, immaterial, irrelevant, and inadmissible!"

Rosalsky turned to Wasservogel and queried: "In other words, you want to have this witness conduct an experiment?"

"I do," the district attorney replied.

Presumably briefed in advance about the strategy, the judge rattled off six examples of legal precedent where in-trial experiments were conducted to confirm or deny part of the prosecution's case. "Now, if you can have experiments conducted in a similar way, that is, under similar conditions," Rosalsky said, "I shall allow you to do so."

After an officer ushered Faurot out of the courtroom, with instructions to monitor the detective at all times, the opposing attorneys tussled over the most accurate way to design the experiment, with Rosalsky offering detailed suggestions from the bench. Ultimately they fingerprinted all twelve jurors and marked each fingerprint with an alphabetic code. One juror—whose prints were represented by the code *I*—was chosen to place his fingers on a piece of glass similar to the one found in the SoHo loft. At that point, Faurot was readmitted to the courtroom.

Wasservogel greeted him with instructions: "Lieutenant, will you step down here, please, at the clerk's desk, and compare these twelve slips with certain finger marks upon the glass, and see whether you can pick out the person who made the one upon the glass from those before you?"

Faurot settled in at the clerk's desk and began the protocol, dusting and examining the print on the glass with a magnifying glass, then turning to the jurors' prints laid out before him. The courtroom remained in a hushed silence as Faurot performed his examination. For the first five prints, he failed to discern a connection to the print on the glass. But when he turned to the sixth, the telltale features popped out at him immediately: a distinctive loop on the index finger and a whorl on the third finger. There was little reason to even glance at the remaining prints, but Faurot was nothing if not methodical.

After completing his examination, Faurot returned to the witness box and offered his analysis to the stunned jury: "The person represented by the letter *I* is the one that made the impression."

Having dazzled the jury with a live demo, Wasservogel returned to his Exhibit 1: the pane of glass removed from the SoHo loft. "How many points of similarity," he asked his lead witness, "do you find in the conceded prints of the defendant of March, 1911 and October

1907—that is, how many similar points do you find on comparison with the prints found on the window, on the pane of glass?"

"Forty-eight points," Faurot replied.

"Are you of the opinion that fingerprints are a better means of identification than the photographs of a human being?"

"Positively, yes, sir," Faurot affirmed. "You can readily see where fingerprints are far superior, as a man's identification, to measurements or photographs. In the Bertillon system of identification, the measurements which we use at police headquarters—and I have had vast experience with them . . . one operator may measure a little tight, that is make a tight or close measurement. I may take a measurement and take a loose measurement. Consequently, there is a slight deviation between our measurements. The deviation means, on looking it up, you have to go over several to allow for that limit of error. [But with] fingerprints, you may take fingerprints, and I may take fingerprints, and we get identically the same result. There is no personal equation. There is no limit of error allowed whatsoever."

Faurot went on to explain that fingerprints had a critical advantage over photography, one that Henry Faulds had originally discerned in calling them "the nature-copy of the forever unchangeable": Unlike the human face, the whorls and loops on the pads of the fingers did not evolve over time. "In photography, you can readily see that yourself, in your own photograph," Faurot noted to the jury. "Take one, say, from fifteen years back and look at it today, and there is a vast difference."

After Faurot left the stand, the defense mounted a half-hearted attempt to build an alibi for Crispi but made no effort to rebut the fingerprint evidence. There were no scientifically trained detectives to call, just a series of slightly shady underworld characters testifying to Crispi's whereabouts. It was clear that Wasservogel and Faurot's parlor trick had won over the jury. When the trial resumed on the morning of May 11, Crispi's attorney announced that they were withdrawing their plea of not guilty and would plead guilty to the crime of unlawful entry.

Recognizing the significance of the case, Rosalsky immediately framed the plea as a validation of the new science. "Crispi, I want you to make a full confession," he told the defendant. "It is important to the cause of justice that you do so. It is important to the cause of science to know whether or not the expert testimony is valuable or valueless. Fingerprint experts are of the opinion that this science is more exact than photography, and that experts are able to identify persons by fingerprints with a greater degree of accuracy than under any other system of identification. Did you remove the pane of glass which was offered in evidence here?"

"Yes, sir."

"Well now, Crispi, while you knew you committed this crime, why was it that you agreed to furnish Lieutenant Faurot with your fingerprints?"

"I didn't believe that the fingerprints would hurt me in any way at all."

"You did not believe that?"

"I knew they had already taken my fingerprints, and I didn't think these would in any way hurt me at all."

"Well, have you changed your opinion upon that subject now?"

"I have, very much."

Rosalsky then commended Faurot for his "important work," going on to add his personal endorsement of the fingerprint methodology.

"I believe this country should develop this science, and it ought to be accepted," he announced. "I know it is rather difficult for a burglar to use gloves in his work." Turning to the defendant, he asked: "Crispi, would you not find it rather difficult to use gloves in burglary, that is, in handling your implements?"

Crispi nodded in affirmation.

"The law must keep pace with the ingenuity and skill of the criminal," Rosalsky proclaimed, before bringing the trial to a close. "We cannot permit the law to remain at a standstill."

The People versus Charles Crispi would go down in history as the first successful conviction based primarily on fingerprint evidence in the United States. The courtroom theatrics generated a flood of publicity for Faurot himself. For the first time, a new theme began to percolate in the press coverage of the NYPD: the notion that the institution might actually be at the vanguard of law enforcement techniques, and not simply a band of enforcers supporting a corrupt political machine. In June, the *Times* ran an effusive full-page profile of Faurot, including a line drawing of him at his desk, looking more like a prosperous insurance executive than a cop. The headline ran: "Keeping Track of the Criminal by his Fingerprints: the Wonderful Art, Long Used in China, Rapidly being Adopted by the Police of this Country, with the New York Force Leading."

"The fingerprint system will remain the great science of identification long after all burglars have learned to go gloved in midsummer," the *Times* reporter predicted. "Banks are already using it with their illiterate depositors. Perhaps some day the census taker will demand our finger prints along with our age and occupation." Like Arthur Woods before him, Faurot envisioned the system that he had pioneered on a local level in New York extending across the entire country. "Lieut. Faurot hopes that the government will establish at Washington a central clearing house for the finger prints of malefactors, thereby facilitating the work of different cities," the profile noted in its closing lines, "and such a bureau of identification for criminals may foreshadow one for the average man."

CHAPTER 17

The Body and the Blood

The morning of September 5, 1913, was unusually cool and pleasant in New York City, with temperatures in the low sixties and a splendid blue sky overhead. On the New Jersey side of the Hudson River, a sister and brother named Mary and Albert Bann sat on the front porch of their tar paper shack built into the base of the towering basalt cliffs of the Palisades and watched a strange package bobbing upstream, carried along by the rising tide. Several feet across, it appeared to be wrapped in brown paper, tied together with coarse twine. Later in the morning, the tide pulled the mysterious bundle back down past the Banns' house, where it bobbed its way into an eddy of driftwood at the edge of an abandoned dock. Eleven-year-old Albert wandered down to the muddy banks of the Hudson and prodded the package toward him with a stick. The bundle had a surprising heft to it, given its size. Enlisting his sister's help, Albert lugged it up to the porch and untied the knot that held it together. Whatever was inside had been placed into a pillowcase with a cheerful floral design, bound up with a cloth-covered wire. There were still feathers inside the pillowcase, but also some other, bulkier object.

When the two children presented their curious discovery to their parents, Mrs. Bann immediately vetoed the idea of unwrapping the bundle. For hours it sat on their porch unopened. But before long a gaggle of neighborhood boys had arrived to inspect the object, and the curiosity of the children slowly wore down the parental restraint. When Albert and Mary finally peeled back the wa-terlogged fabric, it took the assembled onlookers a few seconds to identify what they were seeing. At first, it seemed to be a fragment of a statue or a department store dummy. But then their eyes regis-tered what they had actually pulled from the river: the upper torso of a woman's body, arms and head cleanly amputated.

The Banns lacked a telephone in their small riverside home, so one member of the group raced to the nearby Trilby Hotel and rang the police in Hoboken. Within a matter of hours, the county physi-cian, Dr. George W. King, was examining the remains at a morgue. Early gossip about the discovery had speculated that the body could have been part of a cadaver used for medical instruction. Or perhaps the arms and head had been amputated as part of a riverboat acci-dent. But it took King only minutes of inspection to recognize the obvious truth. "The woman had unquestionably been murdered," he told the *Times* the next day. "There was almost a total absence of blood in the heart and other organs and in the muscles. This condi-tion made it certain that she bled to death. The heart, lungs, stom-ach, and other organs were intact, so that there is not foundation for the theory that the body had been used for dissection." While the body had been dismembered with some skill, King suspected that the killer was not a trained medical professional, because the lungs had not been punctured. A simple incision would have caused them to fill with water once the torso had been submerged in the river. Instead, the intact lungs of the dead woman had served as a kind of life preserver for her remains, floating them back to the surface so the Bann children could discover them.

Another tantalizing clue lay in the packaging. A close inspection of the pillowcase revealed a tag sewn into its lining, with the words: ROBINSON-BODERS COMPANY, NEWARK, NEW JERSEY.

Two days after the first bundle surfaced, a second one washed ashore a mile downriver in Weehawken, retrieved by a pair of crabbers. Inside was the lower half of the torso, absent the legs. When this new gruesome discovery was brought to Dr. King, the physician declared the amputation to be "one of the neatest pieces of surgical work" he had ever seen. "So closely did the two parts fit together it seemed as if one blow had severed them."

The Weehawken bundle differed from the one that the Bann children discovered in that it was weighed down with about ten pounds of rock. After consulting with mineralogists, the police determined that the rock was Manhattan schist, abundant on the eastern shores of the Hudson but practically nonexistent on the Jersey side.

By Monday morning, the eighth day of September, the police were interviewing employees at the Robinson-Boders Company, who identified the pillowcase as belonging to a line that had only been sold to a furniture dealer in Washington Heights. The killer was acquiring his rocks, and his bedding, in Manhattan. This was a New York City case.

That was how the Hudson murder first came across the desk of Joseph Faurot.

Since the triumph of the Crispi conviction in 1911, Faurot had traveled back to Europe—this time as an expert in the forensic sciences, not a student—and the upper brass had endowed him with a proper detectives school where he could train the next generation of sleuths. It helped that Rhinelander Waldo—the latest police commissioner—was less openly hostile to the European techniques than Bingham had been. But Faurot's increased influence was also aided indirectly by rising anti-corruption sentiment in the city. Faurot's bureau was an island of scientific rigor and integrity in a sea of brute corruption. And the cop who most famously embodied that old-guard mentality was a twenty-year veteran of the force named

Charles Becker, whose wages as a law enforcement officer had long been supplemented by an active involvement in the city's gambling and prostitution underworld.

In the summer of 1912, a prominent member of that underworld, Herman Rosenthal, threatened to turn state's witness and accuse Becker of being a silent partner in a number of illegal operations. The night before he was supposed to offer a deposition to the Manhattan DA, Rosenthal was assassinated outside a Times Square hotel. Within weeks, Becker had been arrested for first degree murder, accused of orchestrating the hit on Rosenthal.

The crime scandalized the city: Not only were members of the NYPD on the take, it seemed, but they were willing to assassinate potential informers if necessary. (The murder of Herman Rosenthal made such an impact that it landed a cameo appearance in *The Great Gatsby* more than a decade later.) In late 1912, Becker was convicted of murder and sentenced to death, but underworld figures convinced the governor to reexamine the evidence with an eye to reversing the decision, an investigation that ultimately resulted in a retrial. Becker's trial was front-page news for months, but it was only the most prominent of the corruption charges that had been leveled against the department. Facing a genuine crisis of legitimacy, Commissioner Waldo turned to Faurot, whose cerebral demeanor and recent high-profile successes with Crispi and other cases made him the perfect antithesis to Becker and his ilk. By September of 1913, when the Manhattan schist and the pillowcase tag in the Hudson murders implicated a New York City–based suspect, Joseph Faurot had been promoted to chief detective of the NYPD.

When the foundation was first dug out for the Church of St. Joseph of the Holy Family in the village of Manhattanville, back in 1860, the landscape that surrounded the new church still resembled the original Dutch farming communities that had settled the northern regions of Manhattan two hundred years before. By the time it was completed, the church seemed strangely out of place: a neo-Romanesque brick building with a five-story bell tower planted incongruously in the middle of dairy farms. But the recently completed Hudson River Line had connected the once remote villages of Manhattanville and Harlem to the growing metropolis to their south, bringing in a wave of new residents, most of them immigrants: Italians, Jews, and the German Catholics who built St. Joseph's. By the beginning of the twentieth century, the Manhattan grid had enveloped the area, but the neighborhood had not yet seen the historic influx of African Americans that would give rise to the Harlem Renaissance in the 1920s. In early 1912, when a young German priest named Hans Schmidt joined the parish as a junior pastor, the neighborhood was still a hub of working-class German and Irish Catholics.

Schmidt had immigrated to the United States several years before, after accusations had surfaced suggesting that he had molested young boys in his parish and consorted with prostitutes. Just a few days before the dismembered body first washed ashore on the banks of the Hudson, he married an Austrian housekeeper named Anna Aumüller, who was pregnant with their child.

Hans Schmidt, circa 1910–1915

From a young age, Schmidt had been driven by an almost

vampire-like erotic obsession with blood. Significant evidence suggests that he had also murdered a nine-year-old girl in Louisville, Kentucky, where he had originally worked as a priest after first immigrating to America, though the crime remains unsolved. Schmidt would later claim that the idea for murdering his wife had been a dictate from God that came to him while having sex with her on the steps of the altar at St. Joseph's. The fact that he had also secretly taken out a life insurance policy on her suggests that there might have been pecuniary incentives alongside the spiritual revelations. But whatever was actually motivating Hans Schmidt, his actions on the night of September 2 were clearly the work of a deranged mind. Schmidt would later recount the evening in gruesome detail to a court-appointed alienist:

> As I went in, the moon was shining. There was no light. I was in such a state. I knelt on the bed. She slightly turned her arm. I kissed her for the last time. She had her nightdress on. That same evening I had bitten her and had tasted some of her blood. I had a desire to taste more. Then I did it. I cut her throat with the right hand. I cut almost through the neck. I did not close her mouth. I didn't think of it. As the blood ran all over her, it excited me greatly. I attempted intercourse with her while the blood was flowing. I was pressing against her. I felt perfectly satisfied. I was not frightened at all. I took some blood from the throat and mixed it with water and drank it . . . like in the saying of the mass.

That night, Schmidt methodically dismembered her body in the bathroom and then discarded her remains in the Hudson, weighing it down with rocks he had pilfered from a vacant lot across the street from their apartment. As the mysterious bundles began their slow drift to the Jersey side of the river, Schmidt calmly made his way to St. Joseph's, changed into his vestments and cassock, and performed morning mass for a small weekday congregation. The familiar lines of the Eucharistic Prayer had a chilling second meaning:

> In humble prayer we ask you, almighty God: command that these gifts be borne by the hands of your holy Angel to your altar on high in the sight of your divine majesty, so that all of us, who through this participation at the altar receive the most holy Body and Blood of your Son, may be filled with every grace and heavenly blessing.

It took Detective Faurot five eventful days to get from the Robinson-Boders Company tag on the pillowcase to the killer priest at St. Joseph's. Detectives scoured the records of the furniture dealer in Washington Heights and discovered that twelve pillowcases matching the one found in the Hudson had been sold to a canal boat captain. "Considering that the pieces of the girl's body had been fished out of the river, that clue looked good," Faurot later explained to a reporter. But an interview with the captain made it clear to the detective that it was a red herring. The investigators turned to another receipt at the furniture store for the purchase of a mattress, bedspring, and pillow, attributed to a Manhattan resident named A. Van Dyke.

The goods had been delivered to a one-room apartment at 68 Bradhurst Avenue. An interview with the superintendent revealed that the room had only been recently rented to a young couple. Faurot ordered twenty-four-hour surveillance on the apartment, but for four days no one came in or out of the place. With a sadistic killer on the loose and pressure mounting from the police commissioner, Faurot decided to take a chance and force his way into the apartment. He later admitted that the legal grounds for a search were shaky at best: "I hadn't any right to do what I did, with no more to go on than I had, but the thought of what might be behind that locked door in those silent rooms was too compelling for me to resist."

Accompanied by another officer, Faurot forced the door open with a broken hammer. Inside, they found a bare bed frame and a closet full of clothes, including two trunks filled with women's garments. "The place had been washed and cleaned," Faurot told reporters. But in the bathroom, they discovered bars of soap, rags, and a scrubbing brush, all marked with the rust-colored stain of human blood. Newspapers on the scene matched ones that had washed ashore with the body parts in New Jersey. Most damning of all, they found a hacksaw in the apartment. "Here was the place where the woman had been killed and cut up," Faurot recalled. But who was the woman? And where was the occupant of the apartment?

In a closet, Faurot discovered a small box filled with letters, many postmarked from Germany, all addressed to a certain Hans Schmidt. But the most recent letters were local: sent by a woman named Anna Aumüller with a return address of 428 East Seventieth Street, eighty blocks south of them. Sensing that they were close on the heels of their suspect, Faurot and his men began a frantic expedition across Manhattan, speeding past the trams and horse-drawn carriages in their open-air police car. At East Seventieth Street, they found the apartment occupied by a Central Park boatman who explained that Anna had lived with him and his wife for several years, but that she had moved downtown for a new job at St. Boniface, a church on East Forty-seventh Street. At St. Boniface, Faurot and his men interviewed the parish priest, who recognized Schmidt's name immediately. He had served as curate there until the spring of 1912, when he had left the parish for a new assignment, at a church uptown on 125th Street. The priest noted that he had been relieved when Schmidt left for the new assignment. "I was mystified by [his] constant changes of expression," he told Faurot.

"The only way I can describe him was that he was like Stevenson's Jekyll and Hyde."

Having traversed hundreds of city blocks in a matter of hours, Faurot and his men finally arrived at the Church of St. Joseph of the Holy Family. It was there, in the early morning of September 13, that Joseph Faurot found himself face-to-face with Hans Schmidt.

At first Schmidt feigned confusion about why the police would have any interest in him, claiming never to have met a woman named Anna Aumüller. But Faurot's unnerving interrogation techniques quickly broke through the façade. Shown a photograph of the young woman, Schmidt recoiled visibly. As Faurot urged him on with his penetrating stare, Schmidt exclaimed, in words that would echo through the media over the coming days: "I killed her! I killed her because I loved her."

The arrest of Hans Schmidt—and the lurid details of Anna's murder—became a national story overnight. Faurot's inspired detective work triggered a surge of good publicity for the NYPD in the fall of 1913, a welcome change for an organization that had suffered through a long season of media abuse thanks to the Becker trial. "At first the case looked hopeless. Students of police methods shook their heads and said the mystery would never be solved," the *New York Press* observed. "[But] by infinite patience the chief of New York detectives added bit by bit to the structure he was building up from the disconnected pieces of evidence." The headline hailed it as a "Police Triumph."

For Faurot, the capture of Hans Schmidt—who would ultimately be convicted of Anna Aumüller's murder and executed in 1915, just a few months after Charles Becker suffered the same fate—was more than just a personal triumph. It was also, crucially, a validation of the scientific, cerebral approach he had been championing inside the force. Another fawning profile of Faurot—this one in the *Sun*—explicitly recast the story of Schmidt's confession as an object lesson in the power of new paradigm:

> A detective getting a confession out of a man in a few minutes without using his fists or so much as a high note, without even a threat of arrest? Why, if your two-handed cop of Byrnes's day had witnessed on the stage the unathletic, quiet spoken scene really enacted in the small parlor . . . where Hans Schmidt confessed to Inspector Joe Faurot after midnight last Sunday morning he would have laughed as hilariously as Inspector Joe Faurot must want to laugh when he sees the old time third degree as presented in the crook plays of to-day.

Newspapers all across the country ran full-page profiles, with photographs of Faurot, occasionally supplemented by pictures of "raven-haired beauty" Anna Aumüller. The New York *Sun* gave its feature the headline: "How New York's Real Detective Solves Criminal Mysteries by Scientific Methods." Faurot was favorably compared to Sherlock Holmes: "No old sleuth of lurid-lidded fiction ever followed a trail more relentlessly or more swiftly to its conclusion than this same Inspector Faurot, when he unearthed the man who betrayed and butchered Anna Aumüller."

Faurot seized the newfound celebrity as a platform to make a national case for his reformist ideas. He began writing regular columns, many of them a strange hybrid of true-crime storytelling and op-ed-style advocacy. "A new era has dawned upon the New York detective, and that is why our men are regarded as second to none in the world," Faurot announced in one of them. "I am an ardent advocate of the new and scientific methods and Commissioner Waldo has given me every help possible to introduce methods here which have practically revolutionized police work."

Faurot would not have the opportunity to rest on his laurels for long. Sleeping in the spare bedroom at his brother's apartment in Hamilton Heights later that fall, Faurot was awakened by a loud noise. He struggled into his uniform and found his way to a blown-out storefront on Amsterdam Avenue and 148th Street. The cause was obvious: dynamite, deliberately planted. There was evidence to suggest that it was the work of an anarchist group loosely affiliated with the Black Hand.

Exploring the carnage left behind in the wake of the blast, Faurot attempted to make his way into the cellar of the building. But the explosion had damaged the rickety stairs, and the detective fell several feet, his body landing in "a mass of broken glass," as the *Times* reported the next morning, cutting his arm so badly that he had to be taken to a nearby physician's home to be stitched up.

Walking back to his brother's apartment that night, Faurot would have had no way of knowing that the Hamilton Heights explosion was just a hint of the turbulence to come. Yes, the anarchists had come to his neighborhood, and yes, he had been personally injured in the aftermath of the attack. But it was just one explosion, and the stitches in his arm were merely an occupational hazard of the investigation.

Soon enough, though, the anarchists would be targeting him directly.

That so many glowing profiles were written about Faurot only highlighted the fact that the "scientific detective" was still an anomaly in American law enforcement. For significant changes to policing to take root across the entire landscape, Faurot needed allies. And he needed crimes to investigate that went beyond burglaries or salacious murders—crimes that had national implications, thus warranting a national response.

Still, as 1913 came to a close, the signs were promising. On November 4, voters elected the thirty-four-year-old reformer John Purroy Mitchel the next mayor of New York—the second-youngest mayor in the city's history, and thanks to his Venezuelan-born grandmother, the first of Latin American descent. Mitchel had campaigned as an aggressive opponent of the Tammany machine, with an ambitious plan to overhaul and modernize the police force. On election night, he hosted an intimate dinner for his closest advisors at his Riverside Drive apartment, watching the returns come in on a stock ticker specially adapted for the occasion. Among the attendees was the confidant who had drafted the blueprints for Mitchel's plan to reinvent the NYPD: Arthur Hale Woods.

There was one other hint that fall of the seismic changes to come, though it was only detectable in hindsight.

In the nation's capital, an eighteen-year-old law student at George Washington University took a day job in the "order division" of the Library of Congress, classifying and sorting the hundreds of new publications that arrived at the library each day. The new employee quickly became an expert practitioner of the Library of Congress's classification system, an organizational scheme that had been first implemented in the previous decade by head librarian Herbert Putnam. Just as Bertillon's system had organized the universe of physical traits into nested groups, the Library of Congress Classification (LCC) scheme carved up the entirety of human knowledge into twenty-one categories, each indexed with a single letter, followed by a second letter that denoted a specific subcategory, followed by additional codes that identified the primary author's name and the publication date.

In time, the young library clerk would make a name for himself in a different field. But the lessons he drew from the Putnam system—the unexpected power of systematized card catalogs and file cabinets—remained an animating principle in the mind of John Edgar Hoover for the rest of his career. Almost forty years after he first took the job at the Library of Congress, Hoover reflected on the formative role his time there played in his own intellectual and professional development. "The job . . . trained me in the value of collating material," he wrote. "It gave me an excellent foundation for my work in the FBI where it has been necessary to collate information and evidence."

Eventually, under Hoover's guidance, the soft power of information science would harden into something far more menacing. And the first place where Hoover would demonstrate that power would be in subduing the threat to national security posed by Emma Goldman and Alexander Berkman.

PART THREE

Detonation

1914–1919

CHAPTER 18

Down Inside the Cave to Sleep

For much of the Cretaceous period, the land that makes up modern-day Colorado was submerged beneath the shallow, warm waters of a tropical sea. Roughly seventy million years ago, the slow but inexorable collision between the North American Plate and the Pacific Plate began driving the land upward, a process that would ultimately give birth to the Rocky Mountain range. Gradually, the tropical sea gave way to an immense expanse of bogs, where mosses, ferns, and shrubs grew in abundance. For eons, those plants captured the sun's energy and stored it in leaves and stalks and roots built out of carbon; for eons, generation after generation of these plants perished and covered the remains of their predecessors faster than those older plants could be decomposed by fungi or bacteria. By the time a geologist named Ferdinand V. Hayden surveyed the foothills east of the Rockies in the late 1860s, those plants had hardened into coal reserves that were, according to Hayden, "inexhaustible and of excellent quality."

In 1880, the Colorado Fuel Company began extracting high-grade bituminous coal from the canyons on the edge of the Sangre de Cristo Mountains, where erosion had long ago brought the coal seams closest to the surface. The Colorado mines were among the most dangerous in the nation, with a fatality rate twice the national average. After merging with another firm, the rechristened Colorado Fuel and Iron Company was purchased by John D. Rockefeller and Jay Gould in 1903, who immediately brought in immigrant

labor from Greece and Italy and Hungary to replace striking workers. For a time, the new workforce kept the mines running, produc-
ing coking coal that could be converted into steel in a blast furnace,
providing the foundation for the railroads, subways, and skyscrapers that were multiplying across the United States. But the harsh
working conditions ultimately proved to be intolerable. In the fall of
1913, eleven thousand striking workers and their families streamed
out of the canyons and settled in tent communities constructed by
their union on the prairie's edge, near the town of Ludlow. In an
uncanny echo of the Homestead Strike, Rockefeller hired a team of
private eyes—the Baldwin-Felts Detective Agency—and covered
the wages of the National Guard in an unsuccessful attempt to
break up the strike. For six months, the workers held their own in
the encampments, strategically situated at the mouths of the canyons to prevent access to the mines.

In early April, John D. Rockefeller, Jr., the presumptive heir to
the Standard Oil fortune, traveled to Washington to deliver an im-
passioned defense of union-busting to the House Committee on
Mines and Mining. "We believe that the issue is not a local one in
Colorado," he explained.

> It is a national issue, whether workers shall be allowed to work
> under such conditions as they may choose. And as part owners of
> the property, our interest in the laboring men in this country is so
> immense, so deep, so profound that we stand ready to lose every
> cent we put in that company rather than see the men we have
> employed thrown out of work and have imposed upon them con-
> ditions which are not of their seeking and which neither they nor
> we can see are in our interest.

Asked by the committee chairman if he would choose to stick to
his anti-union principles, even if it "costs all your property and kills

all your employees," Rockefeller had replied, "It was upon a similar principle that the War of the Revolution was carried on. It is a great national issue of the most vital kind."

In the offices of *Mother Earth*, recently relocated to 119th Street in Harlem, the Ludlow showdown was a constant topic of discussion. The lead essay in the November issue—penned by the Czech émigré Hippolyte Havel—conspicuously invoked the Homestead crisis of 1892:

> In the great Homestead strike of 1892 the millmen made the fatal mistake of welcoming with banner and drum the militia sent to shoot down the rebellious slaves. Times have changed. Today labor has at least learned to recognize friend from enemy. The miners of Colorado, for instance, are giving the invading Hessians of capital—the State militia—the reception befitting the occasion. As Comrade August Spies so well said, "dynamite is the diffusion of power." The robber barons of Colorado and their murderous militia have suddenly been forced to realize that "law and order" is not all on their side. Dynamite is the disseminator of "authority," and part of the latter is now in the hands of the workers. That somewhat equalizes the opportunities.

But as the standoff in Ludlow continued, Alexander Berkman and Emma Goldman had more pressing local issues to focus on. The two had relocated to Harlem and helped found an experimental school and community center named after the Italian anarchist and education reformer Francisco Ferrer, executed in 1909. The Ferrer Center became a central hub for the city's radical intellectuals, and a required stop for esteemed visitors from overseas: Margaret Sanger ran education sessions for young women on birth control; Max Weber, Clarence Darrow, and Jack London made appearances. In the spring of 1914, much of the Ferrer Center crowd was focused on a series of protests organized by a new coalition group known as the Conference of the Unemployed that had triggered major disruptions in the city, and led to the arrest of several of their comrades. On April 4, a police riot broke out at a rally in Union Square. "I was sick at heart," Lincoln Steffens reported the next day. "I was in Union Square yesterday, and saw the unemployed clubbed. I've seen such things for twenty years now, but I can't get used to it. It lifts my stomach every time I see a policeman take his nightstick in both his hands and bring it down with all his might on a human being's skull. And then, when he does it, the crowd come [*sic*] about me and asks me if I won't make a complaint against the cop and have him fired! As if I could!" One of the injured was a new member of the *Mother Earth* clan, Arthur Caron, a French Canadian mechanic with a jovial smile and a dark complexion that led many to suspect that he had Native American roots. Ever the firebrand, Becky Edelsohn—no longer in a relationship with Berkman, but very much in his inner circle—threw herself over the body of the Irish activist Wild Joe O'Carroll to protect him from the police blows.

In the days that followed the Union Square riots, the press hammered against the police overreaction, much of its vitriol directed at the current commissioner, Douglas McKay. John Purroy Mitchel had been entertaining doubts about the commissioner through much of his five-month tenure as mayor; the Union Square debacle made it clear that it was time for a change at the NYPD. And in Mitchel's mind, there was only one obvious choice to replace McKay.

In the late morning of April 8, Arthur Hale Woods walked from City Hall to the NYPD's lavish new beaux-arts headquarters, situated on a triangular lot at 240 Centre Street, and signed the paperwork designating him the next police commissioner. Since his first abortive tenure with the NYPD, Woods had made a half-hearted attempt to fashion himself as an entrepreneur. He moved to Mexico to try his hand in the lumber business, and then returned to his birthplace in Boston for a spell, working as a cotton trader. Neither endeavor provided the same thrills—and the same sense of working for a higher purpose—that he had enjoyed during the heyday of the Italian Squad. And so, when John Purroy Mitchel launched his progressive bid for mayor, Woods had been quick to insinuate himself into Mitchel's inner circle.

The contrast between the nightstick brutality of the Union Square riots and the cool, intellectual mien of the new chief was not lost on the press. "There has never been a Police Commissioner quite like him," the *Times* enthused, perhaps forgetting Woods's patron, Teddy Roosevelt. "He may not succeed in carrying out his ideas, but he can never be charged with a lack of them, or an unwillingness to fight for them."

In the early afternoon of April 17, just a week into his new job, Woods walked with Mitchel out of city hall in Lower Manhattan, accompanied by two other city officials: Frank Polk and George Mullan. Headed to a luncheon a few blocks away on Battery Place, the four men strolled unnoticed past a small crowd assembled around the statue of Horace Greeley, where a handful of soapbox orators thundered against the simmering crisis in Ludlow and the greed of the capitalist magnates. They made their way alongside the cascading water of the Mould Fountain, the centerpiece of the small, bustling park wedged between the imposing structures of the Civic Center district, arriving at an NYPD automobile waiting for them on Park Row. Mitchel wedged himself in the back with Polk and Mullan, while Woods walked around the car to sit in the front passenger seat, alongside a detective named George Neun serving as the mayor's personal chauffeur.

As Woods reached for the door handle of the vehicle, he caught a glimpse over his shoulder of an elderly man with a gray beard, lurching toward the car's rear seat, pulling a revolver from the pocket of his ragged coat. In a split second, Woods spun around and slammed his body against the assailant, driving him away from the vehicle and pinning him to the sidewalk.

Inside the car, Mitchel heard what he thought was the sound of a tire blowing out or a muffler exploding, until Polk leaned forward, clutching at his jaw, crying out: "He got me. He shot me in the mouth."

While Woods struggled to subdue the man on the ground, Detective Neun ripped the assailant's weapon out of his hands before he could fire it again. A throng of pedestrians descended on the scene. After confirming that Polk's wound was not life-threatening, Mitchel flung open the car door and pointed his pistol at the haggard man lying prone on the sidewalk, shouting over the screams of the onlookers: "Why did you try to kill me?"

Mitchel's query would reverberate through police headquarters for the next few hours. With tensions still high after the Union Square riots, Woods initially feared a radical conspiracy to kill the mayor. But the suspect's age and disheveled appearance did not quite fit the part. ("He was an old man," the *Times* reported the next morning, "stooped and worn in appearance. His brown eyes were sunken deep under his shaggy gray brows.") Hauled into the nearby city hall squad house, the assailant was brought to a holding room, where Woods and Faurot interrogated him. At first he refused to even volunteer his name. A search of his coat revealed a seemingly random assortment of newspaper clippings and a pair of incoherent handwritten letters addressed to the mayor. More troubling, though, was a clipping where someone had scrawled: "Remember Homestead 1892!" and "Remember Andrew Carnegie, the man responsible for all this."

At one point in the interrogation, Woods turned to Faurot and asked if he thought the man might be linked to an anarchist organization. Faurot shook his head. "I think he's just a 'bug,' one of those letter-writing cranks."

Faurot's hunch proved correct. After a longer interrogation back at the Centre Street headquarters—and the obligatory visit to the Identification Bureau—Woods and Faurot finally extracted the suspect's real identity: Michael Mahoney, a seventy-one-year-old unemployed blacksmith, with no ties to any formal political organization. Despite the scribbled Homestead allusion on the frayed paper in his pocket, Mahoney had not been attempting a revival of Berkman's original attentat. He was just a drifter with an imaginary grudge against Mayor Mitchel.

It was not lost on Mitchel—and the local press—that the assassination attempt might well have succeeded had the young mayor chosen a different man for police commissioner.

Three days after the city hall shooting, on the morning of April 20, two National Guard units commanded by a Rockefeller deputy began laying down machine gun fire across the tent cities outside Ludlow. Some of the strikers managed to escape into the hills, while others huddled in underground bunkers that had been dug for precisely this situation. That night, the Guard swept into the tent city and set it ablaze.

Initial accounts suggested that, miraculously, only a handful of people had perished in the entire conflict. But the next morning, a telephone linesman inspecting the wreckage heard muted cries beneath an iron cot that had survived the inferno. When he dragged the cot away from the pit it had been designed to conceal, he found two women struggling for survival, huddled together in the earth. Around them were the blackened corpses of thirteen victims. Eleven of them were children.

❋ ❋ ❋

The Ludlow massacre endured as a flashpoint in the progressive mind for generations. The radical historian Howard Zinn wrote his master's thesis about it; in his iconic *A People's History of the United*

Aftermath of the Ludlow Massacre

States, he called Ludlow "one of the most bitter and violent struggles between workers and corporate capital in the history of the country." George McGovern wrote his dissertation on the strike and its aftermath. Woody Guthrie composed a ballad called, simply, "Ludlow Massacre." Its opening verses went:

> *It was early springtime when the strike was on,*
> *They drove us miners out of doors,*
> *Out from the houses that the company owned,*
> *We moved into tents up at old Ludlow.*

I was worried bad about my children,
Soldiers guarding the railroad bridge,
Every once in a while a bullet would fly,
Kick up gravel under my feet.

We were so afraid you would kill our children,
We dug us a cave that was seven foot deep,
Carried our young ones and pregnant women
Down inside the cave to sleep.

But all that was in the future. There in 1914, as the news of the charred bodies of those eleven children traveled east on telegraph wire, Emma Goldman and Alexander Berkman could only think of the past. It was Homestead all over again. Rockefeller's readiness to tolerate bloodshed in the name of his anti-union principles had not just been a negotiating tactic. He was clearly willing to condone burning children alive in order to advance his interests. Why should the oligarchs have a monopoly on political violence? In *Mother Earth*, Berkman made a fevered case for fighting back against the industrialists, landing, naturally enough, on the very weapon he had failed to use against Frick:

What are the American workingmen going to do? Are they going to palaver, petition and resolutionize? Or will they show that they still have a little manhood in them, that they will defend themselves and their organizations against murder and destruction? This is no time for theorizing, for fine-spun argument and phrases. With machine guns trained upon the strikers, the best answer is—dynamite.

CHAPTER 19

The Siege of Tarrytown

In the days after the Ludlow massacre, a constant eddy of protestors swirled among the flow of pedestrian traffic in front of Rockefeller's office at 26 Broadway in Manhattan, while radical groups around the city strategized about the best response to the brutal deaths in Colorado. In early May, the anarchist Arthur Caron—the scars from the Union Square beating still visible on his skull—took the Hudson River train north with a small band of fellow protestors to Tarrytown, where they marched to the gates of the nearby Rockefeller estate in Pocantico Hills. Purchased by Rockefeller, Sr., in the early 1890s, the estate covered more than three thousand acres, with formal gardens, working farms, and a nine-hole golf course. Construction of the elaborate Georgian mansion—known as Kykuit, a derivation of the Dutch word for *lookout*—had just been completed in 1913.

When Caron first arrived at the gates of Pocantico Hills, he was disappointed to find that the property was heavily fortified, with imposing stone walls and armed guards protecting the perimeter. But the appearance of the protestors—wearing black mourning bands on their arms, in memory of the dead Colorado strikers—generated front-page stories in the papers the following morning. "We came here to worry John D., Jr.," Caron told the *Times*, "and it seems that we will have succeeded." The headline was prophetic: "I.W.W. PICKETS PEN ROCKEFELLERS. Attempt to Invade

Their Pocantico Estate, but Are Turned Back by Armed Guards. WILL CALL AGAIN IN FORCE."

Caron took three weeks to make good on his promise, returning to Tarrytown on May 30, with eleven other protestors in tow. One of them was Becky Edelsohn, who had become a minor celebrity in recent months for her fiery speeches and confrontational actions at protests. (At one march, she had flung open the door of a passing limousine to spit on the occupants.) Edelsohn's reputation for sexual adventurousness was outsized even among the free-love crowd of the anarchists, and the press had begun to cover her as something between a sex symbol and a radical leader. (A *New-York Tribune* profile in early May spent almost as much time analyzing her looks as her political agenda: "She is a strong-faced girl, with a good forehead and deep, keen brown eyes, not at all the melting brown eyes of the poet or the soft, passionate brown eyes of the south of Europe. Becky's eyes were built to flash, not to weep.") Now in her early twenties, Edelsohn had retained most of the wild-child energy that she had shown as a teenager in the movement. Goldman had eyed her suspiciously since her underage dalliance with Berkman; now that Edelsohn was attracting the kind of newspaper profiles that Goldman had long enjoyed, she threatened to become the new public face of the anarchist movement—despite having little of Goldman's intellectual stature and experience.

In Tarrytown, Caron and Edelsohn set up a soapbox in the town's main square, next to a public fountain that was a popular meeting spot for locals. It was near twilight on a Saturday; a few dozen residents were passing through the square, on their way to dinner or to a local saloon, when Caron stood up and began his oration: "Did you ever hear the wail of a dying child and the wail of a dying mother? They were murdered in Colorado while the American flag flew over the tents in which they lived, and the murderer was John D. Rockefeller, Jr." Caron was only a few sentences into his speech when a policeman wrestled him off the soapbox. Edelsohn quickly replaced him and denounced Rockefeller as a "multi-murderer." Within a matter of minutes, all twelve protestors were under police custody; by eight P.M. they were standing before a local magistrate. According to the *Times,* Edelsohn "immediately started a furor" by shouting from the dock—presumably satirically—that "the occasion was such a solemn one that she would like to borrow a handkerchief from some kind soul to weep on."

Shortly after noon the next day, Alexander Berkman strode confidently out of the Tarrytown train station, a cane in one hand, dressed in a crisp dark suit, with a white tie and pocket square. (Goldman was on a speaking tour in the West.) Berkman brought a number of reinforcements to replace the arrested protestors. When they arrived at the same fountain where Caron and Edelsohn had made their aborted speeches the night before, a band of local police awaited them. Berkman mounted a chair they had brought for the occasion and began by insisting on his free-speech rights, "as guaranteed by the Constitution, but as suppressed by Mr. Rockefeller, the real owner of the Tarrytown police." At those words, the officers flung Berkman off his chair and began rounding up the protestors. For much of the afternoon, the normally placid streets of Tarrytown were transformed into a violent mêlée, with the anarchists squaring off against the police and a pack of Tarrytown residents taking the side of the local gentry. Several more protestors were arrested, but Berkman managed to slink off and ultimately took an evening train back to Manhattan, promising to return with additional forces to keep the vigil alive.

In the subsequent weeks, the Rockefeller estate in Tarrytown descended into a state of uninterrupted siege. Fifty new officers

Lillian Rubel, Becky Edelsohn, Louise Berger,
and Alexander Berkman, 1914

were appointed to the police force; fire hydrants had hoses perma-
nently attached so that they could be used against the rioters at a
moment's notice. The Rockefellers added dozens of private guards
to their security detail and fortified the main entrances to the estate.
They tested new floodlights that could illuminate the perimeter in
the event of an assault.

The siege of Tarrytown became a national news story. "The most
astonishing situation in the history of the United States exists in
Pocantico Hills," a Chicago paper announced, somewhat hyper-
bolically. "Thirty-six dollars and seventy-five cents have one billion
two hundred million eighty-nine thousand dollars surrounded,
blockaded and balked . . . John D. Rockefeller, the richest man in
the world, and his son, John D., Jr., are today as close prisoners in
their estate as are the convicts in Ossining penitentiary."

On June 8, Caron, Edelsohn, and ten other agitators were finally
released on bail, their trial postponed until early July. An enraged
mob followed them to the train station. Edelsohn refused to stand
down. "You can bet we're coming back," she proclaimed. "We are
going to show them in Tarrytown that we can hold meetings there

in spite of their old police force. We'll answer violence with violence . . . It's a matter of principle now."

Less than a month later, in the first few minutes of July 4, 1914, four men strolled out of a brownstone on East 107th Street in Harlem and said good night to the teenage sentries who had been standing watch on the front stoop. Most of the city had long since gone to sleep, anticipating a boisterous Independence Day celebration, but the men retired to a local bar around the corner, where they sat in deep conversation for another hour.

Two of them were former merchant sailors, Latvian by birth, named Charles Berg and Carl Hanson. Both were in their early twenties. The other two were Arthur Caron and Alexander Berkman. After an hour or so of consultation in the Harlem saloon, Berkman parted ways with Berg, Hanson, and Caron, and retired for the night to his home a few blocks away. The other three took advantage of the city's newly created twenty-four-hour subway system and boarded a train heading up the west side of Manhattan, ultimately transferring to a trolley that ran through the hamlets and gated estates strung out along the Hudson River. All the while they carried, with an unusual amount of caution, a small, wrapped package, a gift of sorts for the most celebrated resident of Tarrytown.

CHAPTER 20

The Blast

As the sun rose on Independence Day, the streets of East Harlem slowly filled with New Yorkers heading off to escape the summer heat at the seashore or in the leafy sanctuary of Central Park. Around eight A.M., a woman named Louise Berger—the half sister of Carl Hanson—strolled out of the seven-story tenement at 1626 Lexington Avenue, on her way to the nearby headquarters of *Mother Earth*, with plans to join a picnic rally with Berkman, Edelsohn, and other anarchists later in the day. With workers off duty for the holiday, the usual clamor of a long-running subway-construction project in front of 1626 Lexington had been silenced, replaced by the rattle of motorcars and carriages.

And then, at 9:06 A.M., the sky above Lexington Avenue exploded.

The first shock is just the sound of the blast. ("Like a broadside from a battleship," according to a later report in the *Times*.) The top three floors of 1626 Lexington are instantly reduced to rubble. Fragments of brick and concrete and shards of glass shower the terrified pedestrians below. The shock wave shatters hundreds of windows in adjoining buildings. Furniture from the top-floor apartments shoot out across the roofline, as though propelled by a trebuchet behind castle walls. The temporary deck that had been built atop the subway project collapses. Inside the ruins of 1626 Lexington, a pile of debris half bury a cigar maker named Vincenzo d'Angelo, breaking his arms. Another resident named Peter Casamento lies trapped beneath the wreckage, both of his legs fractured. Dozens of other occupants of the tenement find themselves suddenly thrust into life-threatening situations.

As the screams from inside the collapsed structure begin to rise, the pedestrians who have been unlucky enough to be strolling past 1626 Lexington realize that the debris raining down on them is not merely fragments of brick and mortar from the top three floors of the building. They are also being bombarded by human remains. Scraps of bloody tissue and bone, barely recognizable, lie on the ground and on the rooftop of a neighboring church. An intact human leg lands in the middle of Lexington Avenue itself. As the dust cloud from the blast slowly clears, a horrifying sight appears in the carnage of the upper floors: the lifeless body of a man dangling from the fire escape, his legs twisted at a grotesque angle, the back of his skull blown out.

Aftermath of the July 4 explosion

For more than a year, the stretch of Lexington Avenue below 110th Street had been a construction site, as the Interborough Rapid Transit Company—commonly known as the IRT—blasted its way through the bedrock and earth below street level, making way for the extension of the Lexington Avenue subway line. Buildings in the neighborhood would shudder with the booms of subterranean explosions carving out the tunnels below. The pace of construction was frantic; the IRT built over a dozen stations and connecting tunnels in only six years. (In contrast, it took the modern-day MTA a decade to add three stations to the Second Avenue line.) By the spring of 1914, workers were already putting together the steel beams that would support the concrete deck above the platforms.

With such intense activity, it was understandable that the subway crews failed to notice, in May and early June, that someone had begun quietly but persistently removing sticks of dynamite from the construction site.

Much mystery remains about the exact manner of the theft. Was there an inside man on the IRT payroll who was fencing the dynamite on the side? Or were the thieves infiltrating the site at night and removing the canisters themselves? But the historical record is clear on one thing: the dynamite ultimately found its way to Louise Berger's apartment on the top floor of 1626 Lexington Avenue. A few sticks from the stolen cache were crafted into a portable device by Caron, Berg, and Hanson in the final weeks of June, wrapped in brown paper, and brought to Tarrytown in the early morning hours of July 4.

The migration of those dynamite sticks from subway construction project to attempted terrorist attack mirrors the journey dynamite had made on a global scale over the previous half century. When Nobel first patented dynamite in 1864, the population of New York City was somewhere around nine hundred thousand. By the time the IRT started working on the Lexington Avenue extension, it was five million. Sustaining that many human lives at that density required dynamite on multiple fronts: blasting out the foundation for the new skyscrapers transforming the downtown skyline, carving the tunnels for subterranean mass transit. Manhattan schist would have never yielded so readily to drills and black powder. Only dynamite could bend bedrock to human will.

The two simple ideas that Alfred Nobel wrapped around nitroglycerin—the blasting cap and the diatomite paste—had transformed the world of engineering and created enough wealth to endow the Nobel Prizes in perpetuity. But they had also endowed individuals or small groups with destructive capacity that had previously been reserved for military battalions. Dynamite was miraculously portable and easily concealed. You could carry a couple of sticks of dynamite in your overcoat, as Émile Henry had done in Paris in 1894. Or you could wrap it in brown paper and carry it on the train to Tarrytown without anyone giving you a second look.

No one knows for certain what had happened at Pocantico Hills when Caron, Hanson, and Berg arrived in the early-morning hours of July 4, 1914. Rockefeller, Jr., had left the estate for the family's summer home in Seal Harbor, Maine, and so it is possible that Caron called off the plot at the last minute, after learning that their intended target was not in residence. Perhaps the three men were rebuffed by the new fortifications that surrounded the property. Whatever the reason, no explosives were detonated at Pocantico Hills that night, and the three men made their final journey back to Louise Berger's apartment on Lexington Avenue.

By the time firefighters eventually pulled the corpse hanging from the fire escape down from its bloody perch above the street, Arthur Woods had already arrived at the scene. With him was Deputy Inspector of Combustibles Owen Eagan. Eagan was fifty-five now, something of a hometown hero in the New York press, which described him as holding "the most unusual and dangerous municipal job in the world." Miraculously, he had survived almost twenty

years on the force dismantling
bombs. He was missing a few
fingers, thanks to an infernal
machine that had detonated
in his hands two years earlier.
(The bomb had been delivered
to the home of Otto Rosalsky,
the judge who presided over the
Crispi fingerprint trial.) "Cutting up a bomb is strictly a one-
man job," Eagan once told a
reporter. "The police get out of
my way when I go into action. I
make them do it, but they're
only too glad to obey me."

Owen Eagan, circa 1915

Searching through the dead man's jacket, the police found a
notebook signed "Arthur Caron." Woods recognized the name immediately from the Union Square riots. This was no gas leak or
construction accident. The agitators who had been threatening violence against Rockefeller, Jr., had not been posturing when they
vowed to answer the "machine guns trained at the strikers" with
dynamite.

Eagan had defused thousands of bombs planted by the Black
Handers, political radicals, or sociopaths; he had analyzed the blast
zones left behind by a comparable number of explosions. But the
wreckage he found at the Lexington Avenue site was unlike anything he had ever seen. "The bomb was of the most powerful construction ever employed in the perpetration of an outrage of this
kind in this city," Eagan told the assembled reporters after a thorough examination of the crime scene. "I cannot understand why
there was not even a greater loss of life. It is my belief that Caron

was making a bomb and that it accidentally exploded. Dynamite is very erratic. Sometimes it goes off and sometimes it doesn't."

When the police brought Louise Berger and Alexander Berkman to the morgue later that afternoon and presented the corpse of their comrade Arthur Caron, they at least had a body to identify. There was no comparable proceeding for Charles Berg and Carl Hanson. Their bodies had been atomized in the blast.

After identifying the body, Berkman was interrogated for over an hour by a deputy police commissioner. The *Times*—which somehow planted a reporter in the interrogation room, or at least secured a detailed transcript of the conversation—described Berkman as "cool and suave" during the interview, going on to note that the anarchist "smilingly answered all questions asked him . . . and appeared hurt when asked if he knew of any plan to make a bomb to be used to injure any person who had incurred the enmity of the organization of which he is a leader."

During the interrogation, Rubin zeroed in on the midnight meeting in Harlem.

"Did you attend a meeting at the Ferrer Association rooms last night?"

"Yes."

"What was the reason of that meeting?"

"To discuss the defense of the persons who are to be placed on trial in Tarrytown the coming week."

"Did you discuss the possibility of taking action of a violent sort against any one?"

"Most assuredly not. It was simply a meeting to discuss the defense of the prisoners and those who are out on bail."

"Was there any talk of bombs?"

"No, of course not."

"Did you know there were any explosives in the apartment occupied by Caron and the others?"

"I did not, and do not know it yet."

The question of what Alexander Berkman knew about the plot has hung in the air mostly unanswered ever since the July 4 explosion. When asked about it directly, Berkman maintained the "cool and suave" demeanor he had shown the police at the time, professing no knowledge of any plot to kill Rockefeller, a posture he continued to hold for the rest of his life. But the circumstantial evidence against him is formidable. To begin with, there was the personal history: The last time a group of guns for hire had attacked an encampment of striking workers, Berkman had attempted to assassinate the industrialist behind it—and despite his fourteen years in the Western Penitentiary, he had never apologized for the act. Berkman had admitted to being with the three men who died in the blast just hours before the bomb went off. And, of course, Berkman was on the record—on multiple occasions—calling for the use of dynamite as a retaliation against the Ludlow Massacre.

No historian explored the question of Berkman's involvement in the plot more deeply than the late Queens College professor Paul Avrich, whose oral history of the anarchist movement—based on interviews conducted over thirty years—is arguably the definitive account of anarchism's rise and fall in the early twentieth century. (His collection of more than twenty thousand papers related to the movement is now a permanent collection in the Library of Congress.) On the question of Berkman's culpability in the July 4 plot, Avrich and his daughter Nancy Avrich write:

"Was Berkman involved?" mused Moritz Jagendorf, director of the Free Theatre at the Ferrer Center, when the question was put to him years later. "Well, he was very straightforward, practical, a man of action and organizing strength. I honestly feel that Berkman was involved, that he helped, at least with the planning." Will Durant, who met Sasha at the Ferrer School in 1912, later wrote that when it came to aggressive acts, Berkman "was unrepentant and still believed that when other avenues of social protest were blocked by the power of wealth, the oppressed were justified in resorting to violence." Some Ferrer Center and *Mother Earth* members were certain of Sasha's guilt. "Berkman," Jack Issacson's wife flatly declared, "was the mastermind of the plot." Charles Plunkett knew the full story, but even six decades later was cagey. "I'm the only one still alive who knows about Lexington Avenue, but I'm not going to tell you or anyone else. Why should I? After all, it was murder." Eventually the details spilled out. "Only a few people were involved," Plunkett said. "Caron, Hanson, and Berg, of course. Louise Berger, Hanson's half-sister, knew about it. Becky Edelsohn knew about it. And Alexander Berkman. It was Berkman who organized it, though the others were to carry it out. Berkman still believed in the necessity of violence."

The facts suggest that Berkman was indeed involved. But what about Goldman? According to her memoirs, Berkman appears to have taken the same line with her as he took with the police, claiming that he had nothing to do with the dynamite plot:

Word came from Sasha that the three men who had lost their lives in the explosion were comrades who had worked with him in the Tarrytown campaign. They had been badly beaten up by the police at one of the Union Square demonstrations. The bomb might have been intended for Rockefeller, Sasha wrote, but in any case the men had kept their intentions to themselves, for neither he nor anyone else knew how the explosion had occurred.

The news of the Lexington Avenue explosion brought her back to those terrifying nights in 1892, when Berkman first began crafting an infernal machine to deploy against Frick:

> Comrades, idealists, manufacturing a bomb in a congested tenement-house! I was aghast at such irresponsibility. But the next moment I remembered a similar event in my own life. It came back with paralysing horror. In my mind I saw my little room in Peppi's flat, on Fifth Street, its window-blinds drawn, Sasha experimenting with a bomb, and me watching. I had silenced my fear for the tenants, in case of an accident, by repeating to myself that the end justified the means. With accusing clarity I now relived that nerve-racking week in July 1892. In the zeal of fanaticism I had believed that the end justifies the means! It took years of experience and suffering to emancipate myself from the mad idea.

And yet still, "the mad idea" of political violence seemed to have an escape clause in Goldman's mind. "I understood the spiritual forces culminating in such Attentats as Sasha's, Bresci's, Angiolillo's, Czolgosz's, and those of others whose lives I had studied," she later wrote. "They had been urged on by their great love for humanity and their acute sensitiveness to injustice." But whatever sympathies she might have had for those actions, something in the July 4 explosion hardened Goldman's opposition to the use of violence: "I felt now that I could never again participate in or approve of methods that jeopardized innocent lives."

Freed for the time being from police custody, Berkman immediately began planning a proper memorial service for his fallen comrades. Their stance against the atrocities at Ludlow had elicited a largely sympathetic response from the press, but the Lexington Avenue ex-plosion had turned popular opinion against the radicals. "It is one thing to sympathize with the struggle for industrial freedom and against industrial oppression," the magazine *Outlook* declared. "It is another thing to commit murder." The backlash only hardened Berk-man's determination to hold a public commemoration of Caron, Berg, and Hanson. On July 5, he announced that a mass funeral would be conducted in Union Square, the scene of the police riot where Arthur Caron had been injured just three months before.

Berkman envisioned a procession that would follow Caron's cof-fin through the streets of Manhattan, winding its way to the ulti-mate ceremony site in Union Square. But Arthur Woods worried that a funeral procession taking over a large swath of the city risked making martyrs of the would-be bombers. He and Mitchel were able to convince the board of aldermen to change the laws, making it a requirement that all parades receive police approval.

Outfoxed by Woods, Berkman abandoned the idea of a funeral procession. Instead, mourners were invited to a memorial in Union Square on Saturday, July 11. The anarchists had dragged together two oversize dry goods boxes to make a podium, which they draped in red-and-black bunting. An arrangement of red roses spelled out the words "You did not die in vain." All across the square, banners were unfurled with a range of slogans: "Capitalism is the evil. An-archism is the cure"; "You want to do away with violence? Then do away with capitalism and government. They provoke and breed vio-lence." Woods dispatched almost the entire standing police force—eight hundred officers in all—to monitor the event, and asked Faurot to command a brigade of detectives on the scene. Woods's orders were clear: This was not to be a repeat of the April riot. The police were there not to do battle with the protestors but to ensure that no violence erupted. The memorial would be a test of the NYPD's new philosophy. "In New York, we not merely permit free speech and free assemblage and picketing," Woods explained, "but we protect it."

By two P.M., five thousand protestors had gathered in the square. Berkman spoke first, his voice straining over the noise of the crowd, perspiration running down his glistening bald head. He began with an interesting twist on the facts of the case: "Fellow mourners, we are gathered here to honor the memories of murdered soldiers who died in the cause of humanity." After claiming, somewhat mysteriously, that Caron, Berg, and Hanson had died "the victims of the capitalistic class," Berkman rolled out two competing theories of what had happened the morning of July 4.

> *First, it is possible that our comrades were murdered by the hired agents of capitalism, and of Rockefeller, for all know that Rockefeller has committed many murders, and he would not stop at anything. In my opinion, no matter whether they made the bomb or not, the Rockefellers and their kind are guilty, and our comrades are murdered martyrs to the cause of liberty. They died in the interests of the working classes of the United States.*
>
> *The second possibility is that our comrades themselves may have been making this bomb or infernal machine or whatever it was, their intention being to use it against the enemies of labor. I say that death in such a cause, which is a cause directed against oppression and tyranny, makes of those who so die martyrs, even though they seek to gain redress by the might of dynamite. I charge capital with being guilty of creating the conditions that made such a possibility as this.*

While Berkman once again refused to admit any knowledge of the plot, he made it clear which of the two scenarios he found the more inspiring. "I want to go on record as saying that I hope our comrades were manufacturing the bomb that caused their death," he bellowed from the dais. "I believe with all my heart in resistance and in warlike action when necessary."

Berkman was followed by a dozen additional speakers who, the *Times* reported dryly, "denounced capitalism in general and John D. Rockefeller in particular." The biggest crowd-pleaser was Becky Edelsohn.

> Why is it that in the twentieth century, men, sensitive men and women can be so goaded by oppression that they are forced to retaliate with violence? Every day that the capitalist system is in existence, it is perpetuated by violence, and that is the only way that it manages to hold its own. They talk about violence! What about the massacre in Ludlow? What about the Triangle fire? What about the thousands and thousands of victims in the factories who are daily crippled and maimed or killed in explosions in the subway, railways and mines? . . . Oh, don't let us hear any more twaddle about violence. All the violence that has been committed by the labor movement since the dawn of history wouldn't equal one day of violence committed by the capitalist class in power.

What Edelsohn was saying that afternoon in Union Square about the body count of the industrial revolution was not untrue. There were an astonishing number of bomb-throwing anarchists in the world at that moment in history, but even when you added them all up, they were an asterisk next to the victims of the Triangle fire, or the Ludlow Massacre, and countless other industrial accidents or labor conflicts that characterized the era. The invention of dynamite had meant that the government and the corporations no longer had a monopoly on devastating violence. But they were still its greatest practitioners. And it was not clear, to those standing there among the roses on the dais in 1914, that the industrial system's destructive force could be contained.

More than a century later, it is not hard to imagine a small band of disaffected New York City residents—in our present moment—spinning themselves into some kind of cyclone of hate and building a dirty bomb or a bioweapon in their basement. What *is* harder to imagine is five thousand people showing up in Union Square to mourn their deaths as martyrs to a greater cause. We still have people willing to kill for political ends in countries like the United States, though far fewer of them than there were back in 1914. But when those beliefs materialize into actual dead bodies, you don't conventionally see a great outpouring of public support for those violent acts. There were no rallies for the Unabomber.

Monitoring the events from the West Coast, Goldman initially thought the memorial had brought the "perilous situation"—as she called it in her memoirs—to some sort of close: The conspirators had been laid to rest and Berkman had seemingly been exonerated by the police. But then the July issue of *Mother Earth*—which Berkman had rushed to the printers—arrived in the post. "I was dismayed at its contents," she wrote. "The Union Square speeches were published there in full . . . The whole number was filled with prattle about force and dynamite. I was so furious that I wanted the entire issue thrown into the fire. But it was too late; the magazine had gone out to the subscribers."

Imagine Goldman reading that issue of *Mother Earth* from the other side of the continent: witnessing Berkman throw his lot in with the Lexington Avenue gang, visualizing Becky Edelsohn rousing the crowd with her "prattle about force and dynamite." Whatever Goldman *really* thought about political violence, it did not look like this, at least not in public. The events surrounding the July 4 explosion would trigger the deepest rift of the long partnership between Berkman and Goldman. But she ultimately chose to stand by him. Perhaps she simply resigned herself to the fact that they had different beliefs when it came to the political efficacy of violence. Perhaps part of her—the part that still saw a "great love for humanity" in the murderous actions of Bresci or Czolgosz—wanted to see the Rockefellers of the world obliterated by dynamite, as long as she herself was not on the record advocating for it. Or perhaps she realized—as Berkman must have as well—that despite the extinguished flame of their sexual relationship, they had simply lived through too much together to imagine a life apart.

The Union Square memorial turned out to be a victory for the new regime at the NYPD. The eight hundred cops that Woods had dispatched had little to do other than observe. No riots broke out. One crucial measure of the success of Woods's strategy was visible in the press coverage that followed. After a week in which the July 4 explosion had dominated the front pages, the *Times* ran its report on the Union Square memorial as a two-column item on page four. By allowing the radicals to give voice to their anger without striking back against them, Woods had kept the story from escalating further.

But this was only one flank of the strategy that Arthur Woods intended to use against the anarchists. The sheer scale of the Lexington Avenue blast zone had made it all too apparent that the anarchists had set their sights on more ambitious acts of mass destruction. Five years before, Woods had outlined a plan to solve the problem of the Black Hand, but Petrosino's death and the Duffy scandal had kept him from implementing it. Now the city confronted a more ominous situation, and this time Woods had popular opinion and a sympathetic mayor on his side.

On August 1, 1914, the very day that war was declared among the European powers across the Atlantic, Commissioner Woods announced the creation of a new group within the force dedicated exclusively to the threat posed by the infernal machines, a group that would employ state-of-the-art forensics and undercover operations to keep the city safe from explosions like the one that had terrified the residents of East Harlem three weeks earlier. It marked a milestone in the history of law enforcement: the first police bomb squad in the United States.

Woods endowed it with an official name that made it clear how closely tied this new innovation in urban policing was to the political movements of the day. He called it the Bomb and Anarchist Squad.

CHAPTER 21

The Italian Squad, Revisited

The NYPD was surprisingly bereft of domain expertise in the science of explosives. There was Deputy Inspector of Combustibles Eagen, of course, but he was something of a free agent. (For understandable reasons, Eagen did not have a long list of apprentices lining up to learn the trade under his tutelage.) The only high-ranking member of the force with anything close to Eagan's knowledge of bombs was Thomas J. Tunney, a broad-shouldered captain who had first joined the NYPD during the Roosevelt years as a beat cop. Arthur Woods had witnessed the quiet authority Tunney enjoyed with the officers. One colleague noted that Tunney earned respect not through physical intimidation but through his willingness "to listen to those around him in thoughtful silence." Tunney had worked as an undercover agent in multiple operations over the years, and through those investigations had become an expert in the dark art of Black Hand bomb-making. "It was an interesting subject for study, and a wicked weapon in use," he would later write.

> I managed to pick up information of bomb-manufacture in several ways: Black-Handers, in prison, told me how they had made their missiles; at the New York office of the Du Pont explosives company I had an opportunity to study blasting; the publications of the Bureau of Mines furnished more information, the practice of the Bureau of Combustibles of our own department proved

interesting and instructive, and I found myself before long forced to become something of a student of chemistry.

This background made Tunney the ideal choice to run the new Bomb and Anarchist Squad. The initial lineup of the squad consisted of roughly twenty men, half of them detective sergeants. In the initial weeks after Woods's announcement on August 1, Tunney and Eagen led a crash course in combustion for the new recruits. Tunney described the unusual syllabus in his memoirs: They discussed the primary types of explosives used by the political activists and the extortionists, "their relative strength, their ingredients, the methods of detonating them, the containers into which they were loaded, and the use of clockwork, fuses, acids and gas-pressure to explode them." Eagen gave detailed instructions about handling unexploded bombs, cautioning the men about submerging bombs with electrical devices in water. Tunney forbade the men to ever carry bombs on mass transit or smoke in their presence. "Altogether," Tunney later recalled, "we conducted a rather thorough course in explosives."

Becoming proficient in the science of combustion was only part of the squad's agenda. From the beginning, Woods had conceived the unit as a vehicle for undercover operations, a successor of sorts to the failed Italian Squad from his original tenure at the NYPD. It was not enough to defuse the bombs once they had been discovered. To restore order to the city, the police would have to infiltrate the anarchist community itself, stop the infernal machines *before* they were assembled.

The *Mother Earth* crowd felt the presence of this new secret police immediately. Swarms of "mosquito spies" would descend on rallies and public meetings, professing interest in the movement. "Naturally they dared not approach experienced people," Goldman later wrote; instead, the agents targeted younger members of the group, attempting to glean information about upcoming attacks, or even—as the anarchists would later argue—planting the idea for attacks that the NYPD could then thwart. An atmosphere of constant suspicion settled over the radicals. Every new recruit to the cause was a potential informant. One agent managed to win the confidence of the group by serving a brief prison sentence after a protest; impressed by the young idealist's commitment to the mission, Becky Edelsohn took him on as one of her lovers. But the detective's cover was blown when his wife got wind of the affair.

Alexander Berkman felt increasingly agitated under the endless threat of surveillance, and Goldman's return from the West Coast in early September did not help matters. Still enraged by the events of July, Goldman discovered on her arrival back in New York that Berkman had run *Mother Earth*'s finances into the ground. "I was dazed by the situation and I felt very indignant with Sasha," she wrote. "Entirely absorbed in his own propaganda, he had given me no thought. He was the revolutionist of old, with the same fanatical belief in the Cause. His sole concern was the movement, and I was to him but a means for it."

They did have one point of solidarity in the late summer of 1914, on an issue that would prove pivotal to the third act of their lives: the outbreak of hostilities in Europe. Like almost all of their comrades, Goldman and Berkman had been vehemently opposed to the war, and adopted an official policy of what you might call hostile neutrality: rooting for both sides to fail equally. But they were shocked to read an essay published by their mentor Peter Kropotkin, emphatically throwing his lot in with the Allies. "I consider that the duty of every one who cherishes the ideals of human progress," Kropotkin announced, "is to do everything in one's power, according to one's capacities, to crush down the invasion of the Germans into Western Europe." Despite his advanced age, Kropotkin rumbled to his family in England about actually enlisting in the fight. Back in New York, Berkman and Goldman struggled to understand his reasoning. Berkman wrote, "Our old comrade and teacher, the clear Anarchist thinker that he is, the uncompromising revolutionist and anti-governmentalist, takes sides in the European slaughter, and thereby gives aid and encouragement to this or that government? Impossible."

Whatever brief alignment Berkman and Goldman might have had over the Great War, the combination of Goldman's ire and the omnipresent police scrutiny convinced Berkman that it was time for a change of scenery. In November he headed west, embarking on what proved to be a dismal lecture tour through the American heartland. "Kansas City is depressing," he wrote in a dispatch for *Mother Earth*.

> The sky is drab, the air smooth, the streets haunted by emaciated and bedraggled unemployed. With thousands of jobless workers facing actual starvation, I have no heart to write of other matters. In Pittsburg, Cleveland, Chicago, Minneapolis, St. Louis—everywhere I find the same situation. Thousands, hundreds of thousands, starving in the midst of plenty. Surely the world is topsy-turvy. Civilization has so perverted our natural animal instincts that we prefer to die of hunger rather than to offend against the sanctity of property.

Eventually, though, Berkman would find his way to San Francisco, settling into an apartment on Dolores Street in the Mission District with his new romantic partner, Eleanor "Fitzi" Fitzgerald, a striking redhead born into a Seventh-Day Adventist family in the Midwest who had subsequently fallen in with the anarchist set. Finally, under the spell of California's charms, Berkman's spirits began to lift. "The climate is great, the country beautiful," he wrote to a friend back east. "The bay and the ocean and the mountains all around you, and the great redwoods with their giant trees."

But the charms of San Francisco did little to temper his "fanatical belief in the cause," or lead him to make amends with Goldman over his incendiary tenure at the helm of *Mother Earth*. One of the first things Berkman did after putting down roots in San Francisco was start a magazine of his own.

He called it *The Blast*.

Back on Centre Street, the new graduates from Tunney and Eagen's school of combustion were confronting blasts of their own. Late in the afternoon of October 13, a bomb detonated at the base of a column in the northwest nave of St. Patrick's, the newly consecrated Gothic cathedral on Fifth Avenue that towered over the still low-rise buildings of Midtown. The explosion flung cast iron slugs that had been encased with the dynamite across the hallowed interior, destroying three nearby pews and ripping a hole in the stone floor more than a foot deep; the iron slugs smashed into the altar of St. Bernard Chapel and shattered a pane in a stained-glass window. Fortunately, the cathedral had been largely empty at the time; the fifty-odd churchgoers kneeling in prayer were unharmed. Owen Eagen's subsequent analysis determined that the bomb had indeed been a powerful one, but the stone column it had been placed against—perhaps with the intent of bringing down the structure itself—had absorbed much of its force.

Eighteen hours later, another bomb exploded outside the rectory of St. Alphonsus Church on the Lower East Side, the site of one of the unemployment rallies that had engulfed the city earlier in the year. The blast shattered almost all the windows in the rectory, sending shards of glass into the neck of a clergyman inside the rectory, and blew out two oversize plate glass windows across the street. Iron slugs similar to the ones found at St. Patrick's were scattered across the blast zone. Four days later, an infernal machine exploded in a Greenwich Village basement that belonged to the Italian consul general.

In early November, two massive explosions destroyed the entire edifice of the newly completed Bronx Borough Courthouse, seemingly in an attempt to kill two judges who had recently been the recipients of a series of threatening letters. One bomb had been placed with apparent symbolic intent at the base of a bronze column, next to a statue representing the scales of Justice. "The explosion blew one of the granite bases into pebbles and so wrecked the other that both bronze columns hung suspended over the main arch," the *Times* reported. "The figure of Justice was cracked and its base wrecked, so that it threatened to topple over." The debris field from the explosion extended hundreds of feet in all directions around the court building. Eagen told the paper that the construction of the infernal machine suggested it had been the work of anarchists, not Black Handers. One of the targeted judges noted that the bomb had exploded on the anniversary of the Haymarket Riot, adding additional weight to Eagen's theory.

The string of attacks—terrifying enough in their own right, simply as a disruption of everyday life—also suggested a troubling rise in ambition for the saboteurs. The bombers were not just targeting specific enemies, like those Bronx judges; they were attacking the *institutions* of authority in the city: cathedrals, churches, courthouses. Woods directed additional security details to protect key figures in the city government, starting with Mayor Mitchel himself; round-the-clock surveillance was implemented at major landmarks and municipal buildings.

But despite the extra watchguards, just two days after the Bronx explosions, the anarchists came calling at Centre Street.

Officers lingering in the back of Magistrate John A. Campbell's courtroom on the morning of November 14 would later report seeing a thin man wearing a gray coat, rising up from the back benches and strolling out of the Tombs—a courthouse complex on Centre Street—with a match in one hand and a cigarette dangling from his lips. At the time, the behavior seemed innocuous: a civilian grabbing a quick nicotine fix before a public hearing began. The occupants of the room—lawyers, police, criminals, reporters, bystanders, next of kin—paid him little notice. In his chambers, Judge Campbell gathered his papers, readying himself for the upcoming session. A policeman from the nearby Mulberry Street station, George O'Conner, sat in the back of the court with four fellow officers. The room buzzed with quiet, anticipatory chatter, until a thin blue trail of smoke began to rise in the back benches.

O'Conner noticed it first. Leaping across the aisle that separated him from the smoke, he barreled through a confused line of new arrivals looking for a seat. On the floor in the second row from the back, where the smoker in the gray suit had sat just seconds before, O'Conner found a small box wrapped in newspaper, bound together with twine. A tiny blue flame flickered across a copper wire fuse, moving steadily toward the contents of the box.

Without thinking, O'Conner extinguished the flame with his fingers and then lifted the box to his chest. A hush descended over the courtroom, all the eyes in the back benches directing their attention to O'Conner's jarring behavior. For a second, he stood in the back of the chamber, cradling the package, unsure of his next move. Then he pressed the bomb against his chest tightly and sprinted through the rotunda of the courthouse, out onto Centre Street. Instinct now overcoming reason, O'Conner threw the package across the pavement, narrowly avoiding a passing streetcar. The box settled at the edge of the curb.

In an instant, the street was flooded with O'Conner's fellow officers and other court officials, bellowing at pedestrians and drivers to get away from the bomb. Before long they had cleared the entire block of Centre Street in front of the courthouse. For several excruciating minutes, O'Conner and the other men stood on the steps across the street, waiting for a detonation. At one point, an elderly Italian woman emerged from a storefront, only a few steps from the bomb. Walking out onto the sidewalk, she encountered a baffling scene: Instead of the normal weekday tumult of Centre Street, the entire block was abandoned, other than a few dozen men huddled on the steps of the courthouse, screaming at her in a language she did not understand. She froze, unable to parse the situation. Sensing her confusion, O'Conner once again put himself in physical peril; dashing toward the unexploded bomb, he flung the woman over his shoulder and carried her to Franklin Street, where she disappeared into the usual pedestrian crowds—presumably with no explanation of what had just happened to her.

Back in front of the courthouse, a clerk crept across Centre Street with a bucket in hand. At the curb's edge, he doused the package with water and immediately fled back to the relative safety of the courthouse steps. By the time Joseph Faurot and Owen Eagen arrived on the scene, roughly twenty minutes after O'Conner first detected the blue smoke wafting up from the courthouse benches, the package had been soaked with a second bucket of water.

When Eagen finally got his hands on the contraption, he found it had been wrapped in pages from the *Forward*, what the *Times* later described as a "Socialist organ published in Yiddish." Unwrapping the package revealed an olive oil can with a perforation in the cap where the fuse had been inserted. Wedged inside the can were two pounds of gunpowder, twenty-five revolver cartridges, and dynamite.

"This is the most unusual sort of bomb, and is unlike anything we have ever seen in this city before," a city official later announced. "Putting loaded cartridges into bombs is a new idea, and it is impossible for us to tell how destructive the new type would have proved."

With his expert's eye, Eagen immediately recalled a bomb he had dissected earlier in the summer, shortly after the Lexington

Avenue explosion, that had targeted the offices of the same Italian consul general whose home had been bombed in the previous month. Eagen had the earlier bomb retrieved from the police evidence room, and the two infernal machines were placed side by side on Faurot's desk. The original device did not have the added lethality of the revolver cartridges, but its basic template was strikingly similar. As Faurot and Eagen scrutinized the two infernal machines, an inevitable conclusion took shape in both their minds. The Yiddish wrapping on the Tombs courthouse bomb had been a feint. This was the work of Italian radicals seemingly intent on making increasingly daring attacks on the icons of state authority.

The Italian strain of anarchism had roots that reached almost as far back as the Russian lineage that Kropotkin, Goldman, and Berkman belonged to. An anarchist flank of the Italian Workingmen's Assocation had formed in 1869, and by the end of the next decade, as the historian Nunzio Pernicone observed, "the Italian anarchists, together with their Spanish comrades, were the most active revolutionaries in all of Europe." On the world stage, they also developed a reputation as the most militant of the radical movements. In one alarming six-year stretch at the end of the nineteenth century, Italian anarchists had murdered four heads of state in Europe, culminating in Bresci's assassination of the Italian king Umberto I in 1900. (While Bresci had been born in Tuscany and murdered Umberto in northern Italy, he lived for several years in Hoboken and Paterson, New Jersey—then hotbeds of anarchist activity.) Leon Czolgosz was Polish, but he had carried a newspaper clipping about Bresci's attentat in his coat pocket the day he murdered William McKinley. By 1914, there were a half-dozen distinct Italian anarchist organizations in New York City, with names like the Gruppo Socialista-Anarchico Rivoluzionario (Revolutionary Socialist-Anarchist Group) and La Nuova Civiltà (the New Civilization). That some of these organizations seemed to be conducting an ever more ambitious campaign against both the church and the government was, to say the least, a security issue for the men and women—starting with Arthur Woods—who had been tasked with protecting those institutions.

If the Ludlow Massacre had triggered flashbacks about the atrocities of Homestead in Alexander Berkman's mind, the bombing campaign that transpired in the fall of 1914 brought Woods back to the problem of the Black Hand that had so confounded him during his first sojourn in the NYPD, that had sent Joseph Petrosino on his ill-fated journey to Palermo. In all his interviews and writings, Woods never probed too deeply into his own qualms or sense of guilt over Petrosino's death, but the burden of that history must have weighed heavily on him in the fall of 1914.

He had already sent one talented Italian-born officer undercover in pursuit of bomb-throwing criminals, and the operation had not just cost the life of his friend and colleague but, ultimately, contributed to the demise of the entire Italian Squad. Did he dare risk making the same mistake again?

Right around the time of the attempted Tombs bombing, a twenty-four-year-old man calling himself Frank Baldo rented a one-room flat at 1907 Third Avenue, just a few blocks from the site of the July 4 explosion. He found a job doing manual labor at a factory in Long Island City, across the East River in Queens. Baldo began attending Sunday night meetings organized by the Bresci Circle of anarchists, generally held in the basement at 301 East 106th Street, "a shabby house in a shabby district east of the New York Central tracks," as Tunney would later call it. Though the Bresci Circle had a disproportionate number of Italian members, it was generally a cosmopolitan group, with Russians, Germans, Austrians, and native-born Americans also attending the basement sessions. There was much overlap with the *Mother Earth* crowd: Goldman, Berkman, and Becky Edelsohn had all delivered talks to the group. But it was no accident that the Bresci Circle named themselves after a man best known for murder, while Berkman and Goldman chose a martyred educator as their group's patron saint.

In reality, the new arrival at those Bresci Circle meetings was named Amedeo Polignani, one of the only detectives on the Bomb and Anarchist Squad of Italian descent. Woods and Tunney had already made one attempt to infiltrate the Bresci Circle earlier in the fall, but the operative—who spoke only English—had raised suspicions inside the group, and ultimately was banned from meetings. It was clear to Woods and Tunney that a different approach was required: Paradoxically, they needed an *inexperienced* officer, someone relatively new to the force who would be less likely to be recognized, and who could do a more effective job of eavesdropping when the Bresci Circle reverted to their native tongue. Polignani had joined the force only a few months before the creation of the Bomb and Anarchist Squad and had been assigned to patrol duty in Midtown, far from East Harlem. In conversations with the young detective, Tunney sensed that he "had the nerve and the resource to carry him through tight places," the *Times* reported, after Polignani's identity became public many months later. "He was short, strong, mild-mannered and unobtrusive," Tunney recalled. "And he knew Italian."

Woods and Tunney gave Polignani three primary directives. "First and foremost, he was to be on the watch for evidence of the man who had committed the two bomb outrages in October," Tunney wrote. "Secondly, he was to cover the activities and intentions of the anarchists in general; thirdly, he was to keep his eyes and ears open and his mouth shut, and to deal with any emergency which might arise.

"We discussed every possible angle of the work in order to anticipate and forestall whatever accident either of omission or commission might occur to make Polignani's position suspicious," Tunney continued. "He was instructed to call me by telephone at certain hours, using a private number, telephoning from a public pay-station in a store in which there was not more than one booth, so that no one might follow him and hear his conversation through the flimsy walls of a booth adjoining. He was to deport himself in a retiring manner, and to throw himself earnestly into the part he was to act."

Polignani assembled a workman's wardrobe—"an old blue suit and a soft shirt," according to the *Times*—said goodbye to his wife and young children in their Bronx apartment, and set off for his new life in East Harlem as Frank Baldo, aspiring anarchist.

Strangely enough, it was Polignani's skills as a wrestler that gave him his first access to the Bresci Circle's inner sanctum. For much of his first month undercover, he had lingered quietly through what Tunney called "bitter speeches" that gestured at "wild plans to overthrow the government"—but offered very little actionable intelligence. But he took mental notes on the Bresci Circle regulars as they debated revolutionary praxis in their dingy basement, dutifully conveying his observations to Tunney during their clandestine phone calls. Over time, Polignani began to discern an informal hierarchy in the group; an Italian shoemaker named Carmine Carbone seemed to have undue influence over the others, and was often seen whispering furtively with two compatriots. One day, in December of 1914, an impromptu wrestling match broke out after one of the talks; Polignani joined in, and his stocky, muscular build had him pinning the other anarchists to the floor with ease. As Polignani smoothed over his ruffled hair after the last of the matches, Carbone clapped him on the shoulder, saying: "You're a strong fellow—I'm glad to see you a member of the Bresci Circle!"

Polignani engaged him in conversation, and the two men strolled out onto the wintry sidewalks of Third Avenue. As the young detective nodded along, Carbone began complaining about the Bresci Circle's fondness for high-minded lectures.

"The trouble with these fellows is that they talk too much and don't act enough," Carbone griped in Italian. "They don't accomplish anything."

"That's right," Polignani concurred.

"What they ought to do is throw a few bombs and show the police something. Wake them up!"

They stopped on a corner illuminated by a streetlamp overhead. "Look," Carbone said, lifting his right hand into the light: Where his fingers had been, only five stumps remained. "I got that making a bomb. Someday I'll show you how to make them."

Polignani recorded the next few weeks' activity in his journal:

> Did not see Carbone again until Sunday the 27th. On this day he spoke to me of a friend named Frank and said that if all anarchists were like his friend they would be all right. He thinks nothing of making and throwing a bomb. On January 1st about 1.45 P.M. Carbone met me as per appointment. We went to where the meeting of the unemployed was being held and both of us shook hands with Louise Berg[er], Mandese, and Bianco . . . He introduced me to his friend Frank.

Louise Berger, whose apartment had been destroyed in the July 4 explosion, was a critical link for Polignani to forge: a direct connection between his new mate Carbone and the original perpetrators behind the Rockefeller plot. But it was his introduction to Frank Abarno that would transform the undercover operation from a scouting mission into a far more perilous affair.

Leaving the meeting in Union Square, Carbone and Polignani embarked on another of their meandering sessions, walking north on Fifth Avenue on the mostly empty sidewalks in the fading afternoon light. At Forty-seventh Street, they paused to watch the churchgoers stream out of afternoon mass at St. Patrick's. According to Polignani's account, Carbone sighed heavily as he gazed at the stone arches of the cathedral, muttering his regrets that he didn't have an infernal machine to detonate right there. For the Italian anarchists, there were few more potent symbols of hierarchical authority than Catholic churches, and with its immense stone spires—which had been just a few decades earlier the tallest structure in the entire city—towering over one of the main arteries in Manhattan, St. Patrick's made an ideal target.

Like almost all of the interactions between Polignani and his new compatriots in the Bresci Circle, the specifics of the conversation on Fifth Avenue would later be contested in court. According to Carbone's version of events, it was Polignani who introduced the idea of targeting the cathedral. "The first time I ever saw St. Patrick's Cathedral," Carbone would later testify under oath, "was when Detective Polignani led me there. It was after a Union Square meeting to which he had invited me . . . After the meeting, we walked uptown, and as we passed the cathedral, Polignani cried out: 'Boom, boom, boom! There's the place to set off bombs.'"

According to Polignani, two days later, leaving a basement lecture on January 3, Carbone whispered to Polignani that he should follow him to the 125th Street IRT station. "It's warm up there and we won't be bothered," Carbone explained. "I'll tell you something about making bombs."

As they walked up Lexington Avenue through East Harlem, making their way along the periphery of the construction site where the July 4 conspirators had stolen their explosives, Carbone explained that he had a ready supply of dynamite, through an uncle who worked as a contractor outside the city. But Carbone was having a more difficult time procuring blasting caps.

"We'll get some dynamite," he told Polignani, "and then you and Frank and me will blow up some churches, see?"

Polignani nodded in agreement and asked which church Carbone had in mind.

"St. Patrick's is the best," Carbone replied. "This time it'll be a good one too—not like before."

Strolling past the ruins of Louise Berger's apartment building, Carbone gestured derisively toward the rubble that remained on the site. "That bomb that killed Caron and Berg and Hanson wasn't made right," he noted. "It was wound too tight—that's why it went off too soon. I can make a bomb from a brass ball off a bed-post that will start something."

When Polignani finally got to his payphone for his regular meet with Tunney several days later, he conveyed the latest twists to the Bomb Squad chief, who immediately brought Woods into the loop. So far, their bet on the twenty-five-year-old seemed to be paying dividends. Just two months into his undercover operation, Polignani had managed to insert himself into an active plot to blow up New York's most celebrated cathedral.

The question for Woods was how long the young detective should be allowed to play it out.

Two weeks went by before the next meeting, which turned out to be another ambulatory conversation, this time joined by Frank Abarno, who proved to have an unusually sadistic streak, launching almost immediately into a fantasy of choking Cardinal Farley to death at the altar of St. Patrick's, and then enjoining Carbone to get busy with his bomb manufacture.

"If I can get those caps I'll make a bomb that will destroy the

Cathedral clear down to the ground," Carbone replied, "but if I can't get the caps then I'll have to make the other kind."

Abarno began sketching out a more specific timeline for the attack. "Well, you make two bombs," he told Carbone and Polignani. "We'll set them off on the outside of the church about six o'clock some morning and then we can get away clean and get to work on time and nobody will know the difference."

Carbone then shifted the conversation toward practical matters: the missing ingredients from his anarchist's cookbook. He handed Polignani a shopping list with only two items written out in Italian: one pound of "Collorate di Potase" and "Andimonio"—potassium nitrate and explosive antimony. Abarno was tasked with acquiring sulfur.

Polignani immediately informed Tunney of his latest assignment and arranged to hand off the list of ingredients for the police to hold as evidence. For Tunney and Woods, overseeing the operation from Centre Street, the shopping list presented a crossroads: Should an officer of the law willingly deliver critical ingredients for making explosive devices to a pair of radicals who had explicitly stated their intention to destroy a prominent public building? There was no guarantee that Polignani would remain in Carbone and Abarno's confidence, after all. And the fact that the undercover operative was supplying the key materials could potentially bolster a case that Polignani was an agent provocateur, inciting the two otherwise innocent Italians into the attack on St. Patrick's rather than following their orders.

In the end, Woods and Tunney decided to continue the operation. Polignani had made so much progress infiltrating the group, it seemed likely he would deliver even more actionable intelligence about the inner workings of the Bresci Circle. Two weeks after receiving the shopping list, Polignani delivered the materials to Carbone. There was only one nerve-racking moment: with the materials now in his possession, Carbone asked Polignani to return the shopping list. Without flinching, Polignani explained that he had torn it up. "I didn't want it to be found on me," he said. "It would have gotten me in trouble."

Woods and Tunney's willingness to stick with the operation was almost immediately rewarded with a significant break in the case. With the ingredients delivered, Carbone told Polignani to drop by Abarno's apartment on Elizabeth Street to pick up a booklet with instructions on manufacturing bombs; he would have ninety minutes to review the document before an evening meeting between the three of them to commence work on the devices.

The Bomb Squad had long suspected that some kind of terrorist instruction manual must have been circulating through the Bresci Circle—perhaps an updated Italian translation of Johann Most's *The Science of Revolutionary Warfare* from the late 1800s. "It was reasonable to assume," Tunney recalled several years later, "that there must be such a book of instruction in existence, that the bombers had not been handling delicate explosives with no better knowledge than word-of-mouth, hearsay chemistry." The increased sophistication evident in the infernal machines that Owen Eagan dissected suggested as much. But the police had never managed to acquire the instruction manual itself—if in fact it even existed. And now Polignani was holding it in his hands.

With no time for the usual subterfuge, Polignani dashed to the nearest payphone to call Tunney as soon as he left Abarno's apartment. Tunney agreed to meet him at Centre Street and rallied the photography unit to be ready for his arrival. (With Xerox machines still decades in the future, books had to be photographed by hand.) Polignani raced down the East Side of Manhattan, arriving in time for Faurot's team to capture the first half of the book, before doing the return loop to his meeting with Abarno and Carbone. (The NYPD would get the remaining pages during another, equally daring rendezvous a few days later.) Somehow Polignani convinced the two anarchists that he had spent the last hour and a half studying the material, and not boomeranging across Manhattan and making copies in a photography studio.

Tunney had the photographed pages translated into English. Just reading the table of contents sent a shiver down his spine:

First principles	Gun cotton
Instruments	Preparation of fuses
Manipulation	Capsule and petard
Explosive material	Application of explosive
Powder	materials
Nitroglycerine	Bombs
Dynamite	Incendiary materials
Fulminate of mercury	

The booklet was sixty pages long: not a translation of Most's *The Science of Revolutionary Warfare* but rather an Italian original, with the odd title *La Salute e' in voi!*—a common toast that translated as "Health is in you." In addition to the detailed instructions for bomb manufacture, the booklet contained extensive lifestyle advice for the aspiring terrorist. "We recommend most earnestly that if you wish to engage in this line of work, you procure, before all else, a sufficient amount of money, otherwise you risk being put out in the middle of the street, only to find your long work and trouble all in vain," the anonymous authors advised. "We recommend at the same time that you do not omit any precaution necessary to avoid attracting the attention of the police, and avoid mixing with the public, nor be seen with known companions. And do not work at it in the house except when necessary . . . Above all

we recommend that you never make explosives for the mere plea-
sure of making them."

Tunney's first thoughts reading the translation went to Polignani's safety—as they must have for Woods as well, given the history with Petrosino. "I am free to confess that my first sight of the
pamphlet brought the plots of the men we were watching very close
to grim reality," he wrote. "I never knew just when we would get an
ambulance call and have to go and pick Polignani out of the wreck
of a premature explosion, and I never heard him report in on the
telephone that I didn't experience a momentary apprehension of his
latest news."

Polignani himself appeared not to share the sense of dread that
lingered over the operation. As the plot grew more substantial—
and more deadly—Polignani remained confident and calm. Tunney
later recalled that he was "enthusiastic over the fact that the trail
was growing hotter all the time." Taking their cues from the pre-
scriptions in *La Salute e' in voi!*, Carbone, Abarno, and Polignani
rented a room at 1341 Third Avenue—about thirty blocks south of
the Bresci Circle headquarters—to serve as their dynamite workshop. Up until that moment, the primary risk facing Polignani had
been the one that had ultimately led to Petrosino's death: the risk of
his cover being blown. But now the young detective confronted a far
more perilous and unpredictable threat, the one that had sent Alfred Nobel to his barge on the Elbe fifty years before: the threat of
an uncontrolled explosion.

Perhaps surprisingly, Carbone's boasts about his bomb-making
prowess turned out to be grounded in reality. Laboring in their improvised lab, the three men delicately placed the explosive material
into tin cans originally containing hand soap, bound the cans with
copper wire and iron slugs, and punched a fuse hole at the top of
each bomb. They contemplated traveling out to Queens to test one
of the devices at the Corona Ash Dump—later made famous as the

"valley of ashes" in *The Great Gatsby*. But Carbone was confident that the bombs would detonate and didn't want to take on the risk of an accidental explosion en route to the test site.

Carbone and Abarno failed to notice that an exact duplicate of the copper fuse that they had designed for each device had gone missing from the Third Avenue lab. Polignani had discreetly pilfered it from the supplies and delivered it to Centre Street. There, Owen Eagen ran tests that established that it would take at least eight minutes for the flame to travel the length of the fuse.

With live explosives now involved, Woods assigned four additional detectives to perform 24/7 surveillance on Carbone and Abarno. In the late afternoon of February 27, detectives followed the two anarchists and their undercover colleague as they made their way up Fifth Avenue to make their final preparations for the attack. Abarno argued for placing the bombs in the vestibule, in the hopes of destroying the entire front edifice of the Cathedral. But Carbone overruled, making the case that depositing two packages at the entrance to the church would be too conspicuous. Instead, they would enter the cathedral disguised as worshippers and leave the infernal machines in the pews, not unlike the strategy employed by the Tombs courthouse bomber in November. Carbone had timed the fuse on each device to ensure that they had enough margin to leave the scene of the crime before the bombs went off. The three men would then scatter for the rest of the day, and reconnoiter at Abarno's apartment at nine o'clock, to toast *La Salute e' in voi!* and celebrate the carnage they had unleashed at St. Patrick's.

When they gathered together for the last time at their Third Avenue workshop, Carbone offered one final warning to his two accomplices. "Now, if anybody squeals," he said, "his body is going to be cut up into little pieces. Understand?"

"All right," Polignani affirmed. "I'm for it. Little pieces it is."

CHAPTER 22

Cathedral

The final day of Frank Baldo's four-month-long existence—Tuesday, March 2, 1915—began with a quick predawn breakfast at a luncheonette on the Upper East Side. It was a brisk, clear morning. Walking down still-quiet Third Avenue to the explosives workshop, the usually unflappable Polignani battled his nerves. Twenty blocks south of him, the doors of St. Patrick's had opened to welcome attendees for an early-morning mass, presided over by Bishop Patrick Hayes. As the organist played a quiet rotation of hymns in the chancel, hundreds of worshippers made their way from the vestibule to the front pews, passing a pair of scrubwomen mopping the checkerboard marble floors near the back of the church.

Polignani arrived at the workshop at 6:30 as planned. Abarno was there already, waiting on the front stoop. But there was no sign of Carbone. For Polignani, Carbone's absence was particularly troubling: He had spent months infiltrating the suspect's world, building his confidence, only to have him disappear on the day of the planned attack. Abarno's mind naturally drifted to the possibility that Carbone had been an undercover operative all along—or had been apprehended by the police and was even now testifying against the two men down on Centre Street. As the minutes ticked by, Abarno grew increasingly agitated; he was due at 7:30 at his typesetting job in Little Italy.

In the end, Abarno decided to continue with the attack. "Come up and get the bombs with me," he told Polignani. "We'll probably meet Carbone on the way down the street."

Minutes later, the two men emerged from the apartment building, each clutching a small package under his overcoat. As they made their way down Third Avenue toward the cathedral, two "shadows"—plainclothes members of the Bomb and Anarchist Squad—emerged from doorways across the street and began walking south as well, keeping an even pace with Polignani and Abarno. A few hundred yards behind them, Tunney sat in the back of a police limousine as it crept along the avenue at a pedestrian's speed. Twice during their journey to the cathedral, Polignani and Abarno encountered uniformed officers on patrol; each time, Abarno ushered Polignani across the street to avoid contact, unaware of the parade of law enforcement personnel trailing behind them.

At Fifty-third Street, just a few blocks north of St. Patrick's, Tunney ordered his driver to take a right turn away from the suspects; the second the limousine was out of Abarno's sight, the driver slammed on the accelerator and carried Tunney to the entrance of the church at top speed. There, the Bomb Squad chief found a darkened corner of the vestibule and waited.

From the altar, Bishop Hayes intoned the Liturgy of the Eucharist in Latin:

Blessed are you, Lord God of all creation, for through your goodness we have received the bread we offer you: Fruit of the earth and work of human hands, it will become for us the bread of life.

Hundreds of worshippers, most of them women, bowed their heads in the front pews and murmured the refrain.

Blessed be God forever.

As the bishop turned to the Eucharistic Prayer, he enjoined the congregation to rise. The muffled sound of several hundred people returning their kneelers to an upright position filled the cathedral. Polignani and Abarno entered through the Fifth Avenue doors, each of them smoking a cigar. From his secluded nook in the vestibule, Tunney watched the two men intently. Abarno gestured to Polignani to take a seat in the tenth row, while he continued on to the sixth, passing an imposing man with a curly white beard and gold-rimmed glasses in the aisle. Abarno sat for a second, head bowed, and then veered toward the northern end of the altar next to the pillar at the entrance to the Chapel of Our Lady of San Loretto, where the infernal machine had detonated six months before.

Ten paces behind him, the two scrubwomen began dusting the seats near the Fifty-first Street entrance.

The Lord be with you.
And with your spirit.
Lift up your hearts.
We lift them up to the Lord.

Altar bells rang out, signaling the moment of transubstantiation. Polignani and Abarno bowed their heads with the rest of the congregation. Stealthily, each man removed the package from under his coat and placed it at his feet. As the words of the consecration—*Sanctus, sanctus, sanctus*—reverberated through the vast interior, Abarno pulled the cigar from his mouth, shook off a few ashes, and placed the glowing embers of tobacco firmly against the copper fuse.

Was there a moment of bewilderment in the mind of young Frank Abarno when he glanced up from his pew at St. Patrick's to see the two elderly scrubwomen toss their mops aside and lunge toward him? Or perhaps, at close proximity, he could discern the telltale stubble and masculine physique of two undercover officers.

Either way, within seconds of lighting the fuse, Abarno was carted away by detectives James Sterrett and Patrick Walsh, both of them still in costume. The bearded gentleman with the gold-rimmed glasses—Detective George Barnitz, also in disguise—swooped in to extinguish the flame trailing down the copper wire.

Sergeant Tunney emerged from the shadows at the back of the church and marched toward Polignani in the tenth row. Tunney made a show of grabbing the detective roughly by the shoulder and carting him out of the cathedral toward the police wagon idling on Fifth Avenue. Inside the church, the morning Mass continued un-interrupted. The entire operation had been conducted without the assembled worshippers realizing anything was amiss.

Detectives Sterrett, Walsh, and Barnitz were finished with their theatrical careers, though the NYPD did arrange a photo shoot of each officer in his disguise, images from which were featured prom-inently in the press coverage that followed the arrests.

Polignani, on the other hand, had one last scene to play as Frank Baldo.

It remains a mystery to this day what exactly caused Carbone to miss the 6:30 meet at the workshop. But whether he lost his nerve or simply overslept, his absence turned out to be a fantastic break for the police. The elaborate choreography of the St. Patrick's surveil-lance had made it overwhelmingly clear to Abarno that someone in their inner circle had been talking to the cops. In Abarno's mind, the only logical narc in the group was the man who had abandoned the plot at the very last minute: Carbone. But *that* belief depended on Polignani staying in character—hence Tunney's brusque treat-ment of the detective in the cathedral pews.

Woods was waiting on the steps of Centre Street when the of-ficers and their one genuine suspect arrived shortly before eight.

Woods had his men deliver the two infernal machines to Owen Eagan and put Abarno and Baldo in a room together. While the two suspects waited for their interrogators to arrive, Woods dispatched a police car to Carbone's residence on Sixty-seventh Street. When the police arrived, Carbone was walking out the door on the way to work. "He was arrested after a hard struggle on the sidewalk," the *Times* reported, noting that Carbone was only eighteen years of age.

Back at Centre Street, Faurot and Tunney led the interrogation, speaking to both men through translators. At first Abarno and Polignani quarreled with each other, but then something in Abarno seemed to shift, and he offered a partial confession. Yes, he had intended to light a bomb during morning mass at the most prominent religious landmark in New York City. And yes, he had intended to target additional attacks on individual magnates. He mentioned three magnates by name: the two Rockefellers and Andrew Carnegie.

For all his apparent exhaustion, there was some cunning in Abarno's statement to Tunney and Faurot. What happened in the cathedral was close to the dictionary definition of being caught red-handed. It was pointless to deny the obvious facts. But Abarno did have one way out. If he could prove that an agent provocateur on the police payroll had coerced him into bombing the cathedral, he might at least have a chance of a fair hearing. And if there *were* an undercover agent, there was only one possibility, given that his other partner was sitting beside him in the interrogation room. With no other options, Abarno told Tunney and Faurot that a certain Carmen Carbone had masterminded the entire plot.

That is, the same Carmen Carbone who was at that very moment being ushered into a separate interrogation room, where he would be read the entirety of Abarno's testimony accusing him of setting up the bomb plot and spying for the police. Whatever Frank Baldo had said against Carbone, Tunney and Faurot conveniently left out.

And that left Carmen Carbone with an easy decision: to plead utter ignorance of the plot—an argument bolstered by the fact that he had not been at the cathedral—and point the finger at Abarno, the man whose finger happened to be pointing at him.

By the end of the day, Tunney and Faurot had each man on the record testifying to the other's culpability, without either mentioning Polignani as a potential instigator. It wasn't airtight, but it was the foundation of a case.

Enough of a foundation, at least, for Amedeo Polignani to retire the role of Frank Baldo for good.

"It was a splendid piece of work on the part of the police department," Mayor Mitchel told the press, after the arrests had been announced. "This sort of thing is the most important work the police have to do: The prevention of crimes, of violence, and the apprehension of criminals."

In his statement to the media, Woods praised Polignani effusively and took a swipe at his ersatz conspirators. "This was a piece of real detective work," he said. "As to the extent of the plot, these two little fellows haven't the capacity to think far enough to carry out this far-reaching scheme of attacks on wealthy men; but we know they had large intentions." Anticipating criticism that the police had taken on too much risk by allowing Abarno to light an actual explosive in a crowded church, Woods noted: "The bombs were undoubtedly dangerous. But we knew exactly when and where they purchased the ingredients, bit by bit; we had absolute knowledge of every step they took almost as soon as they had taken it."

Writing in *Mother Earth* several weeks after the arrests, Emma Goldman presented the case that Carbone and Abarno would—unsuccessfully—argue in court: that they had been lured into the attack on the cathedral by Polignani:

Heaven only knows that the spy is despicable enough, but the provocateur is the lowest of all criminals. His business is to waylay a suitable subject, and then work upon the mind of his prey through various forms of suggestion so long until his victim is pliable as putty . . . And this damnable business, this rotten system, this outrageous procedure has now found its way into America in the person of the Italian detective, Polignani, the provocateur of the two unfortunate victims, Frank Abarno and Carmen Carbone . . . The Anarchist, the I.W.W. groups and the Ferrer Center have been infested with mesmerists in search of fit subjects. . . . Polignani, evidently anxious to advance himself, was the most persistent of the provocateurs, who operated in radical circles during the past year. He chose for his instruments two workers, with a background so harrowing, of poverty, wretchedness and drabness, that it was an easy task to arouse their discontent.

Goldman went on to have some fun at Woods's expense, mocking his do-gooder, Groton-tutor persona:

But says Commissioner Woods, "an officer will do no wrong." What's the matter with the Commissioner; has he just come out of boarding school? He talks as if he were still in his knickers. If so, the New York Police Department is no place for him. His mother would do well to take him home.

The language hadn't fully developed yet in 1915, but in our modern terminology, Goldman was claiming that the anarchists generally—and the *Mother Earth* crowd in particular—should not be considered part of a terrorist organization. If there were bombers in their midst planting explosives in crowded cathedrals, that was simply because they had been mesmerized by the agents of the secret police. No self-respecting anarchist in her circle would contemplate taking the lives of innocent civilians in the name of the cause.

Once again, Berkman refused to stick to the nonviolence story. Speaking to a crowd in Denver just a few weeks before the St. Patrick's attack, Berkman had all but confessed to his involvement in the July 4 explosion. Of Berg, Caron, and Hanson, he had told the audience:

> They had no definite idea when they would use the missile, but it was their plan to wait for an opportunity and hurl it into the carriage or automobile of the Rockefellers when they were leaving the Tarrytown estate. They wanted to get both of them together, if possible, but would have taken the life of either one. I do not know what their bomb was made of, but the damage it did when it burst prematurely would seem to indicate that they made it as deadly as they could. According to the statements since made to me by Murphy, they had the bomb almost finished when it exploded . . .

The remarks were newsworthy enough that Woods had briefed reporters the following day, alerting them that the July 4 bombing was still an open investigation, and Berkman could still be indicted for his participation in the plot. Berkman had been a central player in the Tarrytown siege with Caron, and he had been observed meeting with the bomb makers the night before the Lexington Avenue blast. And now he had openly confessed to having direct knowledge of the plot.

Woods was frustrated again by the lack of an organized federal police agency. Berkman was on the other side of the continent after all, and Woods only had a local investigative force at his disposal. Trying to arrange a long-distance arrest of Berkman would have been a distraction from Polignani's dangerous operation. Woods

decided the Bresci Circle investigation had to be the priority. Goldman and Berkman remained free agents, for the time being.

With Carbone and Abarno awaiting trial, Amedeo Polignani hung
up Frank Baldo's "old blue suit" and returned to ordinary life as a
uniformed detective. The "handicap of publicity"—as Woods had
called it in "The Problem of the Black Hand"—meant that his short
career as an undercover agent was over. "What was the reward of
those five months invested in patience?" Tunney later wrote of the
Bresci Circle operation:

> The two prisoners convicted and sentenced to terms of from six to
> twelve years, was one result . . . perhaps the most gratifying was
> the discord which grew in the Brescia Circle. The group was
> frightened, and the members began to suspect each other of es-
> pionage. One former anarchist was quoted as saying that he
> wouldn't even trust himself—he had been dreaming the night
> before that he was a spy. The Brescia Circle became disorganized,
> and several other similar groups in the city suffered the same fate.

Also gratifying was the wave of adulatory press coverage that the
NYPD received in the months after the operation. In April, the *Tribune* ran a story commemorating the one-year anniversary of Woods's
appointment as police commissioner that might as well have been
drafted by Woods himself. The headline observed that Woods had
"begun work with a demoralized, suspicious force," but had somehow
managed to turn the organization into a "real peace army." Woods,
the article explained, had taken on the job after "the most notorious
scandal which ever undermined the reputation of the police—the
Becker case. He found the department disorganized, its members
suspicious of each other and of its head, and resentful. At the end of

twelve months, the Police Department possesses an esprit de corps seldom, if ever before, developed in its history. A systematic and zealous effort is being made to prevent crime." A full-length feature syndicated in papers across the country lauded the NYPD's "vast, intricate, and scientific system of identification based on portraits, fingerprints, and Bertillon measurements":

> The police of New York possess the most remarkable gallery of bad men and women in the world. Even Scotland Yard cannot equal it; nor can its equal be found at the prefecture of police in Paris. It is a "Hall of Infamy" . . . located in a large room on the first floor of police headquarters at 240 Centre Street. It is a much littered room surrounded by filing cabinets. In these cabinets are filed by card index records of a great army of men and women. There is a square-jawed, square-shouldered, square-talking man of good height, doing the work of magic which would probably have got him burned at the stake a few centuries back—Inspector Joseph Faurot, head of the detective bureau.

In just a year on the job, with the help of Faurot, Tunney, and Polignani, Woods had elevated the NYPD to the upper echelons of law enforcement agencies worldwide. Faurot's state-of-the-art Identification Bureau and Frank Baldo's daring undercover investigation had finally realized two of the three main objectives that Woods had first proposed in "The Problem of the Black Hand": a scientific approach to establishing the identities of criminals, and an investigative force capable of infiltrating radical organizations.

Only one piece of that original vision was missing: putting those resources to work on a national level. But you couldn't hope to instigate that magnitude of change based on foiling a single urban bombing plot. To justify the federal investigative force that Arthur Woods and Teddy Roosevelt had dreamed of, you needed a war.

CHAPTER 23

A Madman and a Marriage

In his memoirs recounting his years as head of the Bomb and Anarchist Squad, Thomas Tunney claimed that one of the immediate consequences of the foiled plot at St. Patrick's had been "a sharp decrease in bomb-throwing in New York." Whether or not that statement was true in terms of overall incendiary attacks, it was certainly an overstatement in terms of the *perception* of explosive violence in the city, given the number of high-profile bombings that continued to erupt around the city in the months after the arrests at St. Patrick's. What *did* change, however, is that New York City ceased to be the epicenter of dynamite attacks in the United States. It wasn't so much that there were fewer infernal machines being planted in Manhattan. Instead, the New York bombings increasingly had to compete for press attention with a mounting wave of dynamite attacks sweeping the country.

In the afternoon of July 2, 1915, a former Harvard professor named Erich Muenter wandered through the main entrance of the Capitol building in Washington, D.C., holding a suitcase in one hand. With Congress in recess for the Fourth of July weekend, Muenter meandered through the mostly empty halls undeterred for half an hour—attempting at one point to enter the locked Senate chamber—before depositing his suitcase in a reception room nearby, underneath a telephone switchboard. He opened the valise and delicately configured the timing mechanism he had attached to three sticks of dynamite. (Muenter had devised an ingenious fuse that involved a vial of sulfuric acid slowly eating its way through cork, before triggering the explosion.) He then strolled out of the building and made his way to Union Station, two blocks from the Capitol. He waited there patiently well until the evening, roaming out in the later hours to sit on the benches of Columbus Circle.

In the Senate reception room, the sulfuric acid steadily dissolved the cork, creeping ever closer to the dynamite. At 11:23 that night, the sound of a blast reverberated across the deserted plaza where Muenter sat. It was a symbolic act, specifically designed not to injure anyone. But Muenter harbored more deadly plans. As sirens and alarms began to ring out across Capitol Hill, he rose from his bench and entered Union Station, where he purchased a ticket for the 12:10 train to New York.

In New York, Muenter transferred to the commuter line and rode out to Glen Cove, Long Island, where he managed to secure entry to

Damage from the Capitol building bombing

the mansion of J. P. Morgan, Jr. Just two years earlier, Morgan had inherited the family business—and its vast fortune—after the death of his father. In recent months, Morgan, Jr., had loaned hundreds of millions of dollars to the French, indirectly financing the Allied war effort, despite the United States's official position of neutrality.

Carrying three additional sticks of dynamite in his suitcase, Muenter burst past the butler who answered the door and shot Morgan twice in the hip before the butler and Morgan himself restrained the intruder, striking Muenter in the head so fiercely that he briefly lost consciousness. The whole incident played out as a strange echo of Berkman's failed assassination attempt against Frick; Morgan suffered only minor injuries, and Muenter ended up bound with rope and trunk straps on the front lawn, as the household waited for the police to arrive. (Just as in 1892, the dynamite remained undetonated.) When the local police arrived, Muenter begged them to put him out of his misery: "Kill me now, please. You might as well do it and end my suffering. For six months I have lived in hell. I could not rest because of the frightful murders in Europe."

Though the case was technically not in his jurisdiction, Woods called Tunney at his home in Brooklyn and informed him of the attack and dispatched him to Long Island to assist with the investigation. In part, Woods wanted Tunney on top of the case for professional reasons: Protecting the magnates of Wall Street from terrorist attentats was implicitly part of the job description of a NYPD commissioner, no matter where the crime in question had taken place. But there were personal reasons as well: Woods had recently begun courting Morgan's cousin, the nineteen-year-old Helen Morgan Hamilton, a sharp and spirited recent debutante who had been a favorite of J. P. Morgan, Sr. (Helen had been at the patriarch's deathbed in Rome in 1913.) She was also the great-granddaughter of Alexander Hamilton, which meant that with this new relationship, Woods was extending his connection to some of

America's most powerful dynasties, beyond his existing link to the Roosevelts.

At first, the two attacks in Washington and Glen Cove appeared to be unrelated. The only clue in the Capitol bombing was a letter sent to *The Evening Star*, signed by an R. Pearce, justifying the bombings as, paradoxically, a radical contribution to the peace movement: "Europe needs enough non-contraband material to give us prosperity. Let us not sell her EXPLOSIVES! Let each nation make her own mankilling machines." The note rambled its way into something like an apology for both the use of violence and the irony of it all: "Sorry I had to use explosives. (Never again.) It is the export kind and ought to make enough noise to be heard above the voices that clamour for bloodmoney. This explosion is the exclamation point to my appeal for Peace!"

In Glen Cove, on the other hand, the attacker had identified himself to the police as a Cornell professor named Frank Holt. But a sharp-eyed D.C. detective noticed that Holt's testimony retraced the very distinctive logic of the *Evening Star* letter: "My motive in coming here," Holt had said, "was to try to force Mr. Morgan to use his influence with the manufacturers of munitions in the United States and with the millionaires who are financing the war loans to have an embargo put on shipments of war munitions so as to relieve the American people of complicity in the deaths of thousands of our European brothers."

The D.C. detective wired his suspicions to Faurot's office at the NYPD. They were immediately relayed to Tunney in Mineola, the commuter hub at the center of the island where Muenter was being held. Tunney showed Muenter the *Evening Star* letter and demanded to know if he had written it.

"It does look strange, doesn't it?" Muenter replied, a bloodied bandage loosely wrapped around his skull. "It seems that the man who did that thought about it like I did, too, doesn't it? It was rather odd that he used almost the same words as I did. I can't explain it."

Unsatisfied with the response, Tunney reverted to the interrogation tactics of the Byrnes era. "We had to go after him good and strong before he would tell us what he knew," he told the press unapologetically. After two hours, Muenter broke down, admitting that he had planted the Capitol bomb and sent the letter to the *Evening Star*, and intimating that there were other bomb attacks in the works, organized by a German secret intelligence network known as Abteilung III b.

The telegraph machine and switchboard at Centre Street became the hub of a vast network of clues, shuttling across the wires from law enforcement agencies around the country. From Cambridge, Massachusetts, came word that Muenter had been suspected of murdering his wife while still on the faculty at Harvard in 1908. Dallas police wired news that Muenter's current wife had received an enigmatic note from her husband suggesting that he had planted dynamite on a steamship bound for Europe—which set off a frantic effort by radio operators along the Eastern Seaboard to alert all recently departed vessels that they were in peril. Working around the clock, the Bomb Squad team in Manhattan determined that Muenter had recently taken delivery of two hundred sticks of dynamite, far more than the six sticks that had been accounted for in the two attacks. When Tunney grilled him about the location of the remaining explosives, Muenter refused to answer. Cryptically, he promised Tunney that he would reveal all on July 7, seventy-two hours in the future.

But that turned out to be a promise Erich Muenter couldn't keep, for one simple reason. He only had forty-eight hours left to live.

❋   ❋   ❋

At Centre Street, what had promised to be a leisurely Fourth of July weekend had once again descended into complete mayhem. Robert Moses had not yet streamlined the flow of automobile traffic between Manhattan and the suburbs of Long Island; it was an ordeal just shuttling the police limousines from Centre Street to Mineola and back on surface roads. Woods himself had relocated to Long Island to be closer to the Muenter interrogation, while Tunney and his men—including Detective Barnitz, last seen playing the role of the bearded gentleman at St. Patrick's—embarked on a whirlwind investigation across Manhattan and New Jersey that ultimately took them to a storage unit on the West Side, where they discovered a trunk filled with bomb-making materials, including 134 sticks of dynamite, 3 assembled tin-can bombs, 2 boxes of electric fuses, blasting caps, a dry battery, and the usual demonic chemistry lab of compounds: sulfur, fulminate of mercury, rosin, and more. Even Owen Eagen was shaken by the contents of the trunk. He told the press that it was among the "greatest equipment for bomb making ever brought to New York." The math was particularly ominous: Given Muenter's initial order, 60 sticks of dynamite were still at large.

With all the frenzied activity at the NYPD, it is perhaps understandable that none of the officers on duty the night of July 5 noticed a stranger entering the headquarters through the staff entrance on Centre Street, leaving behind a cheap suitcase in a basement doorway beneath Faurot's Identification Bureau.

The Centre Street bomb detonated at 8:58 P.M., blowing a hole a foot deep in the concrete steps leading to a fire exit, destroying several glass doors and windows in the passageway. A three-inch-thick oak door was "reduced to kindling," according to press accounts. Directly above the bomb site, in the Identification Bureau, Lieutenant Edward McNally was thrown out of his chair; a stenographer named Joseph Evans was nearly impaled by a shard of plate glass from a blown-out window that flew over his shoulder, slicing through the paper in his typewriter. Every window on the lower floors of the Centre Street side of the building was shattered in the blast. Across the street, the windows of the downtown offices of *The New York Times* were "blown almost to powder." A yellow, sulfurous smoke poured out onto the plaza in front of the headquarters, enveloping the crowd of onlookers that immediately assembled at the scene.

The fact that the infernal machine had been planted in the basement—and timed to detonate well into the evening—suggested that the culprit had intended more to send a message than to cause real bloodshed. (It helped that so many of the key members of the force were racing around the greater New York area investigating the Muenter case.) There were no injuries reported—just the symbolic violation of a bomber infiltrating the NYPD's inner sanctum. Returning from Long Island to inspect the damage that night, Arthur Woods told the press: "Naturally, an explosion at the very heart and center of the police department is a bad thing for us, but while there is no one whom we suspect at present, we have two or three clues which I hope will result in something definite in two days."

Given the events of the preceding three days, it was natural for the police to assume that the blast had come from some of those dynamite sticks missing from Erich Muenter's trunk. Eagen examined the debris for signs of the distinctive sulfuric-acid-and-cork timing mechanism that had been deployed in the Capitol bombing. After surveying the wreckage, Tunney raced back to interrogate Muenter in Mineola, only to find that the suspect had been relocated to the local morgue. Overnight, Muenter had managed to climb the bars of his cell and fling himself headfirst onto the concrete floor, fracturing his skull from the forehead to the base.

Muenter had one last terrorist act to perform from the grave, though. The day after his death, a second explosion erupted in one of the holds aboard the Atlantic transport steamer *Minnehaha* as it made its way toward Europe in the North Atlantic. At first the captain had radioed concerns that the blaze caused by the explosion might ignite the cargo of armaments on board, but the ship eventually returned safely to Halifax with no casualties, marking the end of Erich Muenter's brief but eventful reign of terror.

Back at Centre Street, Eagan concluded that the police bomb resembled the earlier ones detonated in St. Alphonsus and St. Patrick's. That it had been planted on the one-year-anniversary of the Lexington Avenue explosion—coupled with the string of threatening letters Faurot had received in the preceding weeks referencing the deaths of Berg, Caron, and Hanson—led the police to an obvious conclusion. "It appears to be the work of anarchists," Woods reported, noting drily: "I don't suppose anyone sought revenge on the Police Headquarters for the exportation of arms to the Allies." In its report on the bomb's aftermath, the *Times* included a one-sentence paragraph that observed, without comment: "Inquiry by the police showed that Alexander Berkman was in the West and that Emma Goldman was at her home in New Jersey."

The bedlam of that July 4 weekend proved to be an augury of things to come. As the drumbeat for American involvement in the war grew louder, the Bomb Squad found itself fighting battles on two fronts: not just against anarchists like Goldman and Berkman and what remained of the Bresci Circle, but increasingly against German saboteurs who were working to block arms shipments to the Allies. Woods facilitated connections between Tunney and military intelligence, and renamed the unit the Bomb and Neutrality Squad, to reflect its growing involvement in the international situation. The Muenter case had made it evident that these kinds of threats demanded a coordinated national response. Lacking an institutional framework to provide that structure, Woods expanded the purview of the NYPD. "Although city police forces did not usually take [it] upon themselves to do such distinctly federal work," he later explained, "we felt it was necessary because of the commanding position of New York as the greatest city and the greatest harbor in the country containing thousands of people of different nationalities."

Woods had also been experimenting with a modern surveillance technique that would go on to be much abused by the federal authorities during the twentieth century: wiretapping. While the constitutionality of police officers eavesdropping on private telephone conversations had not yet been established, the practice was almost as old as Alexander Graham Bell's invention itself. As commissioner, Woods regularly encouraged his detectives to deploy the technique. "Criminals have to do long-distance work nowadays," he would later explain. "In the old times . . . there were more haunts of criminals. They stayed together. They could stay together because there was no other way in which they could communicate with each other. Now, there is long-distance work by criminals and they use long-distance methods, and that is the telephone."

Woods's predilection for wiretapping embroiled him in the biggest controversy of his tenure as commissioner. Mayor Mitchel's reform agenda had included a radical overhaul of the city's orphanages, which had historically been outsourced to the Catholic Church, at significant expense. Horror stories proliferated about the conditions the orphans suffered through in these institutions. Mitchel—who was himself Catholic—convened hearings to discuss the issue; Mitchel and his commissioner of public charities, John Kingsbury, instructed Woods (and his NYPD wiretappers) to listen in on the conversations between the main witnesses for the Catholic side, one of whom was a priest. The transcripts were then deployed against the witnesses during the hearings.

When news of the wiretaps broke, the city's Catholic population was outraged—spying on a priest did not play well in the press or in the pews—and Kingsbury was indicted for unlawful breach of privacy. The district attorney intimated to the *Times* that Woods and Mitchel would be next. The legal jeopardy Woods faced was compounded by the fact that the police had also tapped the phones of a law firm called Seymour & Seymour, allegedly at the request of J. P. Morgan, Jr. (Morgan believed the firm had stolen confidential documents from them related to munitions orders that were being sent to France to help support the Allied cause—the very activity that had sent Erich Muenter over the edge into homicidal madness.) Woods maintained that the surveillance operation had come at the request of federal authorities, part of the close collaboration between Washington and the NYPD that the war had necessitated. But the two scandals erupting in the first months of 1916 threatened to undermine the narrative that Woods had crafted so successfully over his first two years as commissioner: For the first time, his embrace of state-of-the-art crimefighting techniques appeared to have crossed over into an invasion of privacy.

The fact that the police department seemed to be working, Pinkerton-style, on behalf of Big Capital was troubling enough. But Woods was caught in a more complicated web. Publicly, the Seymour & Seymour scandal implied that Woods was happily doing the dirty work for the Bank of Morgan. Privately, he was about to be married into the Morgan family itself. Just a month before the Seymour & Seymour controversy erupted, the society pages had celebrated the surprising news that Helen Morgan Hamilton was engaged to marry the "confirmed bachelor" Arthur Woods. One can imagine the awkward dynamics during the wedding planning, with the groom fearing indictment for a crime allegedly committed in the service of his bride-to-be's family.

In late May, New York State Senator George Thompson convened a series of public hearings to investigate the wiretapping scandal. Behind closed doors, Woods lobbied heavily to take the stand to defend the department's actions. There were personal stakes to his testimony—his reputation was on the line, and of course there was the additional pressure of his looming nuptials—but the wiretapping controversy had broader technological implications as well. The telephone was still a relatively novel communications medium, but its adoption rate was skyrocketing. At the turn of the century, less than 5 percent of American households had a dedicated telephone line; by the time Woods took the stand during the Thompson hearings in the spring of 1916, more than a third of the country had integrated phone conversation into their daily routine. But the question of how private those conversations would be was still an unresolved issue. Party lines were still common, particularly in rural areas, and the recent headlines in New York had made it clear that police surveillance—and perhaps even corporate espionage—had flourished on the new platform. Was the telephone closer to the public square, where anyone could listen in on what you said? Or was it a more intimate medium, closer to the conversation you might have over family dinner? "The disclosure of specific instances of promiscuous tapping of private telephone wires in this city," one newspaper editorial observed, "has started in the minds of the telephone-using public doubt and misgivings which ought to be promptly allayed."

On the stand in front of the Thompson Committee, Woods made a persuasive case for wiretapping as an essential asset for twentieth-century law enforcement. "If you permit the criminal to continue to use the telephone and forbid the people that you hire to protect you from criminals to use it," he argued, "you are deliberately putting into the hands of the criminal a powerful weapon which you are withholding from the police." But Woods was also careful to note that the surveillance methods the police used were acceptable only in the context of criminal investigations. He drew an analogy to the low-tech undercover operations that predated the invention of the telephone:

> Shadowing a crook on the street—if we send some of our good shadowers, and we have got some mighty good ones, Mr. Chairman—if we send some of our good shadowers to shadow honest people, it is a wholly unjustifiable thing for us to do. This is a free country, living under constitutional order, and that would be an infringement upon the rights of the honest man. But I maintain that is not an infringement on the rights of a crook . . . He is a crook. He is an outlaw . . . If people would spend less time talking about the rights of the dear criminal and spend more time in backing up the authorities of law and order . . . we would have less criminals to bother with.

To drive the point home, he invoked Amedeo Polignani's infiltration of the Bresci Circle from the preceding year:

> And let me give you one example that you may remember. We prevented an anarchistic explosion in St. Patrick's Cathedral by that very method. A young detective got his way into a group of anarchists and was able to stay with them so that we could prevent that explosion, and instead of a destructive explosion in the cathedral, we prevented it. Do you object to that kind of detective work or do you applaud it? At the time, it was considered a very fine piece of work. The method used would be wholly objectionable if used against honest men.

Woods's defense of wiretapping at the Thompson hearings played well in the press, and his argument received an additional boost in early June when a New York appellate court declared in a separate case that wiretapping was justifiable when deployed in the pursuit of detecting criminal activities. A jury acquitted Kingsbury in the orphanage case, and the looming indictments against Woods and Mitchel never arrived. It was a personal vindication for Woods, as well as a historical turning point that helped cement electronic surveillance as one of the core modern methods of fighting crime, alongside fingerprint analysis and photography.

If the figurative storm clouds of the wiretapping scandal had lifted by the morning of June 10, 1916, the actual weather was less accommodating, with unseasonably cold storms blanketing the mid-Atlantic states. But the damp spring chill was of little concern to the hundred-odd guests gathered in a small stone chapel on the outskirts of Tuxedo Park to witness the marriage of Arthur Hale Woods and Helen Morgan Hamilton. Many of the dignitaries in attendance—including Mayor Mitchel—had traveled to the Hamilton family's grand estate northwest of Manhattan on a private train organized for the occasion. The bride herself—dressed in a white linen gown—arrived in a carriage drawn by four hackneys sporting white linen rosettes, with a footman and coachman in full livery.

All the elements of the bride's side of the wedding invoked the aura of American royalty, from her fairy-tale entrance to the reception held afterward for nine hundred guests at her family's gothic mansion, Table Rock. But the groom's contributions provided an unusual twist. During the processional, the main aisle of the chapel was lined with twenty-three inspectors from the New York City police department—among them Chief Detective Joseph Faurot—who lifted their batons to honor their commissioner as he made his way to the altar. Afterward, the assembled officers presented Woods with a silver cup, and Mitchel informed him that he had been promoted from sergeant to lieutenant "in recognition of his faithful and meritorious service." In the society pages that later reported on the wedding, much was made of the adorable sight of five young boys dressed in inspector uniforms who also stood at attention during the ceremony, all of them members of the Junior Police Force that Woods himself had founded.

Arthur Woods had been an English tutor and a journalist and a businessman, a dabbler in things, and a confidant of the financial elite. But there in the hills above Tuxedo Park, as he uttered his vows in front of the magnates and the detectives, there was no ambiguity about his professional identity. He was a policeman now, through and through.

CHAPTER 24

They Are Fine and Beautiful Characters

While Woods and Mitchel were skirting indictments in the wiretapping scandal, the increasingly ominous developments in Europe threatened to trigger an internecine battle in the anarchist community between long-standing comrades. For Emma Goldman and Alexander Berkman, the opposition to the war was a given. With the United States increasingly rallying behind the "Preparedness" movement, which assumed that it was only a matter of time before American troops would head to the European front lines, Goldman began delivering antiwar talks with titles like "Preparedness: The Road to Universal Slaughter." But then, in February of 1916, Peter Kropotkin and a group of other European anarchists issued "The Manifesto of the Sixteen," offering close to a full-throated endorsement of the Allied war effort. "Without doubt," they wrote, "despite the war, despite the murders, we do not forget that we are internationalists, that we want the union of peoples and the disappearance of borders. But it is because we want the reconciliation of peoples, including the German people, that we think that they must resist an aggressor who represents the destruction of all our hopes of liberation."

For Goldman in particular, it was "distressing to turn against the man who had so long been our inspiration," the man who had welcomed her so warmly to his carpentry studio in Bromley two decades earlier. But her commitment to pacifism—or whatever strange form of pacifism she believed in that left the door open for the occasional political murder—was stronger than her intellectual and personal allegiances. She kept quiet on Kropotkin's statement in the pages of *Mother Earth*, but she and Berkman stood behind the antiwar statement they had co-signed the year before, released by the Anarchists International organization:

> We are determinedly against any war between peoples, and, in the neutral countries, like Italy, where those in government are seeking once again to push more peoples into the inferno of war, our comrades have opposed, oppose and always will oppose war with every ounce of energy they possess. No matter where they may find themselves, the anarchists' role in the current tragedy is to carry on proclaiming that there is but one war of liberation: The one waged in every country by the oppressed against the oppressor, by the exploited against the exploiter. Our task is to summon the slaves to revolt against their masters.

Worn down by a dreary winter, Goldman traveled out to San Francisco to visit Berkman and Fitzi on Dolores Street. But the refuge in the Bay Area proved temporary. On July 22, as Goldman, Fitzi, and Berkman ate breakfast in the Mission, almost a hundred thousand people gathered in downtown San Francisco to participate in a Preparedness parade through the streets of the city. Just as the march was beginning, a suitcase bomb placed against the wall of a saloon on Market Street exploded, killing ten people and injuring dozens more. "As usual in such cases, the local authorities immediately raised the cry of 'Anarchist,'" Berkman told readers of *The Blast*. Harkening back to the Haymarket Riots, he noted: "The enemy is athirst for blood; it is planning to transplant to San Francisco the [Haymarket] gallows of 1887 when five of Labor's best and truest friends were strangled to death in Chicago."

The police swiftly arrested four men and one woman in association with the bombing, some of them tangentially related to *The Blast*. But suspicion continued to swirl around Berkman. A few days after the explosion, a district attorney accompanied by three detectives showed up at the offices of *The Blast*, confiscating their list of subscribers. "The degree of intelligence the raiders showed," Berkman jeered in the magazine, "convinced us that they couldn't detect the trail of an elephant on a muddy cowpath." When they asked if Berkman had any weapons in the house, he announced proudly, "Of course I have!"—then handed them his (unloaded) .38-caliber handgun.

The evidence for Berkman's involvement in the Preparedness parade attack was much weaker than the case for his culpability in the Lexington Avenue explosion. But the papers were quick to note that Berkman was the one common denominator shared by the two events, and he was on record as a sworn enemy of the conscription drive that the parade had been staged to champion. "Berkman's Hand Seen in Dynamiting," one local paper announced in a headline. In their articles for *Mother Earth* and *The Blast*, Berkman and Goldman kept up their brave faces, criticizing the case against the five suspects on trial, mocking the local authorities. But it was impossible not to feel that a sea change had occurred in the two years that separated the two attacks, driven by the inevitable upwelling of patriotism that accompanies any war effort. Building a bomb to protest the murder of striking laborers and their children was one thing; it was another to sabotage a Preparedness movement that was marshaling support for young men willing to sacrifice their lives to fight an imperial aggressor.

Just as problematic were the targets of the Market Street attack. You could get five thousand people to mourn your passing in Union

Square if you happened to die while plotting the assassination of a robber baron. But murdering random civilians who were merely rallying in support of America's future soldiers? That was a different kind of crime.

Little more than a week after the Market Street bombing, at two A.M. on July 30, a munitions depot on Black Tom Island in New York Harbor detonated, after three saboteurs working for German spymaster Franz von Rintelen had wired the depot with explosives earlier in the night. The blast was powerful enough to shatter windows miles away in Manhattan and Brooklyn; amazingly, the rumble from the explosion was felt as far as Philadelphia and Baltimore. Later estimates calculated that the explosion—which officially killed five people—would have registered at 5.5 on the Richter scale. In the entire history of New York City, only the collapse of the Twin Towers on 9/11 rivals the intensity of the Black Tom blast.

The scale of the Black Tom explosion triggered cultural aftershocks even more far-reaching than the physical ones. While President Wilson initially tried to downplay the explosion as an unfortunate industrial accident—"a regrettable incident at a private railroad terminal," in his words—evidence quickly accumulated suggesting that it had been the work of saboteurs. (Final proof of Rintelen's plot would not surface for years, though.) The threat of political terror loomed large in the public imagination. The United States descended into a sustained state of anti-radical suspicion that exceeded the future red scares of the McCarthy era. "Not only did the authorities increase scrutiny of anarchists, socialists, Wobblies, and other militants, but private individuals and groups took up the pursuit in the name of patriotism," Karen and Paul Avrich write.

Vigilante activities often were sanctioned by state and local authorities, and "superpatriots" engaged in surveillance of their neighbors. Proprietors of halls and gathering places were pressured by police and civilian groups alike to deny access to radicals, and, as happened to *Mother Earth* and *The Blast,* radical publications were hindered in production or removed from the mail.

For the anarchists, the increased police surveillance added a new layer of tension to all public gatherings. Never ones to water down their rhetorical cocktails, Berkman and Goldman both became more judicious in their public remarks, delicately walking the line between protesting the war effort and advocating violence against it. But the postal crackdown arguably had a more significant impact on their work. They had been trailed by detectives in almost all their public appearances since 1892, but their ability to circulate their ideas through a national network of supporters via platforms like *Mother Earth* and *The Blast* had largely been unimpeded. Those periodicals were a critical source of income as well, through subscription fees and the revenue generated by the books and pamphlets promoted in the back pages. It was yet another sign of a growing sophistication in the methods used by the government to suppress the anarchist movement, fighting the battle with the tools of information management rather than physical force. Rather than subduing the radicals with police nightsticks or hired guns, the state leaned instead on postal clerks, to great effect. As Tunney observed wryly in his memoirs, "The business of being an anarchist became surrounded with more and more difficulty as the year drew toward a close."

Another raid on the offices of *The Blast* and a string of convictions in the Market Street bombing trials convinced Berkman that it was time to give up on the West Coast and return to their long-term base in New York. "The political sky in the United States was darkening with heavy clouds, and the portents were daily growing more disquieting, yet the masses at large remained inert," Goldman wrote.

But then, in March of 1917, news from Russia changed the political weather overnight. "Unexpectedly, the light of hope broke in the east. It came from Russia, the land tsar-ridden for centuries. The day so long yearned for had arrived at last—the Revolution had come!"

For Berkman and Goldman, whose political identities had been forged by the Nihilists' failed attempts to overthrow the Romanov regime in the 1880s, the abdication of Czar Nicholas—grandson of Alexander II—and the formation of a provisional government in March of 1917 marked the realization of a dream that they had both been chasing for their entire adult lives. The news from overseas triggered a frantic effort among many of their comrades to make the pilgrimage to Mother Russia to participate in the world-historic events unfolding there. For a brief period of time that spring, a significant percentage of all civilians attempting transoceanic travel were card-carrying revolutionaries. Some members of the radical diaspora—including Louise Berger, whose apartment had been destroyed in the July 4 bombing—dared to sail through the treacherous Atlantic waters, still patrolled by German U-boats—traveling to Russia through Sweden on the Scandinavian-American Line. Others crossed the American continent via train to San Francisco or Vancouver, then took a steamship across the Pacific to Japan, crossing the Sea of Okhotsk to Siberia—and then riding east to Moscow on the Trans-Siberian Railway that Peter Kropotkin's youthful expeditions had made possible. Kropotkin himself packed up fifty crates of books from his Bromley cottage and, with his wife, decamped for Petrograd, via Sweden and Finland. On arrival, he was offered the position of minister of education in the provisional government. Ever distrustful of state authority, he declined the offer.

With the situation growing more challenging by the day in the United States, Goldman and Berkman debated a return to their homeland. As Goldman recalled in her memoirs:

Our own old yearning, Sasha's and mine, began to stir again in our hearts. All through the years we had been close to the pulse of Russia, close to her spirit and her superhuman struggle for liberation. But our lives were rooted in our adopted land. We had learned to love her physical grandeur and her beauty and to admire the men and women who were fighting for freedom, the Americans of the best caliber. I felt myself one of them, an American in the truest sense, spiritually rather than by the grace of a mere scrap of paper. For twenty-eight years I had lived, dreamed, and worked for that America.

Events in Washington ultimately convinced Berkman and Goldman to stay put in their adopted land. On April 2, President Wilson asked Congress for a declaration of war against Germany, citing the continued submarine warfare in the North Atlantic and the Kaiser's attempt to forge an alliance with Mexico against the United States. "Then came Wilson's decision that the United States must join the European slaughter to make the world safe for democracy," Goldman wrote. "Russia had great need of her revolutionary exiles, but Sasha and I now felt that America needed us more. We decided to remain."

With the United States now committed to the fight in Europe, Goldman and Berkman hardened their opposition, forming the No Conscription League on May 9, and issuing a manifesto declaring their opposition to the draft:

Every country in Europe has recognized the right of conscientious objectors—of men who refuse to engage in war on the ground that they are opposed to taking life. Yet this democratic country makes no such provision for those who will not commit murder at the behest of the war profiteers. Thus the "land of the free and the home of the brave" is ready to coerce free men into the military yoke. We oppose conscription because we are internationalists, anti-militarists, and opposed to all wars waged by capitalistic governments.

We will fight for what we choose to fight for; we will never fight simply because we are ordered to fight. We believe that the militarization of America is an evil that far outweighs, in its anti-social and anti-libertarian effects, any good that may come from America's participation in the war. We will resist conscription by every means in our power, and we will sustain those who, for similar reasons, refuse to be conscripted.

More than one hundred thousand copies of the manifesto were printed, and chapters of the No Conscription League quickly sprouted around the country. Perhaps sensing that their days as free citizens were numbered, Goldman and Berkman abandoned the rhetorical discretion they had adopted after the San Francisco bombing. At a mass rally at the Harlem River Casino, in front of a crowd swarming with detectives and federal marshals, Goldman thundered from the podium:

We believe in violence and we will use violence. . . . How many people are going to refuse to conscript? I say there are enough. I could count fifty thousand, and there will be more. . . . They will not register! What are you going to do if there are 500,000? It will not be such an easy job, and it will compel the government to sit up and take notice, and therefore we are going to support, with all the money and publicity at our hands, all the men who will refuse to register and who will refuse to fight . . . If there is any man in this hall that despairs, let him look across at Russia . . . and see the wonderful thing that revolution has done.

They were bold words for Goldman to utter in a public forum, knowing the intensity of the spotlight on her (and on Berkman) at that moment, gazing out at the conspicuous law enforcement presence at the event. While Goldman later claimed that she had been deliberately misquoted in her call to violence, there was no ambiguity about their stance advocating draft refusal. That was an increasingly dangerous position to take in public. Between the two of them, Goldman and Berkman would live for a combined forty-three additional years. But these were the final days they would spend on American soil with some semblance of personal liberty.

On June 14, Congress passed the Espionage Act, perhaps the most sweeping implementation of state-mandated patriotism ever produced by the United States government. The act expanded the postmaster general's authority to impound any potentially seditious material and made it a crime to circulate "false reports or false state-

Goldman and Berkman, 1917

ments" that "promote the success" of the United States's enemies. For Berkman and Goldman and other members of the No Conscription League, the most pertinent sections of the act made it a crime punishable by up to twenty years in prison to "wilfully cause or attempt to cause insubordination, disloyalty, mutiny, refusal of duty, in the military or naval forces of the United States, or . . . wilfully obstruct the recruiting or enlistment service of the United States, to the injury of the service or of the United States."

Over the subsequent decades, the Espionage Act (and the Sedition Act, passed the following year) would be invoked to prosecute everyone from Eugene Debs to Charles and Ethel Rosenberg to Pentagon Papers whistleblower Daniel Ellsberg—all the way to Julian Assange, Edward Snowden, and Chelsea Manning in recent years. But the very first people to feel the force of the new law were Alexander Berkman and Emma Goldman. Within hours of the Espionage Act's passage, a group of law enforcement agents, led by U.S. marshal Thomas McCarthy and Lieutenant Barnitz from the Bomb Squad, arrived at the *Mother Earth* offices on 125th Street.

Goldman answered the door. After verifying her identity, McCarthy announced that he had a warrant for her arrest. "I am not surprised," she replied calmly, "yet I want to know what the warrant is based on." McCarthy handed her an essay on the No Conscription League from *Mother Earth*, asking if she was the author. She affirmed that she was, adding that she "stood for everything in *Mother Earth*," the *Times* reported, "because she was the sole owner of the publication."

When Barnitz inquired whether Berkman was on the premises as well, Goldman turned toward the stairs, and cheerfully announced: "Sasha, Fitzi—some visitors are here to arrest us."

The trial lasted less than two weeks. On the final day, July 9, the entire Bomb Squad gathered in the downtown courtroom—both to observe the proceedings and to ensure there were no additional detonations. Supplemented with additional deputy marshals, the squad formed a cordon around the judge and jury box as the prosecution and the defense made their final statements. It was a fitting arrangement: the two anarchists seated together at the defense table, staring down the division of the NYPD that had been formed three years before to subdue the threat they posed to the city. Berkman delivered a solemn address to the jury that carried on for more than two hours. "We are being tried for being lovers of liberty," he announced. "Are you going to suppress free speech and liberty in this country and still pretend that you love liberty so much that you will fight for it five thousand miles away?" Goldman resorted to her usual satirical style: "The methods employed by Marshal McCarthy and his hosts of heroic warriors were sensational enough to satisfy the famous circus men, Barnum & Bailey," she told the jury. "A dozen or more heroes dashing up two flights of stairs . . . only to discover the two dangerous disturbers and trouble-makers, Alexander Berkman and Emma Goldman, in their separate offices, quietly at work at their desks, wielding not a sword, nor a gun or a bomb, but merely their pens!"

In the end, the jury deliberated for all of thirty-nine minutes before returning a unanimous verdict: Berkman and Goldman were both guilty of violating the Espionage Act. The judge handed down a sentence of two years' imprisonment and a $10,000 fine, noting that under the new laws noncitizens convicted of two crimes could now be deported to their home country. Sitting behind Goldman and Berkman in the first row, Fitzi clutched at her handkerchief as the verdict was read out. ("I can't understand it at all," Fitzi had told the press after the initial arrest, "for they are fine and beautiful characters, and are hundreds of years ahead of their time.") Fitzi and a few other members of the *Mother Earth* scene huddled for a few minutes with Berkman and Goldman as the courtroom emptied. "Through it all Emma sat dry eyed, even proud of the part she was taking," the *Sun* reported, "and far more calm than the younger admirers who were crowding around her."

Shortly after the trial's end, Goldman and Berkman were informed that they were to be transported separately to penitentiaries in Missouri and Georgia that night. But as the arrangements for the transport were being made, U.S. Marshal McCarthy allowed the prisoners to mingle with supporters and the press for a few minutes in an anteroom in the Federal Building. Berkman had seemed anxious throughout most of the day's proceedings, but as the marshals finally escorted them to a patrol car at ten o'clock that night, he took a jaunty tone in his last words to the reporters: "We're going straight to Russia," he quipped with a tip of his cap, "via Atlanta and Jefferson City."

Ten days after the trial ended, a blindfolded Secretary of War Newton D. Baker pulled a number from a bowl, representing the first group of more than 1.3 million men selected for service in the inaugural draft lottery conducted that day. Six days after that, a twenty-two-year-old J. Edgar Hoover—a recent graduate of George Washington University School of Law—began work at the Department of Justice. It was an entry-level position, with an annual salary that paid only $150 more than Hoover had earned as a librarian, but it gave an ambitious young patriot a unique opportunity to defend the nation's interests against the radical element that had caused so much trouble over the preceding years.

And there was this other perk that happened to come with the job: a draft exemption.

CHAPTER 25

The Radical Division

A little more than five months after Berkman and Goldman held their anti-conscription rally at the Harlem River Casino, three thousand New Yorkers traveled up the East Side of Manhattan to the same venue to hear another legendary orator of the age: the old lion Teddy Roosevelt, now fifty-eight and at the very end of his career in public life. The occasion was a rally in support of Mayor Mitchel, who was locked in a fiendishly complex four-way race for reelection involving the Tammany Hall candidate, Judge John Hylan; the antiwar Socialist candidate, Morris Hillquit; and a Republican named William Bennett. The mood at the casino was boisterous as Roosevelt began his address, with the crowd waving American flags and hissing at the mention of Mitchel's opponents.

"First, from the standpoint of the municipal administration, I have been acquainted with the life of New York City just as long as I can remember, and I state the exact truth when I say that not for half a century have we had any Mayor who has been as efficient and as upright in administering on the principles of straight-out democracy as this city government," Roosevelt told the crowd. Delineating the mayor's many accomplishments, Roosevelt began with the transformation of the institution he had once helmed. "I could tell you of the reduction in the number of murders, as showing the efficiency of the Police Department. I could tell you about the reduction of the death rate."

In his closing remarks, Roosevelt turned to the threat posed by Judge Hylan, and the real risk of the city regressing to the machine politics that Mitchel (and Arthur Woods) had done so much to eliminate. "You are voting for a symbol if you vote for Mr. Hylan," Roosevelt warned. "You are putting the city back into the grip of Tammany."

Ultimately, the electoral fragmentation of a four-way race did in fact deliver the city back to Tammany Hall. Mitchel and Hilquist split the progressive vote, and Judge Hylan won in a landslide. The election put Arthur Woods in a delicate position. He had spent three years transforming the NYPD into a world-class urban police force, increasingly working in concert with federal agencies. Many of the NYPD's most high-profile actions—like the arrest and prosecution of Berkman and Goldman—had relied on tight coordination between the Bomb Squad and the federal marshals. Under Faurot's leadership, the Identification Bureau had become the de facto hub of a national network of crime information.

Arthur Woods had been a man of promise for twenty years, but the NYPD he had created during the Mitchel administration was the first tangible realization of that potential. But what would become of his creation if it returned to Tammany?

In early December, just weeks before he resigned as commissioner during the transfer of power to the Hylan administration, Woods convened an all-hands meeting of the Bomb Squad in his Centre Street office. After praising them for their heroic work over the previous years, he informed the men that at the request of War Secretary Baker, the Bomb Squad was going to be transferred to a military intelligence unit inside the War Department. Tunney would be commissioned as a major, supported by Barnitz, who would be appointed a captain in the new arrangement. As Woods later explained to the *Times*, "For more than three years, Inspector Tunney and those working under his command had been working in closest cooperation with the Federal authorities, and the value of the work accomplished had many times been brought to the attention of the authorities." He didn't spell it out directly in his remarks, but the subtext was clear: Delivering the Bomb Squad to the War Department would also protect them from the corrupting influence of the incoming Tammany machine.

U.S. Marshal McCarthy—who had led the arrest of Berkman and Goldman—told the *Times*: "This is a splendid move, because I know of the very effective work done by the Police Department and by the Bomb Squad in particular, since the beginning of the European war. These men under Tunney are experts in handling the alien enemy problem."

Almost a decade earlier, in the final days of his first, troubled tenure at the NYPD, Woods had made the case for a national police force sophisticated enough to combat crime syndicates and terrorist networks, echoing the argument that his old mentor Teddy Roosevelt had made in the wake of the McKinley assassination. For the past three years, Woods had cultivated an elite group of detectives, trained in forensics and undercover surveillance techniques, within the confines of the NYPD. The arrangement Woods crafted with Secretary Baker in the waning days of 1917 marked the logical culmination of that long effort. The members of the Bomb Squad had come of age on the payroll of a municipal police force. But they were federal agents now.

Several weeks later, seventy-four new graduates from the NYPD's police academy, along with six hundred of their relatives, gathered in the drill room of the Centre Street headquarters to celebrate their admission to the ranks of police officers. The ceremony featured a display of the physical training that had become a priority under the Woods regime. According to the *Brooklyn Times*

Union, the audience was treated to exhibitions of "drill work with rifles and police clubs, calisthenics, the jiujitsu, and the methods of reviving a drowning man and handling the law-breakers of the city." The *Sun* brought along a visitor from Scotland Yard who had not been to the city for more than five years, who noted the dramatic change in the physique of the new recruits compared to his memory of the old-guard NYPD. "They're not so big in the girth," he told the *Sun* reporter. "In fact, I should say . . . they're very fit and trim."

But the excitement of the drill work and jiujitsu was overshadowed by a quiet, emotional moment near the end of the ceremony, when the officers presented Arthur Woods with an engraved plaque to commemorate his tenure at the helm of the NYPD. It featured illustrations of the Centre Street headquarters, as well as sketches of policemen on the beat. The testimonial read:

> Whereas for three and one-half years Arthur Woods, as Police Commissioner, has shown a deep interest in the welfare of the entire force; whereas, in work and deed he has been a humane, kind and impartial executive to all members of the force; therefore let it be resolved that the members of the entire force of the New York Police Department do hereby express their appreciation of the sterling qualities of Arthur Woods as a man and as Police Commissioner.

The plaque had been paid for by the rank and file of the NYPD, with all 10,790 men and women on the force contributing five cents each.

Visibly moved, Woods took the podium, looking, as the *Sun* noted, every bit as "fit and trim" as the new graduates. "I want you men always to remember that the very fact that you know your strength and power would make you dangerous to the public unless you know how to use that strength," he told them. "You must maintain the reputation that the Police Department is now the terror of the evil-doer. Unless you do your work as it should be done, the regular life of the city cannot go on." Rumors swirled for weeks that Woods would shortly be appointed as the director of a new federal police force, but as it turned out, his tenure as police commissioner would mark the last stretch of his professional life devoted to law enforcement. He briefly joined Wilson's propaganda arm, the Committee on Public Information, before transferring to the Aeronautical Division of the War Department. John Purroy Mitchel, meanwhile, signed up for the newly formed Air Service and died six months after leaving office, flung from his plane during a routine training flight in Louisiana.

Back at Centre Street, Faurot and Eagen continued their work at the city level. But the vanguard of the revolution that they had all helped bring about—the suppression of political violence and sedition through information science and methodical detective work—had moved one step up the ladder, both to the military intelligence units where Tunney and Barnitz and the rest of the Bomb Squad now found themselves working and to the Department of Justice, headed by Attorney General Mitchell Palmer.

Of all the information management operations launched by the federal government during the early days of World War I, the most sweeping involved the registering of German-born noncitizens, sometimes known as the Enemy Alien Registration drive, which began in February of 1918. Across the country, German nationals reported to registration sites where they were fingerprinted and photographed; each filled out a three-page form detailing their current residence, immigration history, military involvement, and any criminal records. The sheer scale of the operation was breathtaking.

Over two decades of work at the NYPD Identification Bureau, Joseph Faurot had managed to collect roughly 10,000 photographs and 150,000 sets of fingerprints. In just a few years, the Justice Department assembled records for 480,000 Germans.

Thanks to his training at the Library of Congress, J. Edgar Hoover was appointed to run the Alien Records operation in New York, in cooperation with the NYPD. It was the first significant break of his career in law enforcement. "He excelled at the work," Hoover's biographer Beverly Gage writes. "Throughout the spring and into the summer, his office maintained a relentless focus on registration: Forms and lists needed in triplicate, affidavits to be signed, 'indistinct' photographs to be retaken. Hoover seemed to have boundless energy for counting and recounting, then seeking out additional files."

As impressive as the Alien Enemy Registration effort was, for Hoover it was just the beginning. The real pièce de résistance of Hoover's career as a librarian turned crimefighter would not emerge in response to the war being fought across the Atlantic. It was infer-

Example of an Alien Record file, 1917

nal machines being detonated on the home front that would ultimately turn J. Edgar Hoover into a household name.

The first hint of the terror to come arrived in the form of a package,
neatly wrapped in brown glazed paper, stamped with the name and
address of the Gimbel Brothers department store in Manhattan,
delivered by mail to the offices of Seattle mayor Ole Hanson on the
morning of April 27, 1919.

The war had ended six months earlier with the final armistice
signed by Germany, but Hanson was in Colorado promoting the
final Victory Loan campaign to raise money to support peacetime
rebuilding in Europe. And so the Gimbel's box was opened by an
assistant who, in a stroke of enormous good fortune, happened to be
holding the box upside down as he unwrapped it.

The bomb inside the box had been wired with a detonation device similar to the one Erich Muenter had deployed in the Capitol
bombing: rigged so that removing the top of the package would
shatter a small vial of sulfuric acid, which would then drip down
onto the dynamite caps and instigate the explosion. Opening the
box the wrong way up inadvertently foiled the plan, causing the acid
to spill out onto the floor and leaving the dynamite undetonated.

The press reported that the device "was of sufficient power to
blow out the entire side of the County-City Building." Some reports also noted that the wrapping had been stamped with the additional word *novelty*—a seemingly irrelevant detail at the time, but
one that would ultimately prove to be the difference between life
and death for some of the most powerful men in America and their
inner circles.

Twenty-four hours later, two thousand miles away in Atlanta, a
household employee of Georgia senator Thomas Hardwick—
identified by the *Times* only as "a colored woman servant," though

her name was Ethel Williams—would not be so lucky. It fell to her to unwrap the package that had arrived from the New York department store, the one stamped *novelty*. Only, she opened the box right side up. Her hands were mangled so brutally in the blast that they both had to be amputated.

Like the Seattle mayor the day before, the official recipient of the package was unharmed in the explosion—Hardwick was at his office when the Gimbel's box arrived—but his wife suffered severe burns and cuts to the face. Her name might not have been on the parcel paper, but it was there implicitly, as was Ethel Williams's. Whoever had sent those bombs had printed out a home address on the package. By definition, the entire household was the target.

Early in the morning of April 30, a postal clerk named Charles Caplan, riding the IRT up to East Harlem after a late shift at work, noticed a newspaper headline about an averted mail bombing in Seattle. It wasn't often that the postal service made the front page in such tumultuous times, and so the story caught his eye. A few paragraphs into the piece, the description of the Gimbel's wrapping sent a shiver of fearful recognition down his spine. Just a few days earlier, he had seen a package matching that exact description at work.

In fact, he had seen sixteen of them.

It was the word *novelty* that had originally drawn Charles Caplan's attention. Earlier in the week, while sifting through packages in the parcel post sorting room in the general post office across the street from Penn Station, Caplan had come across the sixteen packages— all wrapped in identical fashion, and posted the same day. They had been mailed at parcel post rates, with twelve cents' worth of stamps on each package. But at the time, the lower parcel post rate applied only to certain kinds of merchandise—soaps, medicines, canned foods, and other items—as long as the nature of the merchandise was clearly marked on the outside of the package. Caplan was not certain whether novelty items were legitimate merchandise under the parcel post regulations, and so he had put the sixteen boxes aside, awaiting further interpretation from his superior.

It was well past midnight when Caplan read the newspaper account of the Seattle bomb. He jumped off the train at the next stop and switched to the downtown platform, then hurtled back down to West Thirtieth Street. Back at the post office, he located the night superintendent, and together the two men made their way to the parcel post storage room and cautiously examined the exterior of the sixteen packages, confirming that they were all exact duplicates of the Seattle bomb. The postal inspector for New York was telephoned; he in turn notified the NYPD; in a matter of hours, Owen Eagan was on the scene. With the help of inspector John Dickson, Eagen removed one package to a nearby firehouse, and settled in to do the work of disassembly. It took six hours in total to render the bomb harmless. Dickson and Eagan told the press that they had "never examined a bomb of more skillful construction or deadlier possibilities."

Telegrams were sent to law enforcement agencies and post offices across the country. Within days, thirty-six separate packages were intercepted before they could be delivered to their intended targets. Just as shocking as the scale of the operation, though, was the list of addresses ultimately released by the authorities. The bombs had been mailed to Attorney General Palmer, Oliver Wendell Holmes, Mayor Hylan, J. P. Morgan, John D. Rockefeller, among multiple other lawmakers and tycoons. Notably, two of the district attorneys who had led the case against the San Francisco bombers were targeted as well, along with a Bureau of Investigation field agent who had pursued an Italian anarchist group known as the Galleanisti, a spin-off of the original Bresci Circle group. The full list of targets left little doubt that anarchists had been behind the campaign. For once, Alexander

Berkman was not a suspect, given that he was still locked behind bars in the Atlanta Federal Penitentiary.

Faurot and Eagan set up a dedicated room in the basement of police headquarters, not far from where the 1915 bomb had detonated, to analyze four of the devices recovered from the post office. The bomb mechanism was photographed, and Faurot's direct reports from the Identification Bureau scrutinized the disassembled parts for fingerprints. While they failed to find clear evidence pointing to the culprits behind the bombing campaign, the swift action taken after Charles Caplan's late-night epiphany on the subway meant that, in the end, only one of the thirty-six bombs actually exploded. Given the power and influence of the men on the target list, the course of American history could well have been altered had the bombers chosen to affix just a few extra pennies' worth of stamps to their parcels.

But the thirty-six Gimbel's boxes were only the first wave.

A few minutes before midnight on the night of June 2, Mitchell Palmer prepared for bed in his elegant four-story townhouse just off Dupont Circle in Washington's affluent West End neighborhood. Two blocks away, Palmer's next-door neighbors, the thirty-seven-year-old Assistant Secretary of the Navy Franklin Delano Roosevelt and his wife, Eleanor, strolled under the looming oaks, returning home from a late dinner. It was a warm late-spring night in the capital city; Palmer had the windows open and could hear the quiet bustle of traffic on R Street below him. It was background noise, really, almost soothing. But then Palmer heard the sound of a motorcar coming to a stop at his gate, the engine idling as hurried footsteps raced toward his front door.

Down at street level, the midnight visitor's pace proved to be a little too hurried for his own good. Under the low light of the streetlamps, he tripped over an iron bar next to the steps and stumbled to the ground, just a few feet short of Palmer's front door. The package he was carrying slammed into the stone steps and set off the split-second chain reaction that Alfred Nobel had spent so many years perfecting in the previous century.

The blast destroyed the first-floor edifice of Palmer's home and punched a two-foot hole in the heavy stone steps where the bomb had been dropped. The sitting room at the front of the house, closest to the blast site, was mangled, paintings and books flung to the ground, debris everywhere. Windows were blown out up and down the block. Still two years away from the polio infection that would paralyze him, Roosevelt raced down R Street at the sound of the explosion. All the windows in the Roosevelts' house had been shattered. On his front stoop, among the plaster and shards of glass, he could make out the bloodied remains of a human collarbone.

When the other neighbors emerged, dazed, from their bedrooms to inspect the damage, they, too, found body parts scattered through their sumptuous parlors and entry halls. A Norwegian envoy two doors down from the Palmers discovered bone fragments strewn next to their infant child's cot. Over time, the police would recover an arm, two legs, a section of scalp, and other bone fragments, along with a fedora manufactured by a Philadelphia milliner, and an Italian-English dictionary. The head of the bomber was never located.

Astonishingly, the Palmer family, despite their close proximity to the blast site, were entirely unharmed in the explosion. After verifying that his neighbors were safe, Roosevelt called a reporter acquaintance at *The New York Times* from his living room, describing the "terrific wreckage" at the site of the house, and noting that "blackhand literature" had been strewn across the block. In this last statement, Roosevelt turned out to have conflated the mobster tactics of the Black Hand with the political violence of the anarchists. The literature turned out to be multiple copies of a single-page statement, black type printed on pink paper, fulminating against the capitalist order:

> The powers that be make no secret of their will to stop here in America the worldwide spread of revolution. The powers that be must reckon that they will have to accept the fight they have provoked . . . There will have to be bloodshed; we will not dodge; there will have to be murder; we will kill, because it is necessary; there will have to be destruction; we will destroy to rid the world of your tyrannical institutions . . . Never hope that your cops and hounds will ever succeed in ridding the country of the anarchistic germ that pulses in our veins. We know how we stand with you and know how to take care of ourselves. Besides, you will never get all of us—and we multiply nowadays.

It was signed, simply: THE ANARCHIST FIGHTERS.

By dawn, the shocking news had spread across the country: the infernal machine at Attorney General Palmer's home had been only one of nine explosives that had detonated that night. The anarchists had targeted a church, several judges, immigration officials, industrialists, a city mayor, and a state congressman. All the bombs exploded within minutes of the D.C. blast—in Boston, New York, Pittsburgh, Cleveland, Philadelphia, and at suburban residences in Massachusetts and New Jersey. In the history of terrorism on American soil, only the 9/11 attacks compare to the June 1919 bombing campaign in the scope and complexity of the operation. While the perpetrators were more successful in detonating their weapons than the Gimbel's mail attacks had been, only one innocent victim lost a life: a nightwatchman in New York City, guarding the home of Judge Charles Cooper Nott, the magistrate who had sentenced Carmine Carbone and Frank Abarno to prison after the St. Patrick's plot four years earlier.

As a nod to the national stature of Faurot's Identification Bureau, the evidence from the Palmer bombing was transported by train up to Centre Street. A string of clues—including initials etched into a tattered fragment of the dead suspect's shirt—ultimately led the authorities to declare that the D.C. bomber had

New York Times front page

been a radical named Carlo Valdinoci. The "blackhand literature" Roosevelt had first noticed scattered across R Street led the police months later to a New York typesetter named Andrea Salsedo who ended up falling out of a fourteenth-floor window at the Bureau of Investigation's Manhattan headquarters, after weeks of brutal interrogation. The death was, predictably, ruled a suicide. Both suspects were disciples of the charismatic anarchist Luigi Galleani, who had escaped from an island prison near Sicily, intially settling in Bresci's old haunt in Paterson, New Jersey, before moving to a stone carver's commune in Vermont.

If you followed the intricacies of radical alliances, it was clear that the Bresci-Galleani wing of the anarchist movement were more unapologetic practitioners of terrorism than the *Mother Earth* crowd. Goldman may well have called for violence at that final East Harlem rally, and Berkman had almost certainly had a hand in the July 4 plot. (And he had undeniably attempted to murder Frick almost three decades earlier.) But in the bombing campaigns of 1919, the Galleanists had attempted something far more ambitious: one of the most elaborately planned terrorist conspiracies in American history. To the general public, it was hard to tell the difference between the factions. Whatever fine line Goldman felt she could walk on the question of political violence was hopelessly blurred by the "anarchist fighters" and their assault on America's elite. Putting an end to the threat to public safety posed by the anarchists—whatever faction they happened to belong to—rose to the top of the national agenda.

Enraged both by the personal attack on his family and the sheer scale of the assault on the nation's most powerful men, Attorney General Palmer put the celebrity detective William Flynn—who, like Faurot, had serialized his crimefighting exploits in newspaper columns around the country—in charge of the Bureau of Investigation. Palmer also created a new unit dedicated exclusively to the revolutionary threat at home, just as Woods had done with the Bomb and Anarchist Squad back in 1914.

This one they called the Radical Division. And Palmer knew just the kid to run it.

When historians catalog the momentous inventions of history—the printing press, the telescope, the steam engine—they rarely include indexing algorithms in their canon of breakthrough ideas. But tools that help us explore ever larger pools of information—and widen the net we can cast in those pools—have often turned out to trigger inflection points in history. The invention of the modern footnote and indexing protocols that developed slowly over the sixteenth and seventeenth centuries made a meaningful contribution to the scientific revolution that emerged during that period. The genius of Alphonse Bertillon's system—arguably the single most important breakthrough in the long history of battling crime—was not just the measurement of physical traits but also the filing system that allowed you to find a match in minutes out of a pool of ten thousand potential suspects. Google was for a time the most valuable company on the planet, in large part because its founders hit upon an indexing algorithm called PageRank.

In just a few months, between August and December of 1919, twenty-four-year-old J. Edgar Hoover put in place a new information-management system that belongs in the pantheon with the Bertillon method and PageRank. He called it the Editorial File System.

There is something almost comically paradoxical about the EFS: It proved to be, over the decades, one of the most menacing expressions of state power in American history, paving the way for now-notorious undercover investigations into Martin Luther King, Jr., the Kennedys, John Lennon, and others. But the thing itself was made of index cards.

Hoover's primary mandate at the Radical Division had been to identify potential subversives—particularly resident aliens, though Hoover quickly strayed into tracking American citizens as well—and compile evidence against them that could be used in deportation hearings. But he soon discovered that the bureau was not up to speed in the latest advances in library sciences. "When the Radical Division was formed," he wrote later that year, "the files of the Bureau of Investigation were found to be in such shape as to be of practically little or no use in the preparation of cases for deportation." Collating information on just a single suspect could take hours, but more complex inquiries—like identifying all the individuals who had attended a particular rally or published in a radical journal like *Mother Earth*—was prohibitively time-consuming. Reorganizing all that information, making it *searchable*, was the sort of problem only a librarian could love.

The crucial innovations that Hoover introduced effectively made the Editorial File System into what we would now call a relational database. When a field report arrived at the Radical Division's headquarters, it would be passed along to one of a team of more than thirty clerks, each of them trained in the sort of file management tasks that Hoover had excelled at as a teenager at the Library of Congress. Each report was classified along seven axes: the names of the subjects under surveillance, the city and state, the organizations involved, the ideological worldview of the subjects, and any events or publications associated with the report. Hoover borrowed Putnam's thematic taxonomy from the library, transforming it into a numeric classificatory system for identifying the type of crime being investigated. Crucially, all the information was cross-referenced on the index cards. If a request came for information about an anarchist group operating out of Springfield, Massachusetts, you could assemble all the relevant field reports in a matter of minutes—at least an order of magnitude faster than an equivalent search in the bureau's shambolic pre-Hoover days.

Once again, the primary unit of measure of law enforcement's prowess became the size of the organization's file cabinets. But unlike Faurot's Identification Bureau, which was heavily weighted toward New York crimes, the Editorial File System was a genuinely national database. In just two months, the Radical Division collected fifty thousand index cards documenting radical activity across the country. Hoover had weaponized library science in the service of subduing the revolutionary threat. And as the field reports began piling up on his desk in the late summer of 1919, he became increas-

ingly obsessed with the idea of using that new power to send Emma
Goldman and Alexander Berkman back to Russia.

"Say this to all our friends, no one need worry about me," Goldman
wrote to a friend, several months into her time at the Missouri State
Penitentiary. "I am quite alright. I have my one Great Love—my
Ideal to sustain me, nothing else matters. There are inconveniences
of course, but what do they amount to compared with the great
events of our time? In moments of depression I look to Russia. She
acts like a ray of sunshine working its way through the black clouds."

The penitentiary was situated on a bluff overlooking the Missouri River; Goldman's quarters were in a newly constructed wom-
en's department: a seven-by-eight-foot cell with a toilet, running
cold water, a steel bunk with a straw mattress and pillow. The work
routine at the prison returned Goldman to her early life as a seamstress doing piecework on the Lower East Side; she found herself
once again spending long, tedious hours operating a cheap sewing
machine, this time assembling jackets in a narrow shop room with
the other female inmates. Unlike Berkman, who had been subjected
to long periods of solitary confinement in Atlanta as a punishment
for protesting prison conditions there, Goldman was allowed some
limited contact with the outside world: She could receive letters and
packages, and the occasional visitor, and was permitted to send
three letters a week. In one of those letters, composed shortly after
her arrival, she described her daily prison routine:

> Awakened at 5 A.M., rather difficult to get used to, but one can do
> so much under pressure. Breakfast 6:15, in Shop 6:30. I rather like
> my work. Poor people and not parasites will wear what I make.
> Also I am not contributing to the war. Lunch 11:30. ½ hour rest in
> cell. Shop again until 4:30. Nine hours in all. So many workers still

striking for nine hours. You see the advantage. Supper until 6 P.M. Then recreation in yard, which is the one worth while thing everybody is looking forward to. Friday after work cell cleaning and bathing. Sunday the arrangement differs. It includes later breakfast and church. Don't be shocked. I shall attend it, today anyway. Want the experience, besides my soul needs salvation, don't you think?

Back in Washington, Hoover began paying regular visits to the commissioner general of immigration, Anthony Caminetti, strolling across the broad avenues of downtown D.C. from the Radical Division's headquarters at Justice to Caminetti's office in the Labor Department. Caminetti was at the end of a long career in politics and was more than forty years Hoover's senior, but the two men had a shared interest in Emma Goldman. Two years earlier, after the Espionage Act arrest, Caminetti had gone as far as preparing papers ordering her deportation, but the request had been shot down by a superior on the grounds that Goldman was likely a United States citizen based on her brief marriage in Rochester three decades earlier. But Hoover had been assembling a formidable dossier on Goldman that made what he considered a compelling case supporting two key facts: that she posed a clear and present threat to the nation's well-being, and that she had never made any attempt to declare herself a U.S. citizen. Hoover had also discovered as part of his research that Goldman was set to be released from prison in late September, with Berkman scheduled for release shortly thereafter. "Emma Goldman and Alexander Berkman are, beyond doubt, two of the most dangerous anarchists in this country and if permitted to return to the community will result in undue harm," Hoover wrote in a memo. Deporting the two anarchists would also provide an early, high-profile victory for his fledgling Radical Division.

With Caminetti's help, Hoover had a deportation warrant delivered to Goldman in prison in early September. A hearing was set for

Berkman at the Atlanta penitentiary, though he refused to participate in it. ("Thought is, or should be, free," he told the authorities.
"The proposed hearing is an invasion of my conscience.") On Saturday, September 28, Goldman was released from prison. She was
transported to New York and brought to the Federal Building in
Lower Manhattan, where she secured a $15,000 bond for her re-
lease on the deportation order. There was still the matter of the
$10,000 fine for the original crimes under the Espionage Act. For
that, she had to sign an affidavit testifying that she possessed insuf-
ficient financial assets to pay the fine. The agent gave her a suspicious look. "You're dressed so swell," he said, "funny you claim to be
poor."

"I am a multimillionaire in friends," she replied.

Those friends were indeed thrilled to see Goldman at large once
again—along with a haggard Berkman, who was released in early
October. Knowing that their days in the United States were probably numbered, Goldman traveled to Chicago to visit with comrades, then to Rochester to see her family, before returning to New
York, where they had spent so much of their adult life out of prison.
There, the grim realization sank in: Their financial and legal status
was perilous. "We had nothing left, neither literature, money, not
even a home," Goldman wrote. "The war tornado had swept the
field clean and we had to begin everything anew."

On an unseasonably warm morning in late October, Goldman
and her lawyer Harry Weinberger took the ferry to Ellis Island to
attend the first session of her deportation hearings. When they arrived in an examination room, just a few steps from the Great Hall,
still flooded with new immigrants, they found J. Edgar Hoover
waiting for them, seated alongside the main examiner, Inspector
A. P. Schell. Goldman was immediately struck by the volume of

documentation stacked in front of her "inquisitors." "The documents, classified, tabulated, and numbered, were passed on to me for inspection," she wrote in her memoirs.

> They consisted of anarchist publications in different languages, most of them long out of print, and of reports of speeches I had delivered a decade previously. No objection had been made to them at the time by the police or the Federal authorities. Now they were being offered as proof of my criminal past and as justification for banishing me from the country.

The material that Hoover had managed to assemble in just a few months was indeed staggering in its scope and attention to detail. His files went back as far as Goldman's Rochester days, including legal documents suggesting that while there was no evidence that she had formally divorced her husband, he was not a naturalized citizen, and thus the marriage did not confer citizenship on her. It cataloged almost every public statement or appearance that Goldman had made that had the slightest connection to political violence. Hoover quoted McKinley's assassin Leon Czolgosz claiming that Goldman had "set his mind on fire"; he noted that Goldman had refused to renounce the young anarchist, even after his conviction and execution. Hoover documented many instances where Goldman had referred to other killers—like Gaetano Bresci—as "martyrs to the cause." He provided a close reading of all the incendiary remarks in the issue of *Mother Earth* that followed the Lexington Avenue explosion—an inclusion that must have infuriated Goldman, given that Berkman had edited that issue without her approval. The files also included stenographic notes from the Harlem River Casino speech that had landed Goldman and Berkman behind bars for encouraging draft resistance. The entire case was supplemented with twenty-five separate exhibits, composed of more than a hundred typewritten pages of curated quotations drawn from pamphlets and old issues of *Mother Earth* and *The Blast*.

Almost two decades earlier, after her arrest in connection with the assassination of President McKinley, the state's case against her had dissolved, in large part because the federal government lacked an investigative body capable of amassing the evidence required for such a prosecution. But times had changed. The great enemy of consolidated state power now found herself confronting the Editorial File System.

Goldman refused to answer questions, choosing instead to make an opening statement that Weinberger then released to the press. She accused the United States government of resorting to the same desperate practice of banishing dissidents that had sent her old mentor Peter Kropotkin into exile during the czarist regime:

> I wish to register my protest against these star chamber proceedings, whose very spirit is nothing less than a revival of the ancient days of the Spanish Inquisition, or, more recently, the defunct third degree of Czarist Russia . . . Today so-called aliens are deported. Tomorrow native Americans will be banished . . . The free expression of the hopes and aspirations of a people is the greatest and only safety in a sane society. The object of deportations and of the anti-anarchist law is to stifle the voice of the people, to muzzle every aspiration of labor. That is the real and terrible menace of the star chamber proceedings and of the tendency of existing and banishing everyone who does not fit in the scheme of things our industrial lords are so eager to perpetuate.

As the legal wrangling continued through November, Goldman and Berkman embarked on one last speaking tour, tailed at every stop by operatives from the Radical Division. In early December, while they were enjoying a boisterous dinner with friends in Chicago, a reporter passed along the report that had just come down the wire: Financier Henry Clay Frick had died of a heart attack at his Fifth Avenue mansion at the age of sixty-nine. Berkman took in the news with a wry smile and then proclaimed: "Deported by God!"

Weinberger continued to fight the deportation order in court. But Hoover's prodigious skills as an archivist had convinced Goldman that staying in the United States was increasingly unlikely. And the deportation of Berkman, who had a long history of even more incendiary words, not to mention an attempted murder conviction, was practically a fait accompli. It didn't help matters that Hoover and Palmer had orchestrated the first of the notorious "Palmer Raids" in early November, sweeping up more than a thousand radicals—many of them friends and comrades of Berkman and Goldman—and threatening them with deportation as well.

A few days after Frick's death, the Supreme Court ruled that Berkman was to be deported immediately but allowed Goldman several weeks to put her affairs in order, leaving open the possibility of further delays. Goldman, though, knew her loyalty lay with Berkman. "I decided that if Sasha was to be driven out of the country, I would go with him," she wrote. "He had come into my life with my spiritual awakening, he had grown into my very being, and his long Golgotha would forever remain our common bond. He had been my comrade, friend, and co-worker through a period of thirty years; it was unthinkable that he should join the Revolution and I remain behind." She turned herself into the authorities on Ellis Island, where she was, as she later wrote, "photographed, fingerprinted, and tabulated like convicted criminals."

The following day, Berkman and Goldman crossed paths during one of the recreation periods the detainees were allowed. Berkman was shocked to see her. "You are staying to make the fight, aren't you?" he asked, incredulous. She was too valuable to the cause, he warned, to leave the country of her own volition.

Goldman smiled and thought to herself: *The same old Sasha, always thinking of the Great Ideal first.* Grasping his hand in the bitter chill of the courtyard, she shook her head. "It's no use, old scout," she said. "You can't get rid of me so easily. I have made my decision and I am going with you."

CHAPTER 26

Ellis Island

The SS *Mississippi* took its maiden voyage in the late summer of 1890, sailing from London to Baltimore to commence service as a cargo ship owned and operated by the Atlantic Transport Line. Over the decades, the ship performed in many capacities. Purchased by the army in 1898, the vessel was rechristened the *Buford*, its cargo bays converted into berths to transport soldiers. For years it ran a regular service between California and Japan, and it happened to be in the San Francisco harbor during the 1906 earthquake. (By some strange twist of fate, it also showed up in the Galveston, Texas, harbor for a major hurricane in 1915.) But of all the voyages that the *Buford* made over the course of its forty-year career, the most famous would be the journey it began in the closing days of 1919, transporting 249 so-called undesirables—including Emma Goldman and Alexander Berkman—to Finland, where they would then be transported by train to the Russian border.

Technically, the ship made the voyage as the USAT *Buford*, but the press gave it a new name: The *Red Ark*.

The undesirables were awakened only a few hours after midnight on December 21, 1919, and ushered into a commissary on Ellis Island, where they were served a breakfast of sausage, cabbage, and cold coffee as the immigration officials delivered the news: They were leaving the United States in a matter of hours. As the detainees processed the information, they held an impromptu vote and elected Berkman the leader of their expedition. Dressed for the occasion in leather boots, khakis, and a sombrero that invoked the Mexican Revolution, Berkman led the undesirables in a rousing version of "The Internationale."

A few minutes later, the detainees were returned to their quarters to gather their belongings and then brought back to the south wing of the Immigration Center. They squatted on the floor in the glaring electric light, surrounded by their tin trunks, overcoats, the extra boxes of fruit they had packed on the assumption—correct, as it turned out—that the rations on their voyage would be unsatisfactory. A few strummed old Russian folk songs on banjo and guitar. "I expect to go to Petrograd and carry out my ideas," Berkman told a reporter as he wrapped a paper bag of oranges with twine. "I intend to co-operate with Lenin and Trotsky."

Goldman was dozing when the reporter encountered her but quickly snapped into her habitual posture of defiance. "I do not consider it a punishment to be sent to Soviet Russia," she proclaimed. "On the contrary, I consider it an honor to be the first political agitator deported from the United States."

At 3:30 A.M., as a chilling wind whipped across the harbor, Berkman, Goldman, and their 247 fellow travelers were marched from the detention center toward a gangplank lined with armed security forces, where they boarded a ferry that would take them to the *Buford*, currently anchored two miles away at a South Brooklyn pier. As she trudged across the frozen ground, Goldman's mind turned back to the Russia of her childhood: "I felt dizzy, visioning a transport of politicals doomed to Siberia, the *étape* of former Russian days. Russia of the past rose before me and I saw the revolutionary martyrs being driven into exile. But no, it was New York, it was America, the land of liberty!"

Across the harbor at the Battery, a delegation of politicians had gathered to give the *Buford* and its passengers a proper farewell. Surrounded by a gaggle of reporters and congressmen, J. Edgar Hoover gazed out at the harbor with a nervous intensity—"a slender bundle of high charged electric wire," as one onlooker recalled. When the undesirables embarked on their ferry ride across the harbor, Hoover and a few of the others boarded their own vessel to inspect the transfer to the *Buford,* scheduled to take place at a rendezvous point in the Narrows, near Fort Wadsworth on Staten Island.

When Berkman and Goldman boarded the *Buford,* they found the ship teeming with armed soldiers—a special force of 250 marines culled from the military base on Governors Island dedicated to preventing any mutinous activity on board the *Red Ark* during its passage to Finland. As the detainees were escorted to their berths, Hoover feverishly explored the old cargo ship to confirm that the security protocols were correct and up to standards. And then, just a few minutes before the *Buford* was set to raise anchor, Hoover found himself face-to-face with his nemesis, Emma Goldman, the first victim of the Editorial File System that would claim so many others in the coming decades.

"Haven't I given you a square deal, Miss Goldman?" Hoover inquired.

"Oh, I suppose you have given me as square a deal as you could," she sneered. "We shouldn't expect from any person something beyond his capacity."

The delegation was whisked back to their ferry, and the *Red Ark* raised anchor for the long voyage east. The *Times* described its passage out through the Narrows and into the open ocean with unusual lyricism:

Under the guns of Fort Wadsworth, the leaden-colored transport Buford loomed vaguely in the beginning of yesterday's dawn, her port holes blinking out one by one as light came on. Shortly after 6 o'clock, splashing and rasping in the silence of the empty bay, the anchors came up to the bow, the Buford's prow swung lazily eastward, a patch of foam slipped from under the stern and 249 persons who didn't like America left it.

Through their portholes below deck, Berkman and Goldman took in the full sweep of the harbor, the skyline of Lower Manhattan softly illuminated by the early hint of dawn. "The tall skyscrapers, their outlines dimmed, looked like fairy castles lit by winking stars," he wrote, "and then all was swallowed in the distance."

It was the last time Alexander Berkman would ever see New York.

Aftershock

Early in the evening of March 2, 1920, sixty-three-year-old Inspector Owen Eagan was called from his Midtown apartment to examine a suspicious package that had been discovered in Times Square. He threw on his uniform, gathered the tools of his most unusual trade, and headed out into the night. Walking along Lexington Avenue, in the hulking shadows of Grand Central Palace—where Alexander Berkman had triumphantly returned from the Western Penitentiary fourteen years earlier—Eagan's steps became increasingly erratic. Clutching his stomach, he collapsed onto the sidewalk. Onlookers carried him into a nearby drugstore and called for an ambulance, but the efforts to revive him failed. The official cause of death was listed as acute indigestion.

Against significant odds, the man who had managed to dissect seven thousand bombs over the course of his career had died on the job—as he himself had long predicted—of natural causes.

The *Times* ran a one-column item describing Eagan's death, calling him a "bomb wizard" and "anarchist foe" in the headline. The story also noted that Eagan—despite his founding role on the Bomb and Anarchist Squad and his long collaboration with Faurot—had never officially left the fire department: "Contrary to the general impression, Eagan was not an inspector in the Police Department at high salary. He was a member of the Fire Department, and doing work that called him to risk his life almost daily for twenty-five years he received pay of $1,500 a year." The story did note that Eagan had increasingly collaborated with federal authorities in the last years of his life. Of the work itself, the *Times* observed, "He seemed to be the only man who wanted it, and he enjoyed it."

A few months after Eagan's death, Joseph Faurot was promoted a final time, to deputy commissioner. But the increased responsibility did not deter him from continuing his role as in-house innovator. He introduced the first police radio system in 1922 and oversaw a program to fingerprint newborn babies to ensure that they were not accidentally swapped in the maternity ward. He remained an inveterate tinkerer well into his sixties. A full seven years after retiring from the force in 1926, Faurot introduced a new "inkless" fingerprinting technique—anticipating the electronic fingerprint ID systems that would become ubiquitous in the early twenty-first century—at a conference in New York.

After the war, Arthur Hale Woods moved to Washington, D.C., with his wife, Helen Morgan Hamilton Woods. Some of his early progressive idealism—the quest for "social betterment" that had so impressed his peers at the Harvard Club—continued on in his post-NYPD career. He oversaw a program to reintegrate veterans into society in the early 1920s, and chaired committees on unemployment during the Depression. Over time, Woods found himself increasingly playing the role of trusted advisor to some of the most powerful figures of the age, most notably John D. Rockefeller, Jr. Woods oversaw the creation of Colonial Williamsburg, a pet project of the Rockefellers, and served as chairman of the board of Rockefeller Center—constructed in the 1930s across the street from St. Patrick's, the site of his most dramatic operation as police commissioner.

After leaving the force, Woods largely stopped writing or speaking in public about police reform. But he did agree to write an introduction to his old colleague Thomas Tunney's memoir of the Bomb

Squad years. After a few paragraphs praising the "radically effective" work that Tunney and his team had performed under his watch, Woods turned to the broader implications of that tumultuous period:

> The lessons to America are clear as day. We must not again be caught napping with no adequate national Intelligence organization. The several Federal bureaus should be welded into one, and that one should be eternally and comprehensively vigilant. We must be wary of strange doctrine, steady in judgment, instinctively repelling those who seek to poison public opinion. And our laws should be amended so that while they give free scope to Americans for untrammeled expression of differences of opinion and theory and belief, they forbid and prevent the enemy plotter and propagandist.

Arthur Hale Woods died in 1942, within a few months of his old partner Joseph Faurot. Woods had only spent seven years of his career on the payroll of the NYPD. But in its obituary, the *Times* observed that Woods was "largely responsible for the scientific and sociological attitude toward police work today."

In many respects, Woods's long advocacy for a federal investigative force and his track record modernizing the NYPD would have made him the more logical candidate to take the helm of the Bureau of Investigation as it matured into the immense organization that we know today as the FBI. He was far more experienced and well connected than young J. Edgar Hoover, after all. But Hoover capitalized on his dramatic success deporting Goldman and Berkman. Just five years after the *Red Ark* steamed out through the Narrows, Calvin Coolidge appointed Hoover director of the Bureau, a position he would continue to hold until his death in 1972.

Not everyone embraced the technologies of identification that Woods and Faurot had spent so many years championing. "The Faurot idea of the millennium will not appeal to the unenlightened," one essayist wrote, shortly after Faurot's promotion in 1920. "We are more and more to the time when every one of us will have a number, wear a tag, be vaccinated, inoculated and sterilized daily, and keep a diary for the inspection of the public morals commission, and ask a written permit whenever we want to smoke a cigar or burn a little gasoline." Still, the vision that had captivated Faurot from his early days on the force—a national "central clearing house for the fingerprints of malefactors, thereby facilitating the work of different cities," as he had described it after the Crispi trial—did in fact come to pass, at a scale that would have astonished him. (And perhaps even impressed J. Edgar Hoover.) Today, the FBI's Next Generation Identification database contains more than seventy million fingerprints of convicted criminals, arrestees, and immigration violators. And, of course, billions of humans around the planet have stored biometric information—including facial recognition data, the descendants of Berthillon's portrait parlé—with private technology companies.

In the middle of the nineteenth century, the anarchist Pierre-Joseph Proudhon had famously declared, "To be *governed* is to be at every operation, at every transaction noted, registered, counted, taxed, stamped, measured, numbered, assessed, licensed, authorized, admonished, prevented, forbidden, reformed, corrected, punished." However we may assess the costs and benefits of such an arrangement, all of us today—criminals or not—live inside a system of electronic surveillance far more elaborate than anything Proudhon imagined.

After an arduous transatlantic journey on the *Red Ark,* Emma Goldman and Alexander Berkman finally set foot on Russian soil—for the first time in more than thirty years—on January 19, 1920. They were greeted on arrival by an enthusiastic band of soldiers and peasants at a remote village on the border with Finland. Berkman later called it "the most sublime day of my life." But over the ensuing months, the sobering reality of the Soviet regime began to sink in. Having been expelled from their adopted homeland thanks to Hoover's Editorial File System, Berkman and Goldman were appalled to discover the relentless demand for identification papers that characterized the new Russia. "One could not even get in or out of our hotel without a permit, not to speak of visiting any Soviet institution or important official," Goldman later recalled. "Almost everyone carried portfolios stocked with *propusks* and *oodostoverenyas* (identification papers). Zorin had told me that they constituted a necessary precaution against counter-revolutionary plotters, but the longer I stayed in Russia, the less I saw their value. Paper was at a high premium, yet reams upon reams of it were used for 'permits,' and much time was wasted in securing them."

Over time, they learned of more ominous developments. Lenin's henchmen had shut down anarchist collectives across the country, and imprisoned anarchist leaders, accusing them of sabotaging the revolutionary effort. Rumors swirled that some of them had been executed. In Moscow, Berkman and Goldman secured an audience with Lenin himself. Goldman described their journey into the Soviet inner sanctum almost as a scene out of Kafka's *The Castle*:

> An armed guard was at the elevator, evidently already apprised of our coming. Without a word, he unlocked the door and motioned us within, then locked it and put the key into his pocket. We heard our names shouted to the soldier on the first floor, the call repeated in the same loud voice at the next and the next. A chorus was announcing our coming as the elevator slowly ascended. At the top a guard repeated the process of unlocking and locking the elevator, then ushered us into a vast reception hall with the announcement: "Tovarishtchy Goldman and Berkman." We were

asked to wait a moment, but almost an hour passed before the ceremony of leading us to the seat of the highest was resumed. A young man motioned us to follow him. We passed through a number of offices teeming with activity, the click of typewriters, and busy couriers. We were halted before a massive door ornamented with beautifully carved work. Excusing himself for just a minute, our attendant disappeared behind it. Presently the heavy door opened from within, and our guide invited us to step in, himself vanishing and closing the door behind us.

Eventually they found themselves face-to-face with the Bolshevik leader, who immediately began grilling them for intelligence about the American political situation: How powerful were labor groups like the I.W.W.? Did Berkman and Goldman think revolution was possible in the United States? He complimented both of them on statements they had released during their deportation cases, calling them a "clear-cut analysis of the capitalist system" and "splendid propaganda." But the two anarchists were unswayed by Lenin's charm offensive. They broached the recent arrests and the suppression of the Russian anarchist community.

We had fought in America for the political rights even of our opponents, we told him; the denial of them to our own comrades was therefore no trifle to us. I, for one, felt, I informed him, that I could not co-operate with a regime that persecuted anarchists or others for the sake of mere opinion. Moreover, there were even more appalling evils. How were we to reconcile them with the high goal he was aiming at? I mentioned some of them. His reply was that my attitude was bourgeois sentimentality . . . Russia was making giant strides at home and abroad. It was igniting the world revolution, and here I was lamenting over a little bloodletting. It was absurd, and I must get over it.

It took Berkman and Goldman less than two years to give up on the Soviet experiment. "I found reality in Russia grotesque, totally unlike the great ideal that had borne me upon the crest of high hope to the land of promise," she would write in dispatches filed for Joseph Pulitzer's New York *World* and later published in her book *My Disillusionment in Russia,* one of the first renunciations of Lenin's regime to come from the radical left. "I saw before me the Bolshevik State, formidable, crushing every constructive revolutionary effort, suppressing, debasing, and disintegrating everything." They left in late 1921, disillusioned with the Soviet experiment but still committed, as always, to the Great Ideal. The two would go on to spend the rest of their lives in European exile, though Goldman was allowed back to the United States for a brief speaking tour in the 1930s, returning her to Manhattan one final time. Berkman lived until 1936, ultimately committing suicide after a long illness; Goldman survived long enough to be thrilled by the flare of anarchist hope that was Barcelona in 1936, and then suffer through its extinguishing at the hands of the fascists. She died in 1940. According to her wishes, she was buried in a cemetery on the outskirts of Chicago, near the memorial to the Haymarket anarchists who had so inspired her as a teenager in Rochester.

Her tombstone reads: "Liberty will not descend to a people, a people must raise themselves to liberty."

In one of Émile Henry's final statements before his execution in 1894—the head that Alphonse Bertillon had measured with such exactitude severed by the steel blade of the guillotine—the young anarchist had made a striking prediction:

> You will add other names to the bloody lists of our dead. You have
> hanged us in Chicago, decapitated us in Germany, garroted us in

Xerez, shot us in Barcelona, guillotined us in Montbrison and in Paris, but what you can never destroy is anarchy. Its roots are too deep; born in a poisonous society which is falling apart, it is a violent reaction against the established order. It represents the egalitarian and libertarian aspirations which are opening a breach in contemporary authority. It is everywhere, which makes anarchy elusive. It will finish by killing you.

Henry's prediction echoed the lines Andrei Zhelyabov had uttered in his prison cell in Saint Petersburg: "If you kill us, there will be others. Many people are being born these days." Goldman and Berkman had adopted a similar position in a public letter they wrote to their comrades, days before their deportation. "Our enemies are fighting a losing battle," they wrote. "They are of the dying past. We are of the glowing future." But looking back more than a century later, we know that all three prophecies turned out to be false. In the United States, anarchism made a few isolated appearances in the national conversation in the decade that followed Berkman and Goldman's exile. In 1920, a horse-drawn carriage loaded with a hundred pounds of dynamite exploded on Wall Street, killing forty people. The perpetrators were never identified, but they were believed to be members of the Galleanist anarchist group behind the 1919 bombing campaign. The sense of anarchism as a looming threat to the establishment had its final hurrah with the arrest, trial, and execution of the anarchists Sacco and Vanzetti several years later; after that, it was the threat of Soviet-style communism that dominated Hoover's Editorial File System at the FBI. As a politico-economic philosophy, anarchism would surface at other inflection points: in the intentional communities of the 1960s, the leaderless protest movements of the early twentieth century (most famously, Occupy Wall Street), and the rise of open source technology platforms. Some of the most provocative minds of the modern age would call themselves anarchists: Noam Chomsky, James Scott, David Graeber, among many others. Anarchist values underlie the celebrated work of Jane Jacobs and Howard Zinn. But as a sustained force in American political life, anarchism effectively disappeared when the *Red Ark* steamed out through the Narrows at the end of 1919.

The passage of the USAT *Buford* was, as the Hegelians used to say, a world-historical departure. The loss of anarchism as a viable radical vision meant that after 1920, the primary social structures put forward as possible ways of organizing society were all deeply hierarchical and dependent on vast command-and-control systems to operate them. The structure that Kropotkin had argued for—the voluntary associations of mutual aid that he had first glimpsed on the Siberian frontier—was no longer a part of the conversation. The ideological battle of the twentieth century ended up being fought between three worldviews that all relied on top-down authority: state capitalism, state communism, fascism. In part because markets themselves have elements of decentralized order that command economies do not, much of the planet ultimately embraced the least centralized of the bunch. But a large-scale society truly organized around the lateral entanglements of mutual aid? The world never got to run that experiment.

How would the twentieth century have played out if Kropotkin had been adopted instead of Marx as the founding father of revolutionary leftism? If the radical vision had not been central planning and the Gulag, but rather a return to the hill towns and watchmaking collectives of the free cities, only this time with clean drinking water and electricity? That is, by definition, a purely speculative question; the most you can say is that a century dominated by a clash between capitalism and anarchism would have been dramatically different from the one we actually lived through, and that for a time, that alternative twentieth century was a viable possibility.

It can be argued that anarchism was doomed to failure because the guild model would never have been able to scale sufficiently to provide the kinds of consumer goods and scientific advancements that have driven most quality-of-life improvements over the past century. You could make artisanal watches in the Kropotkin system, but could you, for example, produce enough antibiotics in a mutual-aid world to keep up with the health advances of state capitalism?

Certainly, the pace of technological progress would have been slower in a mutual-aid society. The capitalist economies would have enjoyed radio and television and the Internet before the guilds managed to produce those technologies. But it's hard to imagine that such progress would simply stop in its tracks. Perhaps there was a way for humans to advance up the ladder to radio and television and the Internet but over centuries, not decades, without giving up the egalitarian way of life. Or perhaps we would have invented different but equally compelling technologies. A world teeming with immense corporations and factories and military-industrial complexes is a world optimized to accelerate technological change above everything else. If anarchism had been evangelized as a form of social organization designed to slow down the pace of change—and not merely as an excuse to blow things up—it might have found a more enduring constituency, and at least allowed us to test the mutual-aid hypothesis at scale. But that experiment was shut down, in part by the strategic mistakes of the anarchist movement itself, but also by Interpol, and the Identification Bureau, and the Editorial File System. The infernal machines of the anarchists were transformed into a different, more Orwellian machine, less terrifying in its displays of power, but also more pervasive.

What *did* survive from the anarchist movement, though, were the bombs. The guild system did not prosper as a blueprint for social organization in the twentieth century. But terrorism did. There were different political philosophies—and religions—behind the attentats that followed in the wake of the anarchist movement, but the overall numbers are undeniable: a monstrous upward slope in terrorist violence that, for Americans at least, culminated in the 9/11 attacks. In 2014, the deadliest year in the history of global terrorism, almost fifty thousand people died in attacks around the world. And while that death toll is a small fraction of total human mortality, the psychological and political impact of all that violence carries a heavy weight. "A girdle of dynamite encircles the world," Johann Most had announced after the death of Alexander II. Today the means of destruction are more varied—passenger planes, car bombs, AK-47s—but the general tactics of terrorism remain anarchism's most enduring legacy.

Could that legacy have been avoided? If Goldman and Kropotkin had fully renounced violence as a political tactic—if they had adopted the model of peaceful resistance that Mahatma Gandhi was so successfully developing in India during the same period—could they have managed to separate out anarchism from terrorism? Or was the propensity for violence a flaw that had been so deeply forged back in the original furnace of czarist Russia that it was impossible to extricate? For Berkman, Sofia Perovskaya's plot to take the life of Alexander II clearly left too formative an impression for him to ever forswear the propaganda of the deed. Well into his late fifties, he continued to make the case for the attentat in letters to Goldman. "That acts of violence accomplish nothing, I do not agree at all," he wrote. "The terrorism of the Russian revolutionists aroused the whole world to the despotism of the Czars." But Goldman walked a more delicate—and often contradictory—line: declaring that violence did nothing to advance the cause, and yet refusing to publicly renounce Berkman's attack on Frick or Czolgosz's assassination of McKinley. "Acts of violence," she wrote in a private letter to Berkman, ". . . have proven utterly useless. From that point of view Czolgosz's act was as futile as yours. Neither left the slightest

effect." Had Goldman taken that stance more decisively in the public sphere and persuaded more of her comrades to exchange their
infernal machines for nonviolent protest, a world where anarchism
retained its original meaning—the self-organizing mutual aid of
the free cities, and not the carnage of suicide bombers—might have
remained a possible future.

In March of 1920, two months after they had crossed the border
from Finland, Berkman and Goldman took the slow train north of
Moscow to a small village called Dmitrov. Accompanied by a British journalist, they marched through the snowbanks and the savage
cold to a ramshackle cottage in town. A knock on the front door
revealed the beaming face of their old comrade and mentor, Peter
Kropotkin.

Peter Kropotkin, circa 1900

Goldman had not seen Kropotkin
since a European tour thirteen years
before. Thanks to his stay in the Western Penitentiary and the Anarchist
Exclusion Act, Berkman somehow had
never met him face-to-face before. "He
looks remarkably like his photographs,
with his kindly eyes, sweet smile, and
generous beard," Berkman later recalled. "Every time Kropotkin entered
the room it seemed to light up by his
presence. The stamp of the idealist is so
strikingly upon him, the spirituality of
his personality can almost be sensed."

Berkman and Goldman were shocked to find the three
Kropotkins—Peter, his wife Sophie, and their daughter Alexandra—
living on the edge of starvation. Most of the house had been aban-

doned to the freeze; the Kropotkins had confined themselves to a single room to economize on heating. But despite the spartan conditions, Kropotkin—now in his late seventies—still maintained his workbench in the corner of the living space, along with a typewriter that he used to peck out the manuscript for a new book on ethics that he was struggling to finish.

After moving to Dmitrov in 1919, the family had joined a small peasant cooperative society in town that had originally supplied their rations. (Returning to his roots, Kropotkin had served as the chief geologist for the group, organizing a collection of rocks and minerals the community had accumulated.) But the Bolsheviks had shut down the cooperative as part of the anarchist purge and arrested many of its members. Now the Kropotkins were surviving purely on milk from a cow they kept in the backyard, and produce from their garden that they had stockpiled for winter. Sophie Kropotkin explained that her husband had refused any support from the regime, as a matter of principle.

Goldman found Kropotkin "ill and worn-looking, a mere shadow of the sturdy man I had known," but still "gentle and gallant," and eager to talk political philosophy with his comrades. He was resigned to the bleak reality of post-revolutionary Russia. All anarchists, he said, had "foreseen the dangers of Marxism and its theories." Concentrating power in a revolutionary state would inevitably lead to the abuse of that power and a new kind of oppression that shackled the human spirit as effectively as the czarist regime had. Goldman later described the conversation in her memoirs:

> "Is there no one to speak out against it?" I demanded, "no one whose voice would carry weight? Yours, for instance, dear comrade?" Peter smiled sadly. I would know better, he said, after I had been awhile longer in the country. The gag was the most complete in the world.

Berkman returned to visit Kropotkin several months later, and the long days of summer seemed to have improved the aging philosopher's spirits. "The conditions were terrible, as everyone agreed, and the Dictatorship the greatest crime of the Bolsheviki," Berkman recalled Kropotkin saying. "But there was no reason to lose faith, he assured me. The Revolution and the masses were greater than any political Party and its machinations."

In writing that would be published posthumously, Kropotkin drew once again on the language of natural phenomena to explain the forces that had been unleashed in the chaotic years after 1917:

> The revolution we have gone through is the sum total, not of the efforts of separate individuals, but a natural phenomenon, independent of the human will, a natural phenomenon similar to a typhoon such as rises suddenly on the coasts of Eastern Asia. Thousands of causes, in which the work of separate individuals and even of parties has been only a grain of sand, one of the minute local whirlwinds, have contributed to form the great natural phenomenon, the great catastrophe which shall either renew, or destroy; or perhaps both destroy and renew.

Almost a year later, in February of 1921, Goldman and Berkman—now living in Petrograd—received word that Kropotkin was near death. They both immediately caught a train to Moscow, traveling through a "raging storm" to make it to the bedside of their mentor in Dmitrov. But they arrived one hour too late. "I had known Peter for over a quarter of a century," Goldman wrote, "but only his death disclosed his cherished secret that he had also been an artist of unusual quality. I found, hidden away in a box, a number of drawings Peter had made in his all too few leisure moments. Their exquisite line and form proved that he might have achieved as much with his brush as he had with his pen had he cared to devote himself to it."

Despite the purge of anarchist "counterrevolutionaries" that he himself had instigated, Lenin offered to stage a formal state funeral for Kropotkin, but the offer was refused. ("Peter had never sought or accepted favours from any government nor tolerated pomp and display," Goldman wrote.) Instead, Kropotkin's friends petitioned Lenin to temporarily release the anarchists currently imprisoned in Moscow so that they could pay tribute to the man who had long been anarchism's most persuasive advocate. The bureaucracy responded with a declaration that there were no anarchists in Moscow prisons, a statement straight out of Orwell's *1984*.

A grainy silent film capturing the days leading up to the memorial has somehow survived. It depicts the swarm of mourners descending on Dmitrov, flowing through the wintry village streets carrying Kropotkin's coffin to the train station, like the flocks of birds and deer that had so mesmerized Kropotkin on the Siberian steppes as a young man. The film shows Kropotkin's body lying in state in the Hall of Commons in Moscow's trade union headquarters. Berkman can be briefly seen in a dark shirt and tie, while Goldman stands in a black dress next to the coffin. Banners are draped around the hall, most of them inscribed in Cyrillic with political slogans: "There is no poison more villainous than power over people." One banner conveys in English a message from the passengers of the *Red Ark*: "The American deported anarchists share their grief with the American revolutionary proletariat over the death of our great teacher, Peter Kropotkin." Seven anarchist prisoners—released at the last minute by the Kremlin—arrive to warm embraces from their comrades. The film then cuts to the funeral cortège, a mass of black overcoats and ushankas marching past the elegant white marble buildings of Moscow. At the gravesite, onlookers perch in trees, while a sequence of dignitaries from the many factions of the radical left deliver eulogies to the great teacher: representatives from the left-socialist revolutionaries, the Russian

communist party, the social-democratic Mensheviks, the communist international, the Ukrainian anarchist federation—and Emma
Goldman, speaking on behalf of the American anarchists. The
mourners lower Kropotkin's coffin into the grave and there the film
ends.

As if to underscore the triumph of the centralized state, Kropotkin lies buried in Moscow's Novodevichy Cemetery, just a few miles
from the Kremlin, the ultimate emblem of the oppressive authority
he had fought against his entire career. The demonstration that accompanied his burial—all those anarchists and exiles and undesirables streaming through the Moscow streets—also marked the end
of an era. There would not be another legal public demonstration in
Moscow that wasn't celebrating the beneficence and supreme power
of the Communist Party for more than sixty years.

NOTES

All dialogue quoted in the book comes directly from first-person accounts, either captured in newspaper reports or in memoirs and letters written by the participants.

Chapter 1

3   "Few objects": Darwin, 53.

5   "report like a pistol shot": Fant, 32.

7   Headlines around the globe: Ibid., 84–85.

8   "My new explosive": Quoted in Fant, 94.

Chapter 2

10   As a child: Miller, 1976, 17.

11   "Well, go": Kropotkin, 2010, 118.

11   "so struck me": Kropotkin, 2010, 149.

11   "For three months": Ibid.

12   "the first scientific attempt": Davis, 2016, 23.

13   "Real competition and struggle": Kropotkin, 2021, 34.

14   "I lost in Siberia": Kropotkin, 2010, 150–51.

Chapter 3

15   Darwin received an unusual letter: Quoted in Beavan, 74.

16   criminals for life: Rhodes, 13.

19   Even after the official: "There were 86 murders in the city in the year 1857, according to the Board of Aldermen. Another study, published by the National Science Foundation in 2015, showed that New York City murders in that same year totaled 98. A third study, by police historian Eric Monkkonen, showed about 110 murders in 1860. Those numbers, given the population differences between the 1850s and the contemporary era, translate to a contemporary number of murders of about 1,400, or nearly five times today's actual New York City homicide rate (328 murders in 2014)." Chadwick, loc. 1223.

22   "[The detective] must": Quoted in O'Hara, loc. 677.

Chapter 4

25 **"Dynamite was cheap":** Gage, loc. 760.

27 **"did not die in vain":** Radzinskiĭ, 390.

Chapter 5

28 **"Conditions at the palace":** Quoted in https://spartacus-educational.com /RUSpw.htm.

29 **"terrible power of the powerless":** Radzinskiĭ, 309.

29 **"fourth car of the second train":** Ibid., 322.

30 **With democratic revolutions:** As Kropotkin wrote his memoirs: "Yielding for a moment to the current of public opinion around him, he induced men all over Russia to set to work, to issue from the domain of mere hopes and dreams, and to touch with the finger the reforms that were required. He made them realize what could be done immediately, and how easy it was to do it; he induced them to sacrifice whatever of their ideals could not be immediately realized, and to demand only what was practically possible at the time. And when they had framed their ideas, and had shaped them into laws which merely required his signature to become realities, then he refused that signature." Kropotkin, 2010, 128–29.

31 **"It seemed as if":** Radzinskiĭ, 251.

31 **A new mythology:** Merriman, 62–63.

32 **front-page news in New York:** "to outsiders, the talk of bombing and assassination that suddenly pulsed through revolutionary circles in the late 1870s sounded like little more than an indiscriminate call to violence. . . . [But] within the anarchist movement the idea of propaganda by deed . . . had a very specific logic. Among anarchism's founding premises was the idea that capitalist society was a place of constant violence: Every law, every church, every paycheck was based on force. In such a world, to do nothing, to stand idly by while millions suffered, was itself to commit an act of violence." Gage, 2009, 44.

34 **"Among the mounds":** "The Peril of the Czar," *The New York Times*, March 4, 1880.

36 **"That's the best place":** Radzinskiĭ, 390.

37 **"If you kill us":** Ibid., 405.

37 **"three important arrests":** Ibid.

40 **injured in the blast:** There is some dispute in the historical record over this exchange. Some accounts contend that the initial bomber asks about the czar's state.

40 **"Alexander II must die":** Yarmolinsky, 276.

41 **"Doctors prepared to":** "Russia's Dead Monarch," *The New York Times*, March 15, 1881.

41 **"Nihilist Conspirators":** "Nihilist Conspirators at Last Successful," *The New York Times*, March 14, 1881.

Chapter 6

42 **"some profound and radical difference":** Quoted in Yarmolinsky, 286.

42 **"A disdainful smile":** Ibid.

43 **"Believe me, dearest Mummy":** Quoted in ibid., 288.

44   "The voice of dynamite": Quoted in Gage, 2009, 47.

46   "mysterious compassion": Goldman, 2006, 27.

46   "everything . . . was being torn from its old moorings": Quoted in Avrich and Avrich, loc. 157.

Chapter 7

48   "Here, then, is the record": Hard, 5.

49   The younger McCormick's reforms: Gilpin, 50.

50   "Since the death": Quoted in O'Hara, loc. 1560.

51   "a private army": Quoted in ibid., 75.

52   "It seemed lava": Goldman, 2006, 10.

54   "The economic change": Kropotkin, 2002, 248.

55   "I did not know a single soul": Quoted in Avrich and Avrich, loc. 393.

56   "the full manhood conferred": Berkman, 2009, 236.

Chapter 8

57   "After receiving many directions": Goldman, 2006, 4.

59   When Emma Goldman first strolled: Burrows and Wallace, 1117.

60   "There is scarcely anything": Riis, 118.

60   "I had a roof": Goldman, 2006, 5.

61   "She is one of us": Quoted in Avrich and Avrich, 46.

62   "My first impression": Goldman, 2006, 6.

63   Fedya took her to Central Park: Goldman, 2006, 24.

64   "There is great need in our ranks": Goldman, 2006, 25.

64   "less cultivated, more natural": Quoted in Avrich and Avrich, loc. 618.

66   "From the very first": Goldman, 2006, loc. 1642.

66   "your freedom to love": Ibid., 1866.

Chapter 9

72   "The philanthropic Andrew Carnegie": Goldman, 2006, loc. 2024.

72   "Far away from": Ibid., loc. 2055.

72   "in the movement of these men": Avrich and Avrich, loc. 1052.

73   "Three times during the morning": "Mob Law at Homestead." *The New York Times*, July 7, 1892.

73   "I do not recognize": Quoted in Serrin, 92.

74   "After five months": Avrich and Avrich, loc. 1140.

75   "Frick is the responsible"; "A blow aimed at Frick": Goldman, 2006, loc. 2078.

75   "[Dynamite] can be carried": Quoted in Merriman, loc. 1319.

76   "All means are justified": Berkman, 2011, 7.

77   "My sailor girl, comrade": Goldman, 2006, loc. 2137.

77   "Dear Arthur, I appreciate": Quoted in Drinnon and Drinnon, xx.

78   Sensing her unease: All passages from this exchange quoted in Goldman, 2006, loc. 2014–55.

81   "There is a flash": Berkman, 2009, 12.

82   "Confused voices ring": All quotes describing Berkman's experience of the attack on Frick drawn from Berkman, 2011, 33–36.

82   "This incident will not": Quoted in Avrich and Avrich, loc. 1373.

83   "Frick is an enemy": Quoted in ibid., loc. 1378.

83   "the desperate wretch": Quoted in ibid., 71.

83   "Henry Clay Frick": "A Foul Attempt to Assassinate Chairman Frick," *The Pittsburg Dispatch,* July 24, 1892.

84   "men capable of": Quoted in Avrich and Avrich, loc. 1741.

84   "The bullet from Berkman's": Bemis, 386.

85   "There was a time": Quoted in O'Hara, loc. 1990.

Chapter 10

87   "A glance at your face": Berkman, 2011, 150–51.

87   "like a drowning man": Ibid.

88   "The night was black": Goldman, 2006, 81.

Chapter 11

92   Bertillon's innovation can be thought: Rhodes, 93.

94   "One arm had been": Quoted in https://www.theguardian.com/science/the-h-word/2016/aug/05/secret-agent-greenwich-observatory-bombing-of-1894.

95   "My dynamite will sooner": Tagil, https://www.nobelprize.org/alfred-nobel/alfred-nobels-thoughts-about-war-and-peace.

95   "The Merchant of Death": Fant, 207.

96   Almost the entirety of Nobel's fortune: Ibid., 265.

98   By the time he left the force: Lardner and Repetto, 83.

99   "the only city job": "Eagen, Bomb Wizard Dies Going to Duty," *The New York Times,* March 3, 1920.

Chapter 12

100 "If you are hungry": Quoted in Burrows and Wallace, 1187.

101 "You have read of her": All quotes from the Bly profile from "Nellie Bly Again—She Interviews Emma Goldman and Other Anarchists," *The World,* September 17, 1893.

102 "The theater was crowded": "Howls for Emma Goldman; Thalia Theatre Filled with Enthusiastic Anarchists," *The New York Times,* August 20, 1894.

103 "Here I am again": Ibid.

103 "It was not Emma Goldman": Ibid.

104 "He pointed with great pride": Goldman, 2006, 111.

105 "All right, dear comrade": Ibid., 112.

107 "The movement spread": Kropotkin, 2021, 137.

107 "Whole populations are periodically": Ibid., 197.

108 "Europe is up to this date": Ibid., 193.

110 **"Seven men lost a leg"**: Eastman, 1910, 12.

111 **"Because of your power"**: Quoted in Avrich and Avrich, 118.

112 **"They bound my body"**: Berkman, 2011, 409.

Chapter 13

115 **"In a few minutes"**: "How the Deed Was Done," *The New York Times*, September 7, 1901.

116 **"I am an anarchist"**: Quoted in Scott Miller, loc. 5156.

116 **"It is fortunate"**: Goldman, vol. 1, 2006, 179.

116 **"A wrinkled ugly Russian woman"**: Quoted in Avrich and Avrich, 159.

117 **"The attention of the comrades"**: Ibid., 213.

118 **"plainly my duty"**: Goldman, 2006, 180.

118 **Arriving in the city**: Ibid., 182.

120 **"shrewdest crook I ever met"**: Ibid.

120 **"The police are fools"**: "Emma Goldman in Court," *New-York Tribune*, December 12, 1901.

120 **"Strong hopes entertained"**: "A Favorable Turn," *The Washington Times*, September 9, 1901.

121 **"There was no one else"**: Quoted in Scott Miller, loc. 5540.

122 **The anarchist community**: Quoted in Avrich and Avrich, 215.

122 **"In Russia, where"**: Berkman, 2011, 415.

122 **"soul in pain"**: Quoted in Wexler, 108.

123 **"I killed the president"**: "Assassin Czolgosz Is Executed at Auburn," *The New York Times*, October 30, 1901.

124 **"It was the unanimous agreement"**: Ibid.

124 **"When we turn"**: https://www.presidency.ucsb.edu/documents/first-annual-message-16.

126 **"Anarchy is a crime"**: Ibid.

127 **"spying on men"**: Quoted in Weiner, 11.

Chapter 14

128 **"Detective Sergeant Joseph A. Faurot"**: "Brings Report on Investigation," *New-York Tribune*, February 5, 1906.

129 **"His suave, pleasing"**: Martyn, 261.

130 **"The London police"**: "Finger Prints Effective," *The Morning Astorian*, February 6, 1906.

131 **"foreigners, not American citizens"**: Martyn, 262.

132 **"Fresh ink was spread"**: "Latest Developments of Thumb Prints in Detecting Crime," *The New York Times*, February 2, 1907.

133 **"Mother Earth will endeavor"**: Goldman, 1906, 1.

133 **"There is one thing"**: "Assailant of H. C. Frick Set Free," *New-York Daily Tribune*, May 19, 1906.

134 **"I am afraid to cross the street"**: Berkman, 2011, 485.

134 **"His face deathly white"**: Goldman, vol. 1, 2006, 233.

134 The *Times* reported: "2,000 Greet Berkman," *The New York Times,* June 18, 1906.

136 "You dog, spy, informer": Quoted in https://www.boweryboyshistory.com /2015/02/the-big-history-of-little-italy-2.html.

136 "predatory criminals" of all nations: Quoted in Jones, 159.

138 "hundreds of people": "Black Hand Bomb Explodes." *The Sun,* November 6, 1906.

139 "twenty-five absolutely honest men": "New Committee Forming to Improve Police," *The New York Times,* November 23, 1906.

139 "The detective force": "Laws to Improve the Police," *The Sun,* November 23, 1906.

140 "sympathetic and congenial": "Woods to Bring Police Department into the Uplift," *The New York Times,* April 12, 1914.

140 "You will see him": Ibid.

142 "There is no doubt": https://www.theodorerooseveltcenter.org/Research /Digital-Library/Record?libID=o42416.

142 "My Dear Mr. Woods": https://www.theodorerooseveltcenter.org/Research /Digital-Library/Record?libID=o186163.

Chapter 15

144 "While Sasha pored over": Avrich and Avrich, 280.

145 "Having been starved": Goldman, vol. 1, 2006, 235.

145 "His eyes were brown": Ibid., 249.

146 "For fourteen years he had": Goldman, 2006, 247.

148 "The Italians who keep": "Petrosini, Detective and Sociologist," *The New York Times,* December 30, 1906.

150 "You can't regenerate": Berkman, 1908, 69.

151 "It is a secret": "New Secret Service to Fight Black Hand," *The New York Times,* February 20, 1909.

152 "We do not want": Quoted in Moses, 28.

153 "friends in Sicily": "Petrosino Slain Assassins Gone," *The New York Times,* March 14, 1909.

153 "Petrosino shot, instantly killed": Ibid.

154 "It is hoped": Ibid.

154 "I can't say anything": Ibid.

155 "The investigation should have": Reppetto, 2018, 45.

156 "One thing that annoys him": Woods, 1909, 38–43.

158 "While reporters interviewed": Jones, 162.

Chapter 16

161 "Situated upon the palm": All quotes from the Crispi trial based on trial transcripts here: https://dc.lib.jjay.cuny.edu/index.php/Detail/Object/Show /object_id/5116.

168 "Keeping Track of the Criminal": "Keeping Track of the Criminal by Their Fingerprints," *The New York Times,* July 30, 1911.

Chapter 17

170 **"The woman had unquestionably":** "Find Woman's Body in Bundle in River," *The New York Times,* September 7, 1913.

171 **When this new gruesome discovery:** Ibid.

174 **"As I went in":** New York Court of Appeals, 768.

175 **"Considering that the pieces":** "How Murderer of Anna Aumuller was Traced," *The Tacoma Times,* September 19, 1913.

175 **"I hadn't any right":** Ibid.

176 **"I was mystified":** Ibid.

177 **"I killed her because I loved her":** Quoted in Gado, 74.

177 **"At first the case looked hopeless":** "How New York's Real Detective Solves Criminal Mysteries by Scientific Methods," *The Sun,* September 21, 1913.

178 **"A detective getting":** Ibid.

178 **"No old sleuth":** "A True Thrilling Detective Story in Real Life of Today." *The Day Book,* September 17, 1913.

178 **"A new era has dawned":** Joseph Faurot, "A New System of Identification Adopted to Run Down Criminals," 1913.

180 **Library of Congress's classification system:** "Until Putnam's arrival," the historian Beverly Gage writes, "there had been no reliable method of searching and sorting the library's collections. In that sense, his new classification system was nothing short of revolutionary, the Google of its day." Gage, 2023, 41.

181 **"The job . . . trained me":** Quoted in https://www.fbi.gov/news/stories/copy _of_the-hoover-legacy-40-years-after.

Chapter 18

185 **"of excellent quality":** Hayden, 4.

185 **The Colorado mines were:** McGovern and Guttridge, 66.

The Colorado mines themselves were notoriously unsafe, among the most dangerous in the nation, second only to Utah. In the years from 1884–1912, (28 years), 42,898 coal miners were killed in mine accidents in the U.S.; of these, 1,708 were killed in Colorado mines. Miners died in Colorado coal mines at over twice the national average (McGovern and Guttridge, 1972, 66; Whiteside 1991, 74–75), while handpicked coroner's juries absolved the coal companies of responsibility almost without exception. For example, in the years from 1904–1914, the juries picked by the sheriff of Huerfano County, Jeff Farr, found the coal operators to blame in only one case out of 95 (Whiteside, 1990, 22).

186 **"It is a national issue":** Quoted in Jones, 119–20.

187 **"In the great Homestead":** For a full account of the Homestead Riots, see Serrin, 77–85.

188 **"I was sick at heart":** Quoted in Avrich and Avrich, 222.

188 **entertaining doubts about:** As Thai Jones notes, "John Purroy Mitchel had been entertaining doubts. McKay had never matched the profile of a Mitchel

appointee. He made no claims to socio-scientific expertise, had not published any studies, or conducted sensational experiments." Jones, 123.

189   **"There has never been a Police Commissioner"**: "Woods to Bring Police Department into the Uplift," *The New York Times*, April 12, 1914.

189   **In the early afternoon of April 17**: "Identified as Michael P. Mahoney, Man with Many Grievances," *The New York Times*, April 18, 1914.

190   **"He was an old man"**: Ibid.

191   **"letter-writing cranks"**: Ibid.

192   **"one of the most bitter"**: Zinn, 254.

193   **"What are the American workingmen"**: Quoted in Jones, 167.

Chapter 19

195   **"CALL AGAIN IN FORCE"**: "I.W.W. Pickets Pen Rockefellers," *The New York Times*, May 4, 1914.

195   **Edelsohn's reputation for**: As Thai Jones puts it, "[Edelsohn's] sexuality exerted a fascination on outsiders who let their lascivious imaginings cloud their appreciation for her leadership abilities." Jones, 153.

195   **"a strong-faced girl"**: "Becky—her full name is Rebecca—is an anarchist. She was nurtured in the faith of Emma Goldman and Alexander Berkman . . . The blood of Russian revolutionists is in her veins, heated by the experiences of a life on the East and by the fire in her own heart." "Women in Two Kinds of Revolutions," *New-York Tribune*, May 10, 1914.

195   **"Did you ever hear"**: Quoted in Jones, 224.

197   **"The most astonishing situation"**: Ibid., 225.

197   **"You can bet"**: Ibid., 227.

Chapter 20

199   **"Like a broadside"**: "Exploded in Apartment Occupied by Tarry-town Disturbers," *The New York Times*, July 5, 1914.

203   **"Cutting up a bomb"**: Ibid.

203   **"most powerful construction"**: Ibid.

204   **During the interrogation**: All quotes from the Berkman interrogation from "Exploded in Apartment Occupied by Tarrytown Disturbers." *The New York Times*, July 5, 1914.

205   **"'Was Berkman involved?'"**: Avrich and Avrich, 310.

206   **"Word came from Sasha"**: Goldman, vol. 1, 304.

207   **"Comrades, idealists, manufacturing a bomb"**: Ibid., 305.

207   **"I understood the spiritual"**: Ibid.

208   **"It is one thing to sympathize"**: Quoted in Jones, 249.

208   **Outfoxed by Woods**: Ibid., 154.

208   **"In New York, we"**: Ibid., 155.

209   **"Fellow mourners, we are"; "First, it is possible"**: "5,000 at Memorial to Anarchist Dead," *The New York Times*, July 12, 1914.

210   **"Why is it that"**: Ibid.

211   **"I was dismayed"**: Goldman, vol. 1, 306.

Chapter 21

214 "to listen to those around him": Blum, 34.

214 "I managed to pick up": Tunney and Hollister, 8.

215 "their relative strength": Ibid., 10.

215 "Naturally they dared not": Quoted in Jones, 280.

216 "I was dazed": Goldman, vol. 1, 306.

216 "I consider that the duty": Quoted in Avrich and Avrich, 267.

217 "Our old comrade and teacher": Goldman, vol. 1, 309.

217 "The sky is drab": Berkman, "An Innocent Abroad," *Mother Earth*, vol. 10, no. 11.

217 "The climate is great": Quoted in Avrich and Avrich, 341.

219 "The explosion blew": "Slavers' Bombs Rock Bronx Court," *The New York Times*, November 12, 1914.

221 "Socialist organ published": "Lighted Bomb Put in Tombs Court," *The New York Times*, November 15, 1914.

221 "most unusual sort of bomb": Ibid.

222 "the Italian anarchists": Pernicone, 3.

222 a half-dozen distinct: Goyens et al., loc. 1375.

224 "He was short": Tunney and Hollister, 48.

224 "First and foremost": Ibid., 50–51.

225 "You're a strong fellow": All quotes from Polignani's undercover conversations and journal entries from Tunney and Hollister, 50–59.

230 "It was reasonable": Ibid., 58.

231 "We recommend most earnestly": Quoted in ibid., 59.

232 "I am free to confess": Ibid., 58.

Chapter 22

234 "Come up and get": Quoted in Tunney and Hollister, 61.

235 From the altar: "Trap Bomb Layer as He Lights Fuse in the Cathedral," *The New York Times*, March 3, 1915.

238 "He was arrested": Ibid.

239 "splendid piece of work": Ibid.

239 "The bombs were undoubtedly": Goldman, 1915, 74.

240 "Heaven only knows that": Goldman, "The Barnum and Bailey Staging of the 'Anarchist Plot'," *Mother Earth*, vol. 10, no. 2.

241 "They had no definite": "Berkman Reveals Anarchists' Plot," *The New York Times*, February 16, 1915.

242 "The two prisoners": Tunney and Hollister, 64.

242 In April, the *Tribune*: "Woods Ends Year as Police Head," *New-York Tribune*, April 8, 1915.

243 A full-length feature: "New York Boasts of Best Rogues' Gallery," *New Ulm Review*, July 21, 1915.

Chapter 23

246 "Kill me now": "Intruder Has Dynamite," *The New York Times*, July 5, 1915.

246 Rome in 1913: "Niece of J.P. Morgan to Wed New York Police Commissioner," *The Kingston Daily Freeman*, March 21, 1916.

247 "Europe needs enough": "Bomb Explosion at Capitol Perpetrated by Same Man Who Shot J. Pierpont Morgan," *The Sunday Star*, July 4, 1915.

247 "My motive in coming here": Ibid.

247 "It does look strange": Ibid.

249 "greatest equipment for bomb making": "Holt's Dynamite Found by Police," *The New York Times*, July 7, 1915.

250 "blown almost to powder": "Police Headquarters Shaken by Bomb on Red 'Martyr Day'; Holt Insane, Morgan Out Soon," *New-York Tribune*, July 6, 1915.

250 "Naturally, an explosion": Ibid.

251 "It appears to be": "Police Bomb Like One Holt Made." *The New York Times*, July 7, 1915.

251 "Inquiry by the police": Ibid.

252 "Although city police forces": Quoted in Blum, 58.

252 "Criminals have to": New York Legislature, 104.

252 Horror stories proliferated: https://socialwelfare.library.vcu.edu/programs/orphanage-widows-pension/.

254 "disclosure of specific": "Reassure the Public," *The Evening World*, May 27, 1916.

254 "If you permit": New York Legislature, 109–10.

255 "Shadowing a crook": Ibid.

255 "And let me give you": Ibid., 112.

256 hundred-odd guests: "Arthur Woods Weds Miss H. M. Hamilton," *The Brooklyn Daily Eagle*, June 11, 1916.

257 "faithful and meritorious service": Ibid.

Chapter 24

258 "despite the war": Quoted in Kinna and Adams, 42.

259 "We are determinedly": Quoted in Guérin, 35.

259 "The enemy is athirst for blood": "Planning Another 11th of November," *The Blast*, 1916.

260 "a muddy cowpath": "A Raid and a Visit," *The Blast*, 1916.

261 "Not only did the authorities": Avrich and Avrich, 363.

262 "The business of being an anarchist": Tunney and Hollister, 199.

262 "Unexpectedly, the light": Goldman, 2006, 333.

264 "Our own old yearning": Ibid., 336.

264 "Then came Wilson's": Ibid.

264 "Every country in Europe": Goldman, 1917, 112.

265 "We believe in violence": Quoted in Tunney and Hollister, 207.

267 "Sasha, Fitzi—some visitors": Goldman, 2006, 345.

268 "We are being tried": "Convict Berkman and Miss Goldman Both off to Prison," *The New York Times,* July 10, 1917.

268 "fine and beautiful": Quoted in Avrich and Avrich, 369.

268 "Emma sat dry eyed": "Convict Berkman and Miss Goldman Both off to Prison," *The New York Times,* July 10, 1917.

269 "We're going straight to Russia": Ibid.

Chapter 25

270 "First, from the standpoint": "Roosevelt Calls Support of Mayor Duty to Nation," *The New York Times,* October 30, 1917.

272 "For more than three years": "City's Bomb Squad Goes to the Army," *The New York Times,* December 13, 1917.

272 "a splendid move": Ibid.

272 Several weeks later: "38 Brooklynites Police Grads," *Brooklyn Times Union,* December 27, 1917.

273 "not so big in the girth": "Woods's Rookies Receive Diplomas." *The Sun,* December 27, 1917.

273 Visibly moved, Woods: Ibid.

274 Across the country, German nationals reported: Images here: https://catalog .archives.gov/id/291093?objectPage=2.

275 "He excelled at the work": Gage, 2023, loc. 1686.

276 "was of sufficient power": "Bomb for Ole Hanson Sent from East Stirs Home of Seattle's Fighting Mayor," *The New York Times,* April 29, 1919.

276 Twenty-four hours later: "Bomb Injures Ex-Senator's Wife, Maims a Servant," *The New York Times,* April 30, 1919.

278 "or deadlier possibilities": "Police Trail Tools Used in Big Bomb Plot," *The Sun,* May 3, 1919.

280 the "terrific wreckage": "Palmer and Family Safe," *The New York Times,* June 3, 1919.

280 single-page statement: Ibid.

282 anarchist Luigi Galleani: Like Berkman and Goldman, Galleani had become a major figure in the anti-conscription movement. "In 1917, Galleani published 'Matricolati!,' in which he indirectly advised his followers to avoid registering for the draft. Following his counsel, scores of Italian anarchists assumed false identities, changed residences, or went into hiding." Goyens et al., loc. 1543.

284 "When the Radical Division": Quoted in Gage, 2023, 68.

284 Collating information on just: "Hoover thus set out to do for the Radical Division what Putnam had done for the Library of Congress: to make its vast stores of information accessible at a moment's notice." Ibid., 69.

286 "Say this to all": Quoted in Wexler, 247.

286 "Awakened at 5 A.M.": Ibid., 249–50.

287 "Emma Goldman and Alexander Berkman are": Quoted in Ackerman, 88.

288 "You're dressed so swell": Goldman, 2006, 385.

288 "We had nothing": Ibid., 387.

289 "The documents, classified, tabulated": Ibid., 389.

289 **The material that Hoover:** Hoover's full report can be found in the Emma Goldman Archives here: https://archive.org/details /governmentdocum9101emma_7/page/n127/mode/1up.

290 **"I wish to register":** Goldman, 2006, 394.

291 **"I decided that if":** Ibid., 399.

Chapter 26

294 **"go to Petrograd":** "249 Reds Sail, Exiled to Soviet Russia," *The New York Times,* December 22, 1919.

294 **"I do not consider it":** Ibid.

294 **"I felt dizzy":** Goldman, 2006, 396.

295 **"a slender bundle":** Quoted in Gage, 2023, 74.

295 **"Haven't I given you":** Quoted in Ackerman, 160.

296 **"Under the guns":** "249 Reds Sail, Exiled to Soviet Russia," *The New York Times,* December 22, 1919.

296 **"The tall skyscrapers":** Berkman, 1925, 14.

Epilogue: Aftershock

297 **a "bomb wizard":** "Eagen, Bomb Wizard Dies Going to Duty," *The New York Times,* March 3, 1920.

299 **"The lessons to America":** Tunney and Hollister, 4.

299 **"The Faurot idea":** "Fingerprinting." *The News Scimitar,* July 24, 1920.

300 **"To be *governed*":** Proudhon, 293.

301 **"One could not even":** Goldman, 2006, 411.

301 **"An armed guard":** Ibid., 431–33.

302 **"We had fought":** Ibid.

303 **"You will add":** Quoted in Merriman, loc. 3008.

304 **"Our enemies are":** Quoted in Drinnon and Drinnon, 13.

307 **"That acts of violence accomplish nothing":** Berkman, 2005, 109.

307 **"have proven utterly useless":** Ibid., 107.

308 **"remarkably like his photographs":** Berkman, 1925, 74.

309 **"ill and worn-looking":** Goldman, 2006, loc. 8347.

310 **"The conditions were terrible":** Berkman, 1925, 77, and http://dwardmac .pitzer.edu/Anarchist_Archives/bright/berkman/reminiscences/reminiscences .html.

310 **"The revolution we have":** https://www.marxists.org/reference/archive /kropotkin-peter/1910s/19_04_28.htm.

310 **"I had known Peter":** Goldman, 2006, 493.

311 **A grainy silent film:** The footage of Kropotkin's funeral can viewed at https:// www.youtube.com/watch?v=S1Nm64OOPm8.

BIBLIOGRAPHY

Archives Consulted

For the transcripts of the trial of Charles Crispi: the archives of John Jay College of Criminal Justice; for the personal correspondence of Arthur Woods and Theodore Roosevelt: the Roosevelt Papers at the Library of Congress Manuscript Division; for extensive material on Arthur Woods's early life and career: the Arthur Woods Papers at the Library of Congress; for personal correspondence and other documents from the life of Emma Goldman: the Emma Goldman Papers at the New York Public Library; for information about J. Edgar Hoover and other law enforcement issues: the archives at the National Law Enforcement Museum, in particular the J. Edgar Hoover Collection.

Newspaper Articles

"The Peril of the Czar." *The New York Times*, March 4, 1880.

"Nihilist Conspirators at Last Successful." *The New York Times*, March 14, 1881.

"Russia's Dead Monarch." *The New York Times*, March 15, 1881.

"Mob Law at Homestead." *The New York Times*, July 7, 1892.

"Nellie Bly Again—She Interviews Emma Goldman and Other Anarchists." *The World*, September 17, 1893.

"Howls for Emma Goldman." *The New York Times*, August 20, 1894.

"How the Deed Was Done." *The New York Times*, September 7, 1901.

"A Favorable Turn." *The Washington Times*, September 9, 1901.

"Emma Goldman in Court." *New-York Tribune*, September 12, 1901.

"Czolgosz Found Guilty." *New-York Tribune*, September 25, 1901.

"Assassin Czolgosz Is Executed at Auburn." *The New York Times*, October 30, 1901.

"Brings Report on Investigation." *New-York Tribune*, February 5, 1906.

"Finger Prints Effective." *The Morning Astorian,* February 6, 1906.

"Assailant of H. C. Frick Set Free." *New-York Tribune,* May 19, 1906.

"2,000 Greet Berkman." *The New York Times,* June 18, 1906.

"Anarchist Berkman Missing." *The Sun,* October 27, 1906.

"Black Hand Bomb Explodes." *The Sun,* November 6, 1906.

"Laws to Improve the Police." *The Sun,* November 23, 1906.

"New Committee Forming to Improve Police." *The New York Times,* November 23, 1906.

"Suicide Ends a Man Hunt." *The Sun,* December 19, 1906.

"Petrosini, Detective and Sociologist." *The New York Times,* December 30, 1906.

"Blames Foreigners for Crime Wave." *The New York Times,* July 21, 1907.

"Needs More Police to Check Crime." *The New York Times,* July 25, 1907.

"Bomb Kills One; Police Escape." *The New York Times,* March 29, 1908.

"Bomb Zone Shaken for the Tenth Time." *The New York Times,* July 2, 1908.

"New Secret Service to Fight Black Hand." *The New York Times,* February 20, 1909.

"Ambassador Warned Him." *The New York Times,* March 14, 1909.

"Petrosino a Terror to Criminal Bands." *The New York Times,* March 14, 1909.

"Petrosino Slain Assassins Gone." *The New York Times,* March 14, 1909.

"Petrosino Buried with High Honors." *The New York Times,* April 13, 1909.

"Many Pass Exams for Captaincies; 13 to Get Jobs." *The Evening World,* January 26, 1911.

"Seeks to Convict with Finger Print as Sole Evidence." *The Evening World,* May 9, 1911.

"Jury Study Finger Prints." *The Sun,* May 10, 1911.

"Value of Finger-Print Test." *The New York Times,* May 10, 1911.

"Fifth AV. Thief is Identified by Finger Prints." *The Evening World,* May 24, 1911.

"Keeping Track of the Criminal by Their Fingerprints." *The New York Times,* July 30, 1911.

"School of Detectives Here." *The New York Times,* September 6, 1911.

"'Portrait Parle' Latest Method of Finding Criminals." *The Farmer,* September 14, 1911.

"The Coil of Justice." *The Cleveland Leader,* February 1, 1912.

"Bomb Mailed to Rosalsky Bursts." *The Sun,* March 17, 1912.

"Joseph W. Woods Dead." *The Boston Globe,* April 15, 1912.

"New York Police Captain Has Plan to 'Finger-Print' All Americans." *The Sunday Star,* May 26, 1912.

Sanborn, A. C. "Catching Crooks by Their Wrinkles." *The Salt Lake Tribune,* June 2, 1912.

"Parole System Is to be Probed by Rosalsky." *The Washington Herald,* August 31, 1912.

"Had Insane Father." *The Evening Star,* October 16, 1912.

"Mrs. Rosenthal Told Not to Worry." *The Evening Star,* October 16, 1912.

"Schrank, Weak and White, Pleads Guilty." *The Sun*, October 16, 1912.

"Schrank Is a Crazy Man, Say Experts." *The Rock Island Argus*, October 16, 1912.

"Becker Witnesses Weaken Defence." *New-York Tribune*, October 22, 1912.

"Police, Favoring Becker, Aid Prosecutions Case." *New-York Tribune*, October 22, 1912.

"'Steve' O'Brien Out." *New-York Tribune*, October 22, 1912.

"Inspector Faurot Stricken at Desk, Taken to Hospital." *The Evening World*, July 15, 1913.

"Find Woman's Body in Bundle in River." *The New York Times*, September 7, 1913.

"Faurot Tells How He Solves Crimes." *The Washington Times*, September 16, 1913.

Rose, Norman. "A True Thrilling Detective Story in Real Life of Today." *The Day Book*, September 17, 1913.

"How Murderer of Anna Aumuller Was Traced." *The Tacoma Times*, September 19, 1913.

"Schmidt Ready for More Deaths." *The New York Times*, September 19, 1913.

"How New York's Real Detective Solves Criminal Mysteries by Scientific Method." *The Sun*, September 21, 1913.

"Schmidt Purposed to Kill for Money." *The New York Times*, September 23, 1913.

"A Real Detective Story." *The Daily Banner*, October 28, 1913.

"Faurot—The Detective." *The Logan Republican*, November 1, 1913.

"Index Finger Prints of Immigrant." *The Detroit Times*, November 7, 1913.

"Bomb Wrecks Shop, Alarm on Heights." *The New York Times*, November 28, 1913.

Thompson, Charles Willis. "Woods to Bring Police Department into the Uplift." *The New York Times*, April 12, 1914.

"New Head of Police Has Eye on Welfare of Brooklyn Folks." *The Brooklyn Daily Eagle*, April 12, 1914.

"Identified as Michael P. Mahoney, Man with Many Grievances." *The New York Times*, April 18, 1914.

"I.W.W. Pickets Pen Rockefellers." *The New York Times*, May 4, 1914.

"Women in Two Kinds of Revolutions." *New-York Tribune*, May 10, 1914.

"Exploded in Apartment Occupied by Tarry-town Disturbers." *The New York Times*, July 5, 1914.

Stokes, H. W. "Bomb-Makers Make Life Interesting for Owen Eagen." *New-York Tribune*, July 12, 1914.

"5,000 at Memorial to Anarchist Dead." *The New York Times*, July 12, 1914.

"N.Y. City Sleuths in Their New Homes." *The Washington Times*, September 11, 1914.

"Bomb Exploded in St. Patrick's Cathedral, N.Y." *The Farmer*, October 14, 1914.

"Bombs Exploded in St. Patrick's and at a Church." *The New York Times*, October 14, 1914.

"Bomb in Fifth Av. Rocks Apartments." *The New York Times*, October 19, 1914.

"Slavers' Bombs Rock Bronx Court." *The New York Times*, November 12, 1914.

"Lighted Bomb Put in Tombs Court." *The New York Times*, November 15, 1914.

"Berkman Reveals Anarchists' Plot." *The New York Times*, February 16, 1915.

"Berkman Interview Arouses the Police." *The New York Times*, February 17, 1915.

"Bomb Sleuth Lived with Anarchists." *The New York Times*, March 3, 1915.

"Trap Bomb Layer as He Lights Fuse in the Cathedral." *The New York Times*, March 3, 1915.

"Too Many Lawyers Halt Bomb Hearing." *The New York Times*, March 7, 1915.

"Police Had Tested Cathedral Bomb." *The New York Times*, March 30, 1915.

"30 Anarchists Fail to Shake Polignani." *The New York Times*, March 31, 1915.

"In Cell for Threat at the Bomb Trial." *The New York Times*, April 2, 1915.

"Detective Lit Bomb, Abarno Tells Court." *The New York Times*, April 3, 1915.

"Woods Ends Year as Police Head." *New-York Tribune*, April 8, 1915.

"Convict Bomb Men in Cathedral Plot." *The New York Times*, April 13, 1915.

"Woods Begins Busy Day by Capturing Burglar." *New-York Tribune*, May 21, 1915.

"Bomb Explosion at Capitol Perpetrated by Same Man Who Shot J. Pierpont Morgan." *The Sunday Star*, July 4, 1915.

"Attempt to Kill Police by Bomb." *The Washington Herald*, July 6, 1915.

"Police Headquarters Shaken by Bomb on Red 'Martyr Day'; Holt Insane, Morgan Out Soon." *New-York Tribune*, July 6, 1915.

"Bomb Wrecks Detective Bureau as N.Y. Police Probe Morgan Shooting." *The Farmer*, July 6, 1915.

"Holt's Dynamite Found by Police." *The New York Times*, July 7, 1915.

"Police Bomb Like One Holt Made." *The New York Times*, July 7, 1915.

"New York Boasts of Best Rogues' Gallery." *New Ulm Review*, July 21, 1915.

"Objectional Plate Removed from Becker's Coffin." *Norwich Bulletin*, August 2, 1915.

"A World Wide 'Who's Who' of the Wicked." *The Sunday Telegram*, August 15, 1915.

"Light Nemesis of Burglars; Few Gangs of Crooks Remain." *The Washington Herald*, November 30, 1915.

"Bomb Aimed at Police." *The Middletown Transcript*, 1915.

"Hans Schmidt, Priest, Expiates Crime in Electric Chair at Dawn of Day." *Elko Independent*, February 18, 1916.

"Faurot, Crook Expert, Pinched by Sleuths Down South in Dixie." *The Evening World*, February 19, 1916.

"Arthur Woods to Wed." *Times Union*, March 18, 1916.

"Niece of J. P. Morgan to Wed New York Police Commissioner." *The Kingston Daily Freeman*, March 21, 1916.

"Phone Wiretapping Before Grand Jury." *The New York Times*, May 4, 1916.

"The Mayor Has Escaped Indictment for the Present." *The Standard Union*, May 24, 1916.

"Arthur Woods Weds Miss H. M. Hamilton." *The Brooklyn Daily Eagle*, June 11, 1916.

"Society Given Big Prize." *The Daily Republican*, June 14, 1916.

"Society Given Big Surprise." *Rushville Republican*, June 14, 1916.

"Woods Faces Wire Tapping Charges." *The Sun*, July 28, 1916.

Woods, Arthur. "Long Training Needed for War." *The Brooklyn Daily Eagle*, September 17, 1916.

"Vast Number of Finger Prints." *The Brattleboro Daily Reformer*, December 19, 1916.

"800 Girls Have Disappeared in N.Y. in 6 Months." *The Topeka Daily State Journal*, June 20, 1917.

"Woman in Cruger Case Threatened with Death; Police Shakeup Pending." *South Bend News-Times*, June 21, 1917.

"Convict Berkman and Miss Goldman Both off to Prison." *The New York Times*, July 10, 1917.

"Roosevelt Calls Support of Mayor Duty to Nation." *The New York Times*, October 30, 1917.

"City's Bomb Squad Goes to the Army." *The New York Times*, December 13, 1917.

"Scull Quits Police Enters U.S Army." *The Sun*, December 27, 1917.

"38 Brooklynites Police Grads." *The Brooklyn Daily Times*, December 27, 1917.

"Woods's Rookies Receive Diplomas." *The Sun*, December 27, 1917.

"Woods Welcome of Bugher Warm." *The Sun*, January 2, 1918.

"Timely Invention—A Patent Thief-Catcher." *New-York Tribune*, April 13, 1919.

"Bomb for Ole Hanson Sent from East Stirs Home of Seattle's Fighting Mayor." *The New York Times*, April 29, 1919.

"Bomb Injures Ex-Senator's Wife, Maims a Servant." *The New York Times*, April 30, 1919.

"31 Were Marked as Victims by Bomb Conspirers." *The New York Times*, May 1, 1919.

"Finger Print Is Bomb Clew as Big Net Is Set." *New-York Tribune*, May 2, 1919.

"Police Trail Tools Used in Big Bomb Plot." *The Sun*, May 3, 1919.

"Bomb Material from Europe, Experts Assert." *New-York Tribune*, May 4, 1919.

"Fresh Clue to Bomb Plotters." *The Sun*, May 4, 1919.

"Arrest of Two I.W.W. Near in Bomb Plot." *The Sun*, May 6, 1919.

"What Police of New York Found in a Bomb Raid." *The Alaska Daily Empire*, May 26, 1919.

"Palmer and Family Safe." *The New York Times*, June 3, 1919.

"Dead Bomber Identified as Italian Red." *New-York Tribune*, June 7, 1919.

"Flynn Oversees Many Clues to Bombers." *The New York Times*, June 8, 1919.

"Inspector Tunney Retires." *The New York Times*, August 14, 1919.

"Faurot Supplants Cray as Head of Detectives." *New-York Tribune*, September 8, 1919.

"Deportation Defied by Emma Goldman." *The New York Times*, October 28, 1919.

"'Reds'" of Various Hues Light Up Emma Goldman's Cheery 'Coming Out' Party." *The Evening World*, October 28, 1919.

Faurot, Joseph. "Burglars Will Now Seek New Profession." *The South Bend News-Times*, November 19, 1919.

"Annuls Reds' Writ but Grants Respite." *The New York Times,* December 9, 1919.

"Berkman Must Go; Woman Gets Stay." *The New York Times,* December 12, 1919.

"'Ark' with 300 Reds Sails Early Today." *The New York Times,* December 21, 1919.

"249 Reds Sail, Exiled to Soviet Russia." *The New York Times,* December 22, 1919.

"Eagen, Bomb Wizard Dies Going to Duty." *The New York Times,* March 3, 1920.

"Faurot Appointed as Police Deputy in Porter's Place." *The Evening World,* April 7, 1920.

"Diamond Disk Tattles on Auto Thief." *Daily East Oregonian,* May 13, 1920.

"Fingerprinting." *The News Scimitar,* July 24, 1920.

"Bomb Batters Wall St.; 31 Slain, 125 Hurt; Three Plot Warnings Came from Toronto; Public Buildings and Churches Guarded." *The Sun and The New York Herald,* September 17, 1920.

"Jekyll and Hyde Revealed by Fingerprint System." *The New York Herald,* October 31, 1920.

"Women Cops Get Precinct and Station House of Own." *The New York Herald,* March 8, 1921.

"Chiefs to Crack a Safe and Test Faurot's Skill." *New-York Tribune,* May 5, 1921.

Peltz, Hamilton. "New Science Is Hard Blow to Crime." *The New York Herald,* May 15, 1921.

"'Nick Carter' Dead by His Own Hand." *New Britain Daily Herald,* April 27, 1922.

"Baby Finger Tips Are Printed to Insure It Against Being Traded Off." *The Arizona Republican,* June 26, 1922.

"First Police Radio Station Installed." *The New York Herald,* September 10, 1922.

"Faurot to Resign as Police Deputy." *The New York Times,* July 15, 1926.

"McCarter, with Cutting Words, Lunges at Faurot, Who Parries with Smiles." *The Brooklyn Daily Eagle,* November 9, 1926.

"Third Degree's Use Is Laid to Faurot." *The New York Times,* September 8, 1931.

"Ends Fingerprint Stain." *The New York Times,* April 16, 1933.

"Arthur Woods, 72, Is Dead in Capital." *The New York Times,* May 13, 1942.

"J. A. Faurot, Expert on Fingerprints, 70." *The New York Times,* November 21, 1942.

Books and Essays

Ackerman, Kenneth D. *Young J. Edgar: Hoover, the Red Scare, 1919–1920.* Viral History Press, 2011.

Avrich, Karen, and Paul Avrich. *Sasha and Emma: The Anarchist Odyssey of Alexander Berkman and Emma Goldman.* Belknap Press of Harvard University Press, 2014.

Beavan, Colin. *Fingerprints: The Origins of Crime Detection and the Murder Case That Launched Forensic Science.* Hyperion, 2001.

Bemis, Edward W. "The Homestead Strike." *Journal of Political Economy,* June 1894, 369–96.

Berkman, Alexander. "Violence and Anarchism." *Mother Earth,* April 1908, 67–70.

———. *The Bolshevik Myth (Diary 1920–1922).* Hutchinson and Co., 1925.

———. *Now and After: The ABC of Communist Anarchism,* 2nd ed. Freie Arbeiter Stimme, 1937.

———. *Life of an Anarchist: The Alexander Berkman Reader.* Edited by Gene Fellner. Seven Stories Press, 2004.

———. *Prison Memoirs of an Anarchist.* Dodo Press, 2009.

Blum, Howard. *Dark Invasion.* HarperCollins, 2014.

Burleigh, Michael. *Blood and Rage: A Cultural History of Terrorism.* Harper Perennial, 2010.

Burrows, Edwin G., and Mike Wallace. *Gotham.* Oxford University Press, 1998.

Chadwick, Bruce. *Law & Disorder: The Chaotic Birth of the NYPD.* Thomas Dunne, 2017.

Chomsky, Noam. *On Anarchism.* Penguin Books, 2014.

Cole, Simon A. *Suspect Identities: A History of Fingerprinting and Criminal Identification.* Harvard University Press, 2002.

Darwin, Charles. *On the Origin of Species: The Science Classic.* John Wiley & Sons, 2020.

Dash, Mike. *Satan's Circus: Murder, Vice, Police Corruption and New York's Trial of the Century.* Granta Books, 2009.

Davis, Mike. "The Coming Desert." *New Left Review,* January/February 2016.

———. *Buda's Wagon: A Brief History of the Car Bomb.* Verso, 2017.

Drinnon, Richard, and Anna Marie Drinnon, eds. *Nowhere at Home: Letters from Exile of Emma Goldman and Alexander Berkman.* Schocken Books, 1977.

Dugatkin, Lee Alan. *The Prince of Evolution: Peter Kropotkin's Adventures in Science and Politics.* CreateSpace, 2011.

Eastman, Crystal. *Work-Accidents and the Law: The Pittsburgh Survey; Findings in Six Volumes.* Charities Publication Committee, 1910.

Emsley, Clive, and Haia Shpayer-Makov. *Police Detectives in History: 1750–1950.* Routledge, 2006.

Falk, Emma. *Love, Anarchy, and Emma Goldman.* Rutgers University Press, 2019.

Fant, Kenne. *Alfred Nobel: A Biography.* Arcade Publishing, 2014.

Ferguson, Kathy E. *Emma Goldman: Political Thinking in the Streets.* Rowman & Littlefield, 2013.

Fishman, J. E. *Dynamite: A Concise History of the NYPD Bomb Squad.* Verbitrage, 2013.

Gado, Mark. *Killer Priest: The Crimes, Trials, and Execution of Father Hans Schmidt.* Praeger, 2006.

Gage, Beverly. *The Day Wall Street Exploded: A Story of America in Its First Age of Terror.* Oxford University Press, 2010.

———. *G-Man: J. Edgar Hoover and the American Century.* Simon & Schuster, 2023.

Galton, Francis. *Finger Prints.* Perfect Library, 2015.

Gentry, Curt. *J. Edgar Hoover: The Man and the Secrets.* W. W. Norton, 2001.

Gilpin, Toni. *The Long Deep Grudge: A Story of Big Capital, Radical Labor, and Class War in the American Heartland.* Haymarket Books, 2020.

Goldman, Emma. "Anarchism and the Sex Question." *The Anarchist* (London), September 27 and October 4, 1896.

————. "Mother Earth." *Mother Earth* 1, no. 1, March 1906.

————. "The Barnum and Bailey Staging of the 'Anarchist Plot.'" *Mother Earth* 10, no. 2, April 1915, 73.

————. "The No Conscription League." *Mother Earth* 12, no. 4, June 1917, 112.

————. *A Documentary History of the American Years.* Edited by Candace Falk. University of Illinois Press, 2008.

————. *Living My Life: Abridged.* Penguin Books, 2006.

————. *My Disillusionment in Russia.* Dover Publications, 2016.

————. *Nowhere at Home: Letters from Exile of Emma Goldman and Alexander Berkman.* Edited by Richard and Anna Maria Drinnon. Schocken Books, 1977.

Gould, Stephen Jay. "Excerpt from 'Kropotkin Was No Crackpot.'" *International Journal of Epidemiology* 43, no. 6, 2014, 1686–87, doi:10.1093/ije/dyu207.

Goyens, Tom, et al. *Radical Gotham: Anarchism in New York City from Schwab's Saloon to Occupy Wall Street.* University of Illinois Press, 2017.

Guérin, Daniel, ed. *No Gods, No Masters.* AK Press, 1999.

Hayden, F. V. "Preliminary Field Report of the United States Geological Survey of Colorado and New Mexico." Government Printing Office, 1869.

Hoover, J. Edgar. "Criminal Identification." *American Journal of Police Science* 2, no. 1, 1931, 8–19, doi:10.2307/1147300.

Jensen, Richard Bach. *The Battle Against Anarchist Terrorism: An International History, 1878–1934.* Cambridge University Press, 2013.

Jones, Thai. *More Powerful than Dynamite: Radicals, Plutocrats, Progressives, and New York's Year of Anarchy.* Bloomsbury, 2014.

Kinna, Ruth, and Matthew S. Adams, ed. *Anarchism, 1914–18: Internationalism, Anti-Militarism and War.* Manchester University Press, 2020.

Kropotkin, Peter. *Anarchism: A Collection of Revolutionary Writings.* Dover, 2002.

————. *Memoirs of a Revolutionist.* Dover, 2010.

————. *Mutual Aid: An Illuminated Factor of Evolution.* With illustrations by N. O. Bonzo. PM Press, 2021.

————. *The Conquest of Bread.* New York University Press, 1972.

Kuznetsov, Sergey I., and Yury A. Petrushin. "Siberian Community and Nikolay Muravyov-Amursky." *Sibirica* 9, no. 1, 2010, 53–56, doi:10.3167/sib.2010.090104.

Lardner, James, and Thomas A. Reppetto. *NYPD: A City and Its Police.* Henry Holt, 2001.

Ludlow Collective. "Archaeology of the Colorado Coal Field War, 1913–1914." In *Archaeologies of the Contemporary Past.* Edited by Victor Buchli and Gavin Lucas. Routledge Press, 94–107.

McGovern, George S., and Leonard F. Guttridge. *The Great Coalfield War.* NetLibrary, 1999.

McGuire, Randal H., and Paul Reckner. "The Unromantic West: Labor, Capital and Struggle." *Historical Archaeology* 36, 2002, 44–58.

Mele, Andrew Paul. *The Italian Squad: How the NYPD Took Down the Black Hand Extortion Racket.* McFarland, 2020.

Merriman, John M. *The Dynamite Club: How a Bombing in Fin-de-Siècle Paris Ignited the Age of Modern Terrorism.* Houghton Mifflin Harcourt, 2009.

Miller, David. "The Neglected (Ii) Kropotkin." *Government and Opposition* 18, no. 3, 1983, 319–38, doi:10.1111/j.1477-7053.1983.tb00348.x.

Miller, Martin A. *Kropotkin*. University of Chicago Press, 1976.

Miller, Scott. *The President and the Assassin: McKinley, Terror, and Empire at the Dawn of the American Century*. Random House, 2013.

Mitchell, Elizabeth. *The Fearless Mrs. Goodwin: How New York's First Female Police Detective Cracked the Crime of the Century*. Byliner, 2011.

Moses, Paul. *The Italian Squad: The True Story of the Immigrant Cops Who Fought the Rise of the Mafia*. New York University Press, 2023.

O'Hara, Stephen P. *Inventing the Pinkertons, or, Spies, Sleuths, Mercenaries, and Thugs*. Johns Hopkins University Press, 2016.

Oppenheimer, A. R. *IRA, the Bombs and the Bullets: A History of Deadly Ingenuity*. Irish Academic Press, 2018.

"The People vs. Hans Schmidt." New York Court of Appeals, Records and Briefs, 1915.

Piazza, Pierre. "Alphonse Bertillon and the Identification of Persons (1880–1914)." *Criminocorpus,* August 26, 2016, criminocorpus.org/en/expositions/anciennes /suspects-defendants-guilty/alphonse-bertillon-and-identification-persons-1880 -1914.

Pribanic-Smith, Erika J., and Jared Schroeder. "Goldman, *Mother Earth,* and the No-Conscription League." In Pribanic-Smith and Schroeder, *Emma Goldman's No-Conscription League and the First Amendment*. Routledge, 2019, 57–89, doi:10.4324/9781351027984-3.

Proudhon, Pierre-Joseph. *General Idea of the Revolution in the Nineteenth Century*. Cosimo Classics, 2007.

Radzinskiĭ, Ėdvard. *Alexander II: The Last Great Tsar*. Free Press, 2006.

Reppetto, Thomas A. *American Detective: Behind the Scenes of Famous Criminal Investigations*. Potomac Books, 2018.

———. *American Police: A History, 1945–2012*. Enigma Books, 2013.

Rhodes, Henry T. F. *Alphonse Bertillon, Father of Scientific Detection*. G. G. Harrap, 1956.

Ricca, Brad. *Mrs. Sherlock Holmes: The True Story of New York City's Greatest Female Detective and the 1917 Missing Girl Case That Captivated a Nation*. St. Martin's Paperbacks, 2019.

Richardson, James F. *The New York Police: Colonial Times to 1901*. Oxford University Press, 1970.

Riis, Jacob A. *How the Other Half Lives: Studies Among the Tenements of Jacob A. Riis*. Penguin, 1997.

Roosevelt, Theodore. Letter from Theodore Roosevelt to Arthur Woods. October 10, 1903. Letter. Theodore Roosevelt Papers. Library of Congress Manuscript Division. Theodore Roosevelt Digital Library. Dickinson State University. August 31, 2023.

Scott, James C. *Two Cheers for Anarchism: Six Easy Pieces on Autonomy, Dignity, and Meaningful Work and Play*. Princeton University Press, 2017.

Segrave, Kerry. *Wiretapping and Electronic Surveillance in America, 1862–1920*. McFarland, 2014.

Serrin, William. *Homestead: The Glory and Tragedy of an American Steel Town.* Vintage Books, 1993.

Simensen, Anne Synnøve. *The Woman Behind the Nobel Peace Prize: Bertha von Suttner and Alfred Nobel.* Self-pub, 2018.

State of New York. *Minutes and Testimony of the Joint Legislative Committee Appointed to Investigate the Public Service Commissions.* 1916.

Tunney, Thomas J., and Paul M. Hollister. *Throttled! The Detection of the German and Anarchist Bomb Plotters.* Small, Maynard & Company, 1919.

Weinberg, Arthur, and Lila Shaffer Weinberg. *The Muckrakers: The Era in Journalism That Moved America to Reform, the Most Significant Magazine Articles of 1902–1912.* Simon & Schuster, 1961.

Weiner, Tim. *Enemies: A History of the FBI.* Random House Trade Paperbacks, 2013.

Wexler, Alice. *Emma Goldman: An Intimate Life.* Virago, 1985.

Whalen, Bernard, and Jon Whalen. *The NYPD's First Fifty Years: Politicians, Police Commissioners, and Patrolmen.* Potomac Books, 2014.

Woods, Arthur. "The Problem of the Black Hand." *McClures*, vol. 33, no. 1, 1909, 40–47.

———. *Policeman and Public.* Yale University Press, 1919.

Yarmolinsky, Avrahm. *Road to Revolution: A Century of Russian Radicalism.* Princeton University Press, 2014.

ACKNOWLEDGMENTS

Though I have spent nearly all of my adult life as a resident of either Manhattan or Brooklyn, this is the first of my books to be centered around the history of New York City itself. So I should begin by paying tribute to all the ways the city has nourished me as a writer over the years: talking shop with friends and colleagues in cafés and bars not all that different from Sachs's Café on the Lower East Side, where Goldman and Berkman first met; mulling over ideas while walking along the same stretch of Prospect Park where they discussed Sophia Perovskaya's martyrdom early in their relationship. I began my career as a writer about thirty years ago in an office right across the street from the old NYPD headquarters where Joseph Faurot first rolled out his fingerprinting table. Writing about such a turbulent—and sometimes terrifying—stretch of New York City's history was a constant reminder of how much of modern New York is civil and safe and functional, in many ways an ideal environment in which to create and connect.

As it happens, the book of mine with the most material about New York before this one was *Emergence*, which featured a chapter that discussed Jane Jacobs and the sidewalk-centric urbanism that she celebrated in the West Village. *Emergence* actually shares a number of themes with *The Infernal Machine*; it includes a few sections about the guilds of the "free cities" that Peter Kropotkin might have approved of and opens with a discussion of the leaderless organization of ant colonies that could have been lifted from the pages of *Mutual Aid*. So it's fitting that, more than two decades later, I ended up working with the original editor of *Emergence*, Gillian Blake, for this new book. Gillian's vision and enthusiasm—and her unflagging insistence on the value of getting to know the characters in this story—improved the final book in countless ways. I'm grateful, too, for all the support from the team at Crown, starting with Amy Li, who was essential in getting the manuscript in shape and offered some terrific editorial guidance herself. Thanks as well to Yang Kim, Chris Brand, Christine Tanigawa, Patricia Shaw, and Heather Williamson.

I am indebted to a number of friends and fellow authors who were generous enough to read part or all of this manuscript and offer numerous helpful contributions, particularly Mark Bailey, Bill Wasik, Beverly Gage, Thai Jones, Henry Farrell, and my wife, Alexa Robinson. Thanks as well to my agents for supporting this book alongside my various other endeavors: Lydia Willis, Jay Mandel, Sylvie Rabineau, Travis Dunlap, and Ryan McNeily. I'm also grateful to my longtime collaborators at Riverhead—Courtney Young and Geoff Kloske most of all—who offered some helpful advice on early versions of this project. Some of the material on Alfred Nobel was originally developed in a script I wrote for the *American Innovations* podcast; thanks to Marshall Lewy and Nathalie Chicha at Wondery for supporting that deep dive into Nobel's extraordinary life. As always, thanks to the SERJ group, who have listened to me ramble on about anarchism, forensic science, and the history of dynamite for more than five years now.

This book had an interesting twist to it, in that I wrote most of it while simultaneously developing a tool to help people research and write books (among other things) during my tenure as a Visiting Scholar at Google Labs. We weren't able to build the final product in time to actually help me write *The Infernal Machine*, but I can't wait to use NotebookLM for the next one. Thanks to my colleagues past and present at Google Labs for all the camaraderie and inspiring work over the past two years, especially Josh Woodward, Clay Bavor, Raiza Martin, and the rest of the brilliant NotebookLM team. Tailwind forever!

Speaking of research, this book is dedicated to my oldest son, Clay, who served as my research assistant for the last mile, digging through the newspaper archives to uncover details about Arthur Woods's wedding, Joseph Faurot's family life, and much more. Clay was born three days before the deadliest terrorist attack in the history of New York—9/11 was his first day home from the hospital— but despite that horrifying start, he has grown up to become a consummate New Yorker, always ready to go roaming out into the bustling streets in search of new experiences. Thanks to Clay for all his help on this project—and for being such an inspiration to me, both as a city-dweller and a son.

November 2023
Brooklyn

INDEX

(Page references in *italics* refer to illustrations.)

Umberto I, king of Italy, 95, 113, 222
undercover operations, xviii, 213,
    215–16
  Black Hand and, 137, 143, 148, 151,
    155, 157, 158, 214, 223
  Bresci Circle and, 223–43, 255
  of Pinkertons, 21–22, 50
unemployment rallies, 149, 150, 218
Union Square:
  Goldman charged with incitement to
    riot after rally in (1893), 100
  memorial for Caron, Berg, and
    Hanson in (1914), 207–11, 212
  police riot in (1914), 188, 189, 190,
    194, 203, 206
  Silverstein's failed bomb attempt in
    (1908), 149–50
U.S. Capitol bombing (1915), xix, 124,
    244–45, *245,* 247, 248, 250, 276

Valdinoci, Carlo, 282
Vanderbilt, William K., 63
vigilante activities, 261–62

Waldo, Rhinelander, 171, 172, 178
Wall Street bombing (1920), 304
War Department, U.S., 271–72, 274
Washington Times, 120–21
Wasservogel, Isidore, 161–66
Watt, James, 110
Weinberger, Harry, 288, 290, 291
Williams, Ethel, 277
Wilson, Woodrow, 261, 264, 274
Winter Palace bombing (1880), 32–35
wiretapping, 252–56
Woods, Arthur Hale, xi, xvii, xviii,
    139–43, *141,* 149, 151, 168, 202,
    213, 214, 215, 219, 223, 246–47,
    271–74, 298–99
  attempt on Mitchel's life and, 189–91
  background of, 140–42

Bresci Circle operation and, 224, 228,
    229, 230, 232, 233, 237–38, 239,
    241–42, 255
  Detective Bureau reinvented by,
    147–48
  first NYPD position resigned by, 158
  lifestyle and demeanor of, 147,
    188–89
  McClure's essay by ("The Problem of
    the Black Hand"), 155–57, 242, 243
  meteoric rise of, in NYPD, 141–42
  Muenter investigation and, 246–47,
    249, 250
  Petrosino killing and, 152, 154–56,
    223, 232
  position in NYPD created for, 143
  purview of NYPD expanded by,
    251–52
  radical groups' protests and, 150
  return to NYPD as police
    commissioner, 188–89, 191
  Roosevelt's friendship with, 142–43
  wedding of, 253, 256–57
  wiretapping controversy and, 252–56
Woods, Helen Morgan Hamilton, 246,
    253, 256, 298
workplace accidents, xvi, 48–49,
    110–11, 210
World War I, 213, 216–17, 251, 264,
    274, 276
  opposition to, 216–17, 246, 247,
    258–61, 264–65
  Preparedness parades and, 258,
    259–60
  saboteurs and, 219, 251–52, 261

Yarmolinsky, Avrahm, 42–43

Zhelyabov, Andrei, 35, 36, 37, 42–43,
    65, 304
Zinn, Howard, 192

ABOUT THE AUTHOR

Steven Johnson is the bestselling author of fourteen books, including *Enemy of All Mankind, Where Good Ideas Come From, How We Got to Now, The Ghost Map,* and *Extra Life.* He's the host and co-creator of the Emmy-winning PBS/BBC series *How We Got to Now,* the author of the newsletter *Adjacent Possible,* and the editorial director for NotebookLM and Google Labs. He lives in Brooklyn, New York, and Marin County, California, with his wife and their three sons.